THE
MATLAB®
HANDBOOK

THE
MATLAB®
HANDBOOK

Eva Pärt-Enander

Anders Sjoberg

Bo Melin

Pernilla Isaksson

ADDISON - WESLEY

Harlow, England • Reading, Massachusetts • Menlo Park, California • New York
Don Mills, Ontario • Amsterdam • Bonn • Sydney • Singapore
Tokyo • Madrid • San Juan • Milan • Mexico City • Seoul • Taipei

© Addison Wesley Longman 1996
Addison Wesley Longman Limited
Edinburgh Gate
Harlow
Essex
CM20 2JE
and associated Companies throughout the world.

Many of the designations used by manufactures and sellers to distinguish their products are claimed as trademarks. Addison-Wesley has made every attempt to supply trademark information about manufacturers and their products mentioned in this book.
Cover designed by Viva Design Ltd
and printed by The Riverside Printing Co. (Reading) Ltd
Typeset by Express Graphics Ltd, Basingstoke and Meridian Phototypesetting, Pangbourne
Printed and bound by The University Press at Cambridge.

First printed 1996

ISBN 0–201–877570

British Library Cataloguing-in-Publication Data
A catalogue record for this book is available from the British Library.

Library of Congress Cataloging-in-Publication Data is available

Preface

What is MATLAB?

MATLAB is a product of The MathWorks, Inc. and is an advanced interactive software package specially designed for scientific and engineering numerical computation. The MATLAB environment integrates graphics illustrations with precise numerical calculations, and is a powerful, easy-to-use, and comprehensive tool for performing all kinds of computations and scientific data visualization. MATLAB has proven to be a very flexible and usable tool for solving problems in applied mathematics, physics, chemistry, engineering, medicine, finance, and other application areas which deal with complicated numerical calculations. MATLAB is also an excellent pedagogical tool when teaching mathematics, numerical analysis, and engineering. The program is widely used at universities and colleges all around the world, and its popularity for industrial use is rapidly increasing. MATLAB is available on machines ranging from personal computers to supercomputers.

About MATLAB

The commands in MATLAB are expressed in notation close to that used in mathematics and engineering. For instance, to solve a linear system of equations, written as $\mathbf{Ax} = \mathbf{b}$ in matrix form, one first creates the coefficient matrix $\mathbf{A}$ and the right-hand side $\mathbf{b}$ and then simply types x = A\b. In a similar way, one can use short notations for finding, for example, solutions of ordinary differential equations, eigenvalues of a matrix, and interpolating or curve fitting of some given data.

There is a very large set of commands and available functions, also known as MATLAB M-files, that make life easier, since there is no need for programming in an ordinary high-level language such as C or FORTRAN. Hence, solving problems in MATLAB is generally much faster than traditional programming, and the code is clear and self-documented because of the natural notation. The algorithms used are robust and well-known numerical methods, programmed by leading experts in mathematical software. To obtain high performance, the MATLAB software is written in optimized C, with some important inner loops coded in assembly language. MATLAB's two- and three-dimensional graphics architecture is object-oriented, making it a powerful environment for construction of high-quality images and graphs. MATLAB is both an environment and a matrix/vector-orientated programming language, allowing the user to build her or his own reusable tools. With MATLAB code, one can easily create special user-defined M-files, for example, functions and programs, which solve certain problems.

Furthermore, there exists a large set of optional 'toolboxes' of functions for specific application purposes, for example, signal processing, optimization, symbolic math, and image analysis. All of these are written on top of MATLAB, and the toolboxes can be combined to form high performance design and analysis tools.

There are two basic versions of the software, the professional version distributed by The MathWorks, Inc., and the smaller Student edition of MATLAB, distributed by Prentice-Hall. The main restriction in the student edition is that the matrix size is limited to 8192 elements, and the number of rows and columns may not simultaneously be more than 32. Moreover, this version of MATLAB cannot dynamically link C or FORTRAN subroutines, that is, MEX-files. However, the student edition contains two specially designed toolboxes, known as the Signals and Systems Toolbox and the Symbolic Math Toolbox.

The main features of MATLAB are:

- advanced algorithms for high-performance numerical computations, especially in the field of matrix algebra;

- a large collection of predefined mathematical functions and the ability to define one's own functions;

- two- and three-dimensional graphics for plotting and displaying data and for pedagogical, scientific, and aesthetic illustrations and visualizations;

- powerful matrix/vector-oriented high-level programming language for individual applications;

- ability to cooperate with programs written in other languages and for importing and exporting data;

- toolboxes available for advanced problem solving in several application areas.

About *The MATLAB Handbook*

This book provides practical guidance on the use of MATLAB and shows how to create user-defined programs in MATLAB code. It is based on MATLAB version 4.2, but can also be used with other versions. Most of what appears in the text can be carried out with both the professional and student versions of the software. Some things cannot be performed with the student edition, however, and we have noted these at the beginning of sections where the differences occur. It is a concise reference book, but it also gives examples of how MATLAB can be used as a teaching tool in numerical analysis and mathematics and in other subjects where computations are useful. *The MATLAB Handbook* is a source of information that answers many of the frequently asked questions raised by both inexperienced and experienced MATLAB users.

The specific characteristics of the book are:

- it is discipline independent;

- it is a complete and reliable manual written in a succinct style;

- the MATLAB commands and functions should be easy to locate and simple to understand;

- concepts and problem fields should be easy to find;

- conceptually close commands are grouped together in chapters, sections and tables, to assist problem solving;

- each chapter, each section and each table starts with the most basic commands;

- it contains a number of straightforward examples and demonstrations of commands;

- the graphics of MATLAB are integrated into the text together with other commands, but are also covered more fully in two chapters;

- it contains definitions, basic concepts, and theory of linear algebra in an appendix;

- it contains a step-by-step introduction for beginners as an appendix;

- it contains a short description of the Student edition of MATLAB as an appendix.

Audience

The MATLAB Handbook is intended for all MATLAB users, from the beginner to those already familiar with the software. The book can be used by students of mathematics, engineering and natural sciences, but also applies to areas such as economics and statistics. It is also an invaluable reference guide for advanced users, such as scientists and engineers.

How to use *The MATLAB Handbook*

The material is logically organized and presented with examples throughout. It is comprehensive and self-contained. The chapters in *The MATLAB Handbook* can be read almost independently from each other. However, we recommend that a beginner starts with Chapter 1, which is a presentation of MATLAB, and follows on with Chapter 2, to learn the basics. It is recommended that a pure novice starts with Appendix A, a step-by-step introduction to MATLAB. There is also a list of references, a list of command and function tables and an index. Appendix B contains the basic definitions of concepts in linear algebra and Appendix C describes extension programs of MATLAB, that is, the currently available toolboxes and SIMULINK block-diagram modeling and simulation software. Commands and examples specific to the Student edition of MATLAB are covered in Appendix D. A quick reference to all commands and functions can be found in Appendix E.

The History of MATLAB and *The MATLAB Handbook*

MATLAB was originally written by Dr Cleve Moler, Chief Scientist at The MathWorks Inc., to provide easy access to matrix software developed in the LINPACK and EISPACK projects. The very first version was written in the late 1970s for use in courses in matrix theory, linear algebra, and numerical analysis. MATLAB is therefore built upon a foundation of sophisticated matrix software, in which the basic data element is a matrix that does not require predimensioning.

The Department of Scientific Computing at Uppsala University, Sweden, began using MATLAB in 1986 as a teaching tool in numerical analysis, especially in numerical linear algebra. The MATLAB software at that time was an academic version, written in FORTRAN code. Besides preparing exercises and assignments, the Department also wrote a handbook, This handbook which has since then been updated and extended.

This present *MATLAB Handbook*, written for MATLAB version 4.2, is a thoroughly revised edition of the Swedish original, *Användarhandledning för MATLAB*. The first edition has been used by several universities and colleges in Sweden.

Chapter 14, Advanced Graphics, is new, and has been written by Rickard Enander, Department of Scientific Computing, Uppsala University.

Comments and further information

Further information about MATLAB can be found in the WWW home pages of The MathWorks, Inc. The MathWorks, Inc. also maintains an archive of M-files on the anonymous ftp server **ftp.mathworks.com**.

Eva Pärt-Enander	Anders Sjöberg
Bo Melin	Pernilla Isaksson

June 1996

Comments on this book can be sent by e-mail or in an envelope marked 'MATLAB' to the following address:

Department of Scientific Computing
Uppsala University
P.O. Box 120
S–751 04 Uppsala
Sweden
e-mail: matlab@tdb.uu.se
www: http://www.tdb.uu.se

Comments to The MathWorks regarding MATLAB can be sent to

The MathWorks, Inc.
24 Prime Park Way
Natick, MA 01760
U.S.A
phone: (508) 653 1415
fax: (508) 653 2997
e-mail: info@mathworks.com
www: http://www.mathworks.com

Table of Contents

What is MATLAB?

And none of this would have been any fun without MATLAB.

Nachtigal, M. N., Reddy, S. C. and Trefethen, L. N. (1990).
How Fast are Nonsymmetric Matrix Iterations?
In *Proc. Copper Mountain Conference on Iterative Methods,*
Copper Mountain CO, 1–5 April, 1990.

1.1 What can be done in MATLAB?

MATLAB is a program for computation and visualization. MATLAB is widely used and is available on all kinds of computers, ranging from personal computers to supercomputers.

MATLAB is controlled by commands, and it is programmable. There are hundreds of predefined commands and functions and these functions can be further enlarged by user-defined functions.

MATLAB has powerful commands. MATLAB can, for instance, solve linear systems with one single command, and perform a lot of advanced matrix manipulations.

MATLAB has powerful tools for two– and three–dimensional graphics.

MATLAB can be used together with other programs. The graphics capabilities of MATLAB can, for instance, be used to visualize computations performed in a Fortran program.

There are about 25 different MATLAB toolboxes available for special application fields.

MATLAB is a very efficient tool for solving both small and large problems in a wide range of areas:

*   Research and development in industry.

*   Teaching mathematics, especially linear algebra. All basic concepts can be studied.

*   Teaching and research in numerical analysis and scientific computing. Algorithms can be studied in detail and compared with each other.

*   Teaching and research in engineering and scientific subjects, for example electronics, control theory and physics.

*   Teaching and research in all other fields where computational problems occur, such as economics, chemistry and biology.

The building block in MATLAB is the matrix, and the name MATLAB is derived from MATrix LABoratory.

1.2 Some MATLAB examples

The examples in this section are just a brief presentation of what MATLAB can do. In some cases we have given the complete MATLAB command and in other cases, for simplicity, only parts of the command.

The MATLAB code is shown in this book in a specific font to distinguish it from the rest of the text. The MATLAB output is in italics. We thus have:

> `This style for commands that we give to MATLAB.`
>
> *This style for what MATLAB gives as response.*

The percentage sign % is used in MATLAB as a symbol for comments and this is used throughout the book. Other notations we have used are italics for scalars and predefined functions and bold face for matrices, vectors and user-defined functions. Matrices are named with a capital letter first, and vectors with the whole word in lowercase letters.

■ **Example 1.1   Functions in 2D and 3D**

MATLAB can be used to calculate and graphically show functions in two and three dimensions. All elementary mathematical functions and a large number of advanced functions are included as MATLAB functions.

(a) We compute and plot $sin(2x)$, $sin\ x^2$ and sin^2x in the interval $0 < x < 6$ by giving short MATLAB commands.

```
x = linspace(0,6);    %  Creates a vector x.
y1 = sin(2*x)         %  The vector y1 contains the
                      %  sin(2x) values at the
                      %  x-coordinates defined by x.
y2 = sin(x.^2)        %  The vector y2 contains the
                      %  sin(x^2) ditto.
y3 = (sin(x)).^2      %  The vector y3 contains the
                      %  (sin(x))^2 ditto.
```

The command `plot(x,y1)` plots the vector **y1** as a function of vector **x**, the definition of the `plot` command can be found in Chapter 13. Thus we can easily draw the curves of $sin(2x)$, $sin\ x^2$ and sin^2x in a graph and label them correctly (Figure 1.1).

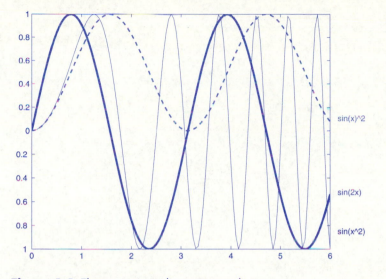

sin(x)^2

sin(2x)

sin(x^2)

Figure 1.1 Three curves in the same graph.

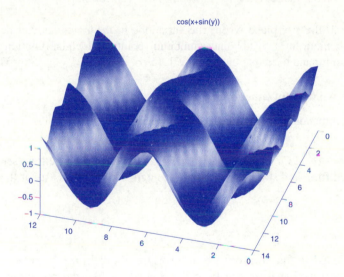

cos(x+sin(y))

Figure 1.2 A surface of a function of two variables.

(b) A function of two variables needs three dimensions to be properly visualized and MATLAB can give very good three-dimensional plots. In Figure 1.2 we show the function $f(x,y) = cos(x+siny)$. The commands used to create the picture are `surf` and `shading interp`. This same function is also shown in Figure C.5 in the color plate section, using `shading faceted` instead, which is the default shading for the `surf` command. This 3-D surface can be

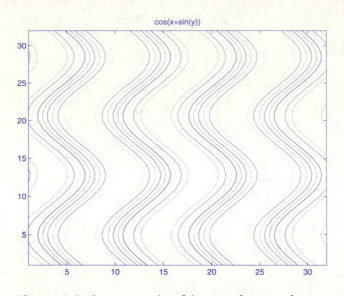

Figure 1.3 The contour plot of the same function of two variables.

projected on to the *x–y* plane where the variations in the functions can be displayed as contour lines, that is, lines combining points with equal function values. The command used to create Figure 1.3 is `contour`. ∎

■ **Example 1.2   Analysis of functions**

The MATLAB commands `fzero` and `fmin` can be used to find zeros and minima of a function.

The function $xe^{x^2} - e^{x^2} - \sin x^3$ can be written as a user-defined function (see Section 2.9) called **func** and stored as an M-file **func.m**. This file consists of the following lines:

```
function y = func(x)
y = x.*exp(x.^2) - exp(x.^2) - sin(x.^3);
```

If this M-file is saved in the directory we are working in, or in a subdirectory called **matlab**, the function **func** can be called upon just like the predefined MATLAB functions, for example, the call `xiszero = func(0)` gives us the answer:

xiszero =
  –1

With this function defined, MATLAB provides an instrument to find the zeros of the equation $xe^{x^2} - e^{x^2} - \sin x^3 = 0$. The command:

`xsolv = fzero('func',3)` gives us:

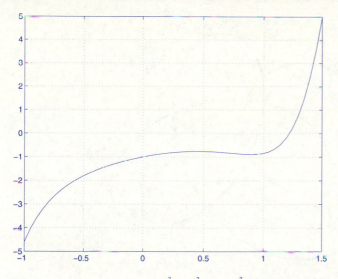

Figure 1.4 The function $xe^{x^2} - e^{x^2} - \sin x^3$ plotted in the interval $-1 < x < 1.5$.

> *xsolv =*
>
> *1.2194*

The second argument in the command, in this case with the value *3*, is a first guess we put into MATLAB.

If we plot the function in $-1 < x < 1.5$ we see that the answer is correct (Figure 1.4).

The function seems to have a minimum between *0.5* and *1*. To find out exactly where we can give the command `mpoint = fmin('func',0.5,1)`. The result is:

> *mpoint =*
>
> *0.8954*

The commands for examining user-defined functions in MATLAB can be found in Chapters 10 and 11. ∎

■ **Example 1.3   Parametric curves in 2D and 3D**

(a) It is also possible to plot a parametric curve, for instance:

$$\begin{cases} x = \cos t - \sin 3t \\ y = \sin t \cos t - \cos 3t \end{cases}$$

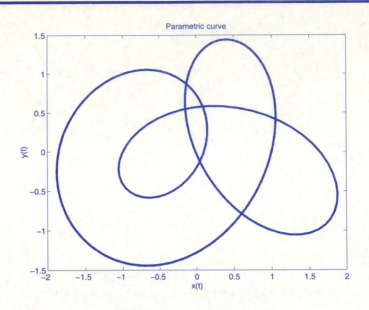

Figure 1.5 A parametric curve.

The plot in the *x-y* plane will be Figure 1.5.

(b) It is also possible to draw parametric curves and surfaces in three dimensions, such as the helicoidal surface in Figure 1.6 that is described by the parametric equations:

$$\begin{cases} x = \dfrac{t}{30}u\cos t + 10 \\[2mm] y = \dfrac{t}{55}u\sin t + 10 \\[2mm] z = t \end{cases}$$

Without the parameter *u*, which varies between *0* and *1*, we would only get a helicoidal curve drawn in three dimensions. Figure 1.6 is made with the commands `surf` and `shading flat`.

In MATLAB we can choose to show only the surface of the function without the x, y, z-axes as we have done in Figure 1.6. MATLAB's graphical facilities are described in Chapters 13 and 14. ∎

■ **Example 1.4   Linear systems and eigenvalues**

(a) MATLAB can solve linear systems with one single command line. Let the coefficient matrix **A** and the right-hand side **b** be defined as:

Figure 1.6 A helicoidal surface.

$$A = \begin{bmatrix} 3 & 1 & -1 \\ 1 & 2 & 4 \\ -1 & 4 & 5 \end{bmatrix} \qquad b = \begin{bmatrix} 3.6 \\ 2.1 \\ -1.4 \end{bmatrix}$$

This correspond to the linear system $A\,x = b$ which looks like:

$$\begin{cases} 3x_1 + x_2 - x_3 = 3.6 \\ x_1 + 2x_2 + 4x_3 = 2.1 \\ -x_1 + 4x_2 + 5x_3 = -1.4 \end{cases}$$

and is solved by the command:

```
x = A\b
```

The result is:

```
x =
```

$$1.4818$$
$$-0.4606$$
$$0.3848$$

(b) There is also a large number of matrix manipulation commands. For instance, the eigenvalues of the matrix **A** from the example in (a) can easily be found by the command:

```
[eigenvectors,eigenvalues] = eig(A)
```

which gives:

eigenvectors =

−0.9482	−0.3129	−0.0553
−0.2887	0.7756	0.5613
0.1328	−0.5482	0.8258

eigenvalues =

3.4445	0	0
0	−1.2305	0
0	0	7.7860

The columns of the matrix **eigenvectors** are the eigenvectors of **A** and the elements on the diagonal of **eigenvalues** are the eigenvalues. Since the matrix **A** is symmetric all eigenvalues are real and the three eigenvectors are mutually orthogonal.

An essential concept in MATLAB is the matrix. Basic matrix instructions are presented in Chapter 3, and further commands are given in Chapters 4, 7, 8 and 9. ■

■ **Example 1.5   Curve fitting and interpolation**

(a) If we have a set of points in the *x*–*y* plane represented by two vectors **x** and **y**, then we can interpolate the points or fit a curve to them. Let

$$\mathbf{x} = \begin{bmatrix} 1 & 1.5 & 3 & 4 & 5 & 6 & 6.5 & 7 & 8 \end{bmatrix}$$

$$\mathbf{y} = \begin{bmatrix} 1.2 & 1 & 1.7 & 2.5 & 2 & 2.3 & 2.5 & 3 & 3.1 \end{bmatrix}$$

correspond to *9* points in the *x*–*y* plane. First, we show the linear function that fits the data in the least square sense. This is obtained by three simple command lines in MATLAB:

```
p1 = polyfit(x,y,1);    %   p1 = A vector containing the
                        %   coefficients for a polynomial
                        %   of degree one.
linc = polyval(p1,x);   %   linc = A vector containing the
                        %   values of the polynomial p1 in
                        %   the points x.
plot(x,linc,x,y,'x')    %   Plots the polynomial and the
                        %   data marked by 'x'.
```

See Figure 1.7 (a), for the result.

We can fit polynomials of higher degrees to the set of points in least square sense. The command lines from above will have to be changed a little to obtain a polynomial of degree seven instead:

```
p7 = polyfit(x,y,7);   %   p7 = A vector containing the
                       %   coefficients for a polynomial
                       %   of degree 7.
xx = 1:.25:8;          %   xx = All points in which we
                       %   want the polynomial computed.
polc = polyval(p7,xx)  %   polc = A vector containing the
                       %   values of the polynomial p7 in
                       %   the points xx.
plot(xx,polc,x,y,'x')  %   Plots the polynomial and the
                       %   data marked by 'x'.
```

The result of this is shown in Figure 1.7 (b).

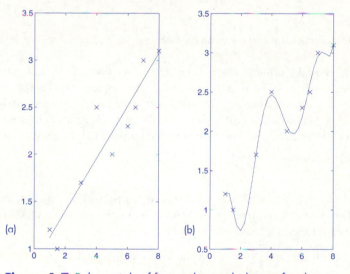

(a)   (b)

Figure 1.7 Polynomials of first and seventh degree fitted to the set of data consisting of nine points in the *x*–*y* plane.

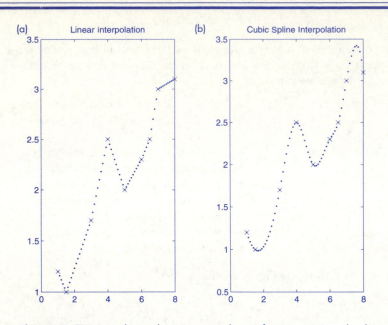

Figure 1.8 Interpolation by piecewise linear functions (a) and cubic splines (b).

(b) MATLAB provides interpolation functions for both two and three dimensions. Given a set of points, (x_i, y_i) and some intermediate points, $\tilde{x}_i$, MATLAB can return the values in those intermediate points by interpolating the data. This can be done in different ways. As an example we will use the set of points from (a) to give the interpolated values in the following points:

$$\tilde{x} = \begin{bmatrix} 1 & 1.1 & 1.2 & 1.3 & \dots & 7.9 & 8 \end{bmatrix}$$

In Figure 1.8 we show piece-wise linear and cubic spline interpolation respectively. The 'x'-marks represent the original set of data, and the dotted lines are the interpolated functions in the intermediate points.

More about interpolation and curve fitting can be found in Chapter 10.   ■

■ **Example 1.6   Statistics**

MATLAB conains statistical commands. For example, we can easily find mean and median values out of experimental data and also plot histograms or bar graphs.

Figure 1.9 displays the age of everyone in Littletown. Section (a) is a histogram where the number of persons of every age is shown. For instance, we can see that the two oldest persons are 92 years old. The histogram also shows that there is no one in Littletown of age 11 or 12 and seven children of age 7.

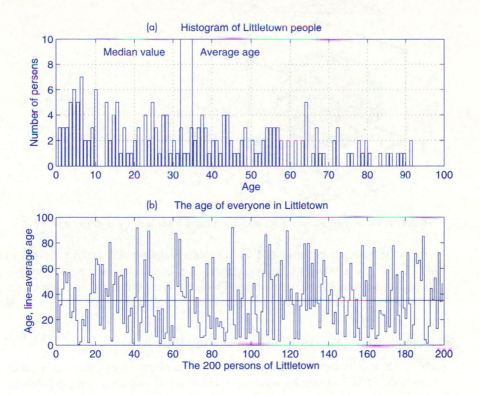

Figure 1.9 A histogram and a bar graph of data from Littletown.

We can also see that there are as many people aged over 32 as there are aged under, since the median age is 32. Furthermore, the average age is 35. This is also marked in Section (b).

Figure 1.9 (b) shows the age of all inhabitants in Littletown. For example, if we knew the eleventh person to be listed we would also know that this person is just a baby, since the eleventh bar touches the x-axis. This kind of plot is called a stairstep graph, that is, a bar graph with no internal lines.

The statistics commands are presented in Chapter 6.   ■

■ **Example 1.7   Geometrical illustration**

MATLAB can be used to visualize complicated geometrical figures, for instance a sphere inside a cube inside a sphere (see Figure 1.10). The program which produced this diagram is presented in Chapter 14.

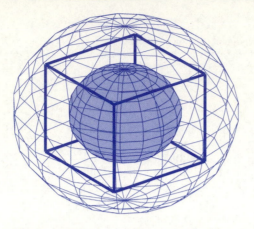

Figure 1.10 A unit sphere inscribed by a cube inscribed by a larger sphere.

Any shape that can be described by mathematical formulas can be viewed in MATLAB. For complicated figures there are other alternatives. Try typing `makevase` in your MATLAB command window! That command is a part of the MATLAB `expo`. See also the command `ginput` in Section 13.3.   ■

■ **Example 1.8   Fourier transform and signal analysis**

MATLAB can compute a discrete Fourier transform using the fast Fourier transform, FFT. This can be used in signal analysis and in solving differential equations.

To demonstrate the Fourier transform in MATLAB we perturb the function $5\sin(x) + 2\sin(5x)$ using random numbers with expectation value 0 and variance 1:

```
x = linspace(0,2*pi,64);
signal = 5*sin(x) + 2*sin(5*x) + randn(x);
```

The perturbed and the original signal are shown in Figure 1.11 (a). Then we transform the signal and delete all high frequencies in the transformed signal, that is, the central part of the coefficient vector is set to zero.

```
transf = fft(signal);
filttransf(1:9) = transf(1:9);
filttransf(56:64) = transf(56:64);
```

The real part of the Fourier transform is shown in Figure 1.11 (b) and the Fourier transform with the high frequencies deleted in Figure 1.11 (c).

The vector with only the low frequencies is retransformed:

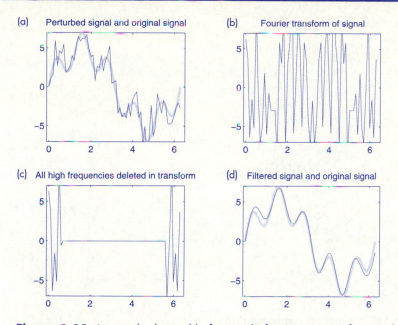

Figure 1.11 A perturbed signal before and after Fourier transform and filtering. The discrete Fourier transform has the high frequencies represented in the middle of the vector.

```
filtsig = ifft(filttransf);
```

This filtered signal along with the original signal are shown in Figure 1.11 (d). The filtered signal is smooth, as expected. It is not equal to the original signal since the perturbation also affected the low–frequency part of the signal.

In Section 10.5 the Fourier transforms that come as a part of MATLAB are presented. For more information about the Signal Processing Toolbox see Appendix C. ∎

■ Example 1.9 Ordinary differential equations

MATLAB can solve ordinary differential equations numerically. As an example we show the solution of the classical prey–predator problem:

$$
\begin{cases}
\dfrac{dx_1}{dt} = x_1 - \dfrac{1}{10}x_1x_2 \\[2mm]
\dfrac{dx_2}{dt} = x_2 - \dfrac{1}{40}x_1x_2 \\[2mm]
x_1(0) = 20 \\[1mm]
x_2(0) = 20
\end{cases}
$$

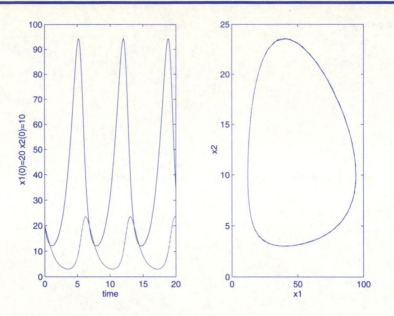

Figure 1.12 A prey–predator problem.

The number of prey is represented by the function $x_1(t)$ and the number of predators by the function $x_2(t)$. The solutions and their phase portrait can be seen in Figure 1.12. In Section 11.2 we show how to use MATLAB for ordinary differential equation problems in general. ∎

■ **Example 1.10   Partial differential equations**

There are toolboxes in MATLAB for different applications. Here we give as an example the PDE Toolbox, which can solve elliptic, parabolic and hyperbolic equations in two-dimensional geometry by using the Finite Element Method. The region is divided into a large number of triangular subregions. For each triangle the solution is approximated by a simple function and the error will be smaller the more triangles we use.

We have solved the elliptic problem

$-\Delta u = sin(2\pi y + \pi/2)\ cos(2\pi x + \pi/2)$ in the region shown in Figure 1.13.

The Laplace operator Δ is $\dfrac{\partial^2}{\partial x^2} + \dfrac{\partial^2}{\partial y^2}$. On the boundaries we have Dirichlet conditions $u=0$. The triangulation made by PDE Toolbox is also shown.

The solution of the problem can be visualized as a 2D plot with contour lines as in Figure 1.14.

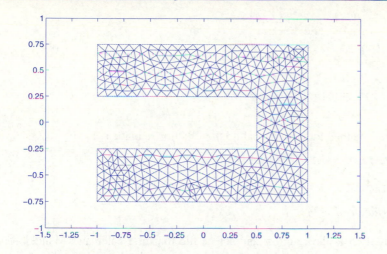

Figure 1.13 Triangulation for FEM by PDE Toolbox.

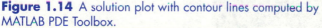

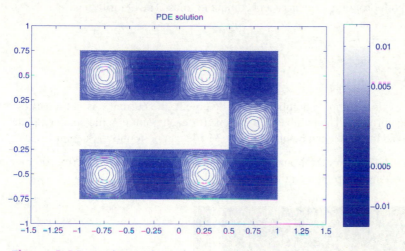

Figure 1.14 A solution plot with contour lines computed by MATLAB PDE Toolbox.

▪ Example 1.11 Programming in MATLAB

MATLAB is programmable. Sequences of commands can be written in a text editor and then the user-defined function or program from the MATLAB command window can be called. The name of the file must have the extension .m and the file is called an M-file. These M-files can be used in the same way as all the standard MATLAB functions.

(a) The factorial, $n! = 1 \cdot 2 \cdot 3 \cdot \ldots \cdot n$, can be computed in different ways. Here we show a user-defined function which is recursive:

```
function p = factorial(nn)
% Computes the factorial of nn.
if (nn == 1)
    p = 1;
else
    p = nn*factorial(nn - 1);
end
```

The M-file is named **fac.m** and a call to the function is made by:

```
fourfactorial = factorial(4)
```

The result is:

fourfactorial = 24

(b) Figure 1.15 is the result of another M-file that first calculates Mandelbrot values in a grid defined by the user in the complex plane according to an algorithm and thereafter visualize the result. Thus, an M-file can contain both program sequences and command lines. The algorithm is:

$$\begin{cases} z_0 = 0 \\ z_{i+1} = z_i^2 + c \end{cases}$$

where c is a complex number. If z_i is divergent, the current c is not a part of the Mandelbrot set. The number of iterations for each point c in the complex plane is saved so the result can be plotted. This M-file can be found in Section 13.3.

Figure 1.15 shows the Mandelbrot fractal with a resolution of *100 × 100* points in a rectangular region on the complex plane.

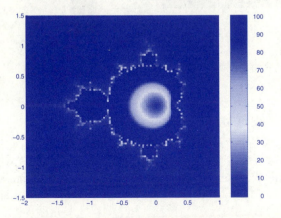

Figure 1.15 Mandelbrot fractal computed by MATLAB.

For more about programming MATLAB, see Chapter 12. ∎

∎ Example 1.12   Graphical user interface

MATLAB offers an opportunity to design easy-to-use programs. Program can be manipulated by push buttons, pop-up menus, editable text, and so on, in a control figure. This is described in Section 14.4. In Figure 1.16, we show an example of such a graphical user interface designed by a Swedish scientist. The program is used for solving a model equation on non-equidistant grids.

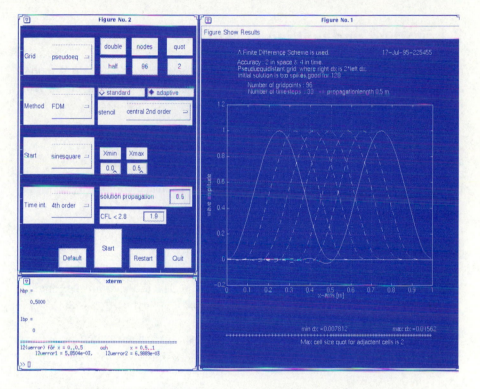

Figure 1.16 A MATLAB program with graphical user interface applications. ∎

2 Getting Started

Firstly, we describe how to start and, just as important, how to quit MATLAB. Then we describe how assignments and computations are made. We also demonstrate how to save results, get help and how to define your own functions. Some of the contents of this chapter can be skipped by inexperienced MATLAB users. However, we recommend a quick browse of the chapter. We also recommend the step-by-step introduction in Appendix A.

2.1 Starting and quitting in MATLAB

How MATLAB is started varies between different computer systems. In Windows and Macintosh systems, the program is usually started by clicking on an icon. In UNIX systems the program is started by typing:

```
matlab
```

at the command line prompt.

If none of the suggestions above work, ask the systems manager.

To quit MATLAB type `quit` or `exit`.

Command 1	EXIT AND INTERRUPTION

`exit, quit`	ends the MATLAB session. The program finishes and values of variables are lost if not explicitly saved; see Section 2.8.
`Ctrl-c`	interrupts a MATLAB task, for instance when MATLAB is computing or printing, but the session is not ended.

Apart from this there are menu options specified for some systems. As an example, the option `quit` can be found under the `file menu` in Windows and Macintosh systems.

The following keyboard shortcuts are very useful when editing or executing MATLAB. When alternatives are given, it is usually because different keys are valid on different platforms. Try these keys on your system, and note which key combinations apply.

Command 2	SPECIAL FUNCTION KEYS

↑ or `Ctrl-p`	recalls previous commands.
↓ or `Ctrl-n`	recalls commands typed later than the current command.
→ or `Ctrl-f`	moves one character right.
← or `Ctrl-b`	moves one character left.
`Delete`, `Backspace`	deletes character.
`Ctrl-l` or `Ctrl-←`	moves one word left.
`Ctrl-r` or `Ctrl-→`	moves one word right.
`Ctrl-a` or `Home`	moves to first character of line.
`Ctrl-k`	deletes to end of line.
`cedit`	toggles between different shortcuts. Type `help` `cedit` for more information.

2.2 Introduction to matrices in MATLAB

The basic format for data in MATLAB is the **matrix**. A matrix is a rectangular table with the elements ordered in **rows** and **columns**. If it has m rows and n columns the matrix is said to have the **size** $m \times n$, or is of type $m \times n$.

■ **Example 2.1**

A 2×3 matrix can look like:

$$A = \begin{bmatrix} 1 & 2 & 3 \\ 4 & 5 & 6 \end{bmatrix} = \begin{bmatrix} a_{11} & a_{12} & a_{13} \\ a_{21} & a_{22} & a_{23} \end{bmatrix}$$

The first row is $\begin{bmatrix} 1 & 2 & 3 \end{bmatrix}$ and the second column is $\begin{bmatrix} 2 \\ 5 \end{bmatrix}$　■

The **elements**, that is the numbers a_{ij}, of the matrix are usually real, but can also be complex numbers. An element a_{ij} is referred to by the row index i and the column index j. In Example 2.1, we have $a_{21} = 4$.

When the matrix consists of only one row it is a special case; then it is a **row vector**. If the matrix has only one column, we have a **column vector**. Vectors are special cases of matrices. The number of elements in a vector is called the **length** of the vector.

If the matrix is of size *1 × 1* it is a **scalar**, that is, a number.

A variable is defined in MATLAB by assigning it a value. This is done as follows:

```
variable = expression
```

After *expression* press the carriage return key. The *expression* can consist of numbers, variables, operators, functions, and so on.

An alternative way of defining a variable is to enter the term *expression*. MATLAB then assigns the value of the expression to the predefined variable **ans**, an abbreviation of 'answer'.

Assignment of a matrix can be done in several ways, the easiest of which is to give the elements row by row surrounded by brackets, `[]`. Brackets are not needed when a scalar is defined.

Elements in the same row are separated by one or more blanks or a semicolon `;` or 'carriage return'. Each command given without a finishing semicolon displays the result on to the screen. With a semicolon at the end, the computation is performed, but the result is not displayed.

The value of a variable is obtained by printing its name and pressing carriage return. MATLAB answers by displaying both the variable name and the value. If the variable does not exist, an error message is displayed. An alternative way to display the contents of a variable is given in Section 5.3.

A specific element of a matrix or a vector is referred to by specifying its indices:

```
variable(rowindex,columnindex)
```

If the variable is a vector, only one index is needed.

■ **Example 2.2**

(a) Assignment of a scalar. If x = 7 is written the following is printed on the screen:

$x =$
    7

(b) If only 7 is written the result becomes:

ans =
    7

(c) The definition of a matrix, in this case of size 2×3, can be made by giving the elements row by row:

```
A = [1 2 3
4 5 6]
```

which gives the following on the screen:

A =

1	*2*	*3*
4	*5*	*6*

(d) It is also possible to give all the elements on the same line with semicolons to separate the rows:

```
A = [1 2 3;4 5 6];
```

A semicolon after the command suppresses the print-out of the result.

(e) Definition of a row vector and a column vector:

```
rowvec = [1.2 3.2 4];
colvec = [2.7; 3.4; -9.2];
```

(f) Displaying the value of a variable. By writing `colvec` MATLAB displays:

colvec =

   2.7000

   3.4000

 −9.2000

(g) Assignment of a matrix element by element:

```
B(1,1) =   1;
B(1,2) =   7;
B(2,1) =  -5;
B(2,2) =   0
```

gives us the result:

B =

1	*7*
−5	*0*

MATLAB allows several variables to be defined on the same command line. It is also possible to continue a large assignment on the next line by typing three dots before pressing carriage return.

■ **Example 2.3**

(a) Several commands on the same line:

```
x = 7; y = 4.6735567; z = x^y;
```

(b) A long command divided into several lines:

```
mat1 = [1.2 1.1 −1.1 1.4 1.1 −1.1 −1.2 ...
−1.1 −1.3 1.7];
```
■

MATLAB remembers the sizes of the different matrix variables. To obtain the size of a certain variable the commands `size` and `length` are used.

Let **A** now be an $m \times n$ matrix and **x** an $m \times 1$ matrix (a column vector) or a $1 \times n$ matrix (a row vector). MATLAB has the following commands:

Command 3   SIZE OF VARIABLES

`size(A)`	gives a row vector containing the size of **A**. The first element in the returned vector is the number of rows, and the second is the number of columns.
`[m,n] = size(A)`	gives the size of **A**, as the number of rows m and the number of columns n, that is two scalars.
`size(A,p)`	gives the number of rows in **A** if $p <= 1$ and the number of columns in **A** if $p >= 2$.
`size(x)`	gives a row vector with the size of the vector **x**. If **x** is a column vector, the first element will be m and the second 1. If **x** is a row vector the first element is 1 and the second n.
`length(x)`	gives the length of a vector, that is n if **x** is a row vector and m if **x** is a column vector.
`length(A)`	gives the largest number of m and n.

Note: Sometimes the word 'dimension' is used instead of size and length. It is also common for length to be associated with vector norm, and for size of matrix to be associated with matrix norm. However, in this handbook size and length are used in the same meaning as `size` and `length`. When the concept length is used in the other sense, this is specified to avoid misunderstandings.

■ **Example 2.4**

The command `thesize - size(A)`, where **A** is the same as in Example 2.2(c) above, returns

    thesize =

       2   3   ■

2.3 Variables in MATLAB

Names of variables can be *19* characters long in MATLAB. Letters A–Z, a–z, numbers, and the underscore sign can be a part of it, but the first character has to be a letter. The name of a predefined function can also be used as a variable name, but this is not recommended since the function cannot be used until the variable is deleted by the command `clear`.

Normally, MATLAB makes distinctions between uppercase and lowercase letters, for example the matrices a and A are not the same. MATLAB commands are normally written with lowercase letters. As an example, the command `abs(A)` gives the absolute value of **A**, but `ABS(A)` results in the following error message being displayed on screen:

    ??? Undefined variable or function ABS; Caps Lock may be on

But it is possible to make MATLAB accept both uppercase and lowercase letters in commands to cancel distinctions between upper and lower case in names of variables. This is done by the command `casesen`.

Command 4	CAPITAL LETTERS IN IDENTIFIERS

`casesen on`	MATLAB makes a distinction between uppercase and lowercase letters.
`casesen off`	makes no distinction between uppercase and lowercase letters, everything is considered to be lowercase. If the same letters are used in names using both uppercase and lowercase letters only the one using lowercase letters will be accessible.

There are a number of predefined variables in MATLAB as follows:

Command 5	PREDEFINED VARIABLES IN MATLAB

`ans`	is assigned the value of the latest computed expression if this is not given a name.
`eps`	returns the machine accuracy, defined as the distance between *1* and the next representable floating point value. The number *eps* is used as tolerance in some commands. The user can assign a new value to *eps,* but note that the value of *eps* is not restored by the command `clear`.
`realmax`	returns the largest floating point number the computer can handle.
`realmin`	returns the smallest floating point number the computer can handle.
`pi`	returns π, that is *3.141592653589793*, with an accuracy of about *16* decimals if *eps* is small enough.
`inf`	is defined as *1/0*. When division by zero occurs MATLAB returns *inf* and continues to compute without interrupting the execution.
`NaN`	is defined as 'Not a Number'. This non-number is either of the type `0/0` or `inf/inf`.
`i,j`	are defined as $\sqrt{-1}$, the imaginary unit. We can assign *i* and *j* other values, and they will no longer be predefined constants. They are restored by the `clear` command; see below.
`nargin`	gives the number of input arguments in a function call (see Section 12.3).
`nargout`	gives the number of output arguments in a function call (see Section 12.3).

To find which variables are defined the following commands can be used:

Command 6	LIST OF VARIABLES

`who`	gives a list of the defined variables.
`who global`	as above, but only the global variables are listed (see Section 12.3).
`whos`	gives a more detailed list than the command `who`, for example the sizes of the matrices are shown.

Command 6	**LIST OF VARIABLES** (continued)

`whos global`	as above, but only the global variables are listed (see Section 12.3).
`exist(namestr)`	returns different values depending on how the variable in the string **namestr** is defined. (For more information about strings see Chapter 5.) For now it is only important that the name of the variable should be given between quotation marks ' '. The function returns the value:

    1.   if **namestr** is the name of a variable;

    2.   if **namestr** is the name of an M-file (see Section 2.9);

    3.   if **namestr** is the name of a MEX-file (see Chapter 15);

    4.   if **namestr** is a compiled SIMULINK function;

    5.   if **namestr** is the name of a predefined MATLAB function.

Every variable that is defined will remain throughout the whole session if it is not deleted or renamed by the user. To delete variables, which is advisable when dealing with very large matrices, for example, the command `clear` is used.

Command 7	**DELETING VARIABLES**

`clear`	deletes all variables and restores all predefined variables except *eps*.
`clear name`	deletes only the variable *name*.
`clear name1,name2...`	deletes the variables *name1, name2, ...*
`clear value`	gives different results depending on *value*. Type `help clear` for details.
`pack`	rearranges and compacts the allocated memory, a so-called 'garbage collection'. When MATLAB's memory is full you can obtain more space with the command `pack` without clearing any variables. What happens is the following:

    1. all variables are saved on disc in a temporary file **pack.tmp**;

    2. the contents of the primary memory are deleted;

    3. all variables are loaded in primary memory from **pack.tmp**;

    4. the file **pack.tmp** is deleted;

Command 7	DELETING VARIABLES (continued)

`pack filename`	rearranges and compacts the allocated memory by using the file *filename* as temporary file.

Type `help clear`, `help memory` and `help pack` to get more information on how to save memory space in MATLAB.

Remark: Commands in MATLAB are actually considered to be functions, taking strings as arguments. This means that the two statements

```
command argument
```

and

```
command('argument')
```

are equal. For instance, `clear name` gives the same result as `clear('name')` and `who global` is equivalent to `who('global')`. Other examples can be found in several parts of the book, for example `axis square` and `axis('square')` in Section 13.3. The possibility to use the function/string formulation makes the MATLAB programming language very flexible, since command arguments may be created using string manipulation commands (see Chapter 5).

2.4 Arithmetic expressions and mathematical functions

Common conventions are used to write numbers in MATLAB. The decimal point is used and scientific notation makes it possible to write very large and very small numbers. Examples are *3.14* and *1.23E–6*, where the second stands for $1.23 \cdot 10^{-6}$.

MATLAB has an extended set of **arithmetic operators**, and these are:

1. ^   power

2. *   multiplication

    /   right division (ordinary division)

    \   left division

3. +   addition

    –   subtraction

The operators are given in order of precedence, where 1 is of highest precedence. In expressions with the operators of the same precedence they are executed from left to right. Parentheses, ( ), can be used to change the order of precedence.

In Section 3.3 we shall see that it is useful to have two different kinds of division. For scalars the right division $2/5$ giving *0.4* is the same as the left division $5\backslash2$. It is the expression or number that the slash 'leans' on that is the denominator.

■ **Example 2.5**

If we write $a/b + c$ MATLAB reads it as $\frac{a}{b} + c$ but the expression $a/(b+c)$ is read $\frac{a}{b+c}$.

If we use left division $a\backslash(b+c)$, MATLAB interprets it as $\frac{b+c}{a}$. ■

MATLAB contains predefined mathematical functions which can be used in arithmetic expressions. If the argument is complex, so in most cases is the answer.

MATLAB can also compute expressions containing predefined variables, for example an expression can be used as an argument for a function.

The predefined mathematical functions are listed in Command 8. Even if these functions are described for scalar arguments, we shall see in Section 3.6 that they can handle vectors and matrices as well. Note that all trigonometric functions require that the arguments are given in radians.

| **Command 8** | **MATHEMATICAL FUNCTIONS** |

`abs(x)`	gives the absolute value of x, that is $|x|$.
`sign(x)`	gives the sign of x, *1* if positive, *−1* if negative and *0* if zero.
`sqrt(x)`	gives the square root of x, that is $\sqrt{x}$.
`pow2(x,f)`	gives $x*2^f$. This is a very efficient operation since it is performed as an addition of f to the exponent in the floating point format of x.
`exp(x)`	gives the exponential function of x, that is e^x.
`log(x)`	gives the natural logarithm of x, that is *ln x*.
`log10(x)`	gives the base 10 logarithm of x, that is $log_{10} x$.
`log2(x)`	gives the base 2 logarithm of x, that is $log_2 x$.
`sin(x)`	gives *sin x*, x in radians.
`cos(x)`	gives *cos x*, x in radians.
`tan(x)`	gives *tan x*, x in radians.
`cot(x)`	gives *cot x*, that is *1/(tan x)*, x in radians.

Command 8	MATHEMATICAL FUNCTIONS (continued)
`asin(x)`	gives *arcsin x*, that is $sin^{-1}x$.
`acos(x)`	gives *arccos x*, that is $cos^{-1}x$.
`atan(x)`	gives *arctan x*, that is $tan^{-1}x$.
`atan2(x,y)`	gives *arctan (x/y)* and the result is in the interval $[-\pi,\pi]$.
`acot(x)`	gives *arccot x*, that is *1/ (arctan x)*.
`sec(x)`	gives *1/(cos x)*.
`csc(x)`	gives *1/(sin x)*.
`asec(x)`	gives *1/(arccos x)*.
`acsc(x)`	gives *1/(arcsin x)*.
`sinh(x)`	gives *sinh x*.
`cosh(x)`	gives *cosh x*.
`tanh(x)`	gives *tanh x*.
`coth(x)`	gives *coth x,* that is *1/(tanh x)*.
`asinh(x)`	gives *arcsinh x*.
`acosh(x)`	gives *arccosh x*.
`atanh(x)`	gives *arctanh x*.
`acoth(x)`	gives *arccoth x*, that is *1/(arctanh x)*.
`sech(x)`	gives *1/(cosh x)*.
`csch(x)`	gives *1/(sinh x)*.
`asech(x)`	gives *1/(arccosh x)*.
`acsch(x)`	gives *1/(arcsinh x)*.

■ **Example 2.6**

   (a) If we type `sinepi = sin(pi)` we get:

      sinepi =

      1.2246e–16

      The result is not exactly *0* since `pi` is an approximation of π and since we have round-off errors in the computation.

   (b) `logarithm = log10(100)`

      logarithm =

        2

   (c) `e = exp(1)`

      e =

        2.7183

There are several commands for rounding numbers. In Command 9 below x is a floating point number or a matrix with floating point elements.

Command 9	ROUNDING COMMANDS AND RELATED COMMANDS

`round(x)`	gives the integer closest to x. If x is a vector this holds for all components.
`fix(x)`	gives the integer closest to x in the direction towards 0, that is upwards for negative x and downwards for positive.
`floor(x)`	gives the closest integer below x.
`ceil(x)`	gives the closest integer above x.
`rem(x,y)`	gives the remainder of the integer division x/y.
`gcd(x,y)`	gives the greatest common divisor of the integers x and y.
`[g,c,d] = gcd(x,y)`	gives g, c, d such that $g = x\,c + y\,d$.
`lcm(x,y)`	gives the least common multiple of positive integers x and y, and can be used to determine the least common denominator.
`[t,n] = rat(x)`	gives an approximation of x by the rational number t/n, where t and n are integers. The relative error is less than 10^{-6}. See also `rats`, Section 5.2, that gives the corresponding string.
`[t,n] = rat(x,tol)`	gives two integers of a rational number as the previous command but the relative error is *tol*.
`rat(x)`	gives the continued fraction representation of x.
`rat(x,tol)`	gives the continued fraction representation of x with relative error *tol*.

■ **Example 2.7**

(a) Rounding can be done in several ways:

The commands $x = -1.49;$

`rdx = round(x),fixx = fix(x), flx = floor(x), clx = ceil(x)`

return

rdx =
    −1
fixx =
    −1
flx =
    −2
clx =
    −1

(b) We approximate $\sqrt{2}$ by a rational number t/n:

```
[t,n] = rat(sqrt(2))
```

t =

    1393

n =

    985

To compare with the true value we type `differ = sqrt(2) − t/n` which gives:

differ =

3.6440e–07

As we can see, the difference is not large and will be even smaller if we specify a smaller value for the parameter *tol* in the function `rat`. ■

Complex valued expressions are allowed in most applications in MATLAB. The built-in variables *i* and *j* return the **imaginary unit**, that is the value of $\sqrt{-1}$, and can be used to generate complex numbers. It is possible to use the names *i* and *j* as names of variables and a new complex unit can be generated by:

```
ii = sqrt(−1);
```

One has to be careful with blanks when writing complex elements in a matrix since blanks will separate the elements (see Example 2.8(c) below).

■ **Example 2.8**

```
(a) z = 3 + 4 i
```

z =

    3.0000 + 4.0000i

(b) A more complicated expression can look like:

```
w = r*exp(i*theta); comp = z*w;
```

where `r` and `theta` are already defined variables.

(c) Vectors can be complex as well:

```
complexvector = [1−i 2−2i 3 −3i] returns:
```

complexvector =

    1.0000 − 1.0000i   2.0000 − 2.0000i 3.0000 0   − 3.0000i

The blank between `3` and `−3i` forces MATLAB to read them as two separate complex numbers. ■

There are some functions dealing with complex numbers and functions.

Command 10	FUNCTIONS ON COMPLEX NUMBERS

`real(z)`	gives the real part of z.
`imag(z)`	gives the imaginary part of z.
`abs(z)`	gives the absolute value of z, that is $\|z\|$.
`conj(z)`	gives the complex conjugate of z, that is $\bar{z}$.
`angle(z)`	gives the phase angle of z, that is θ in $$z = x + iy = re^{i\theta}.$$
`unwrap(v)`	gives a vector of the same length as **v**, where the differences in phase angle between two consecutive elements have been changed so that the difference is at most π.
`unwrap(v,k)`	gives a vector just as above, but uses jump tolerance k instead of π.
`cplxpair(v)`	gives a vector where the elements of **v** have been sorted by increasing real part and the complex numbers have been ordered in pairs with their complex conjugate. In one pair the negative imaginary part stands first. Real elements are sorted at the end in the vector. If a complex element of **v** has not got its complex conjugate in **v**, an error message is displayed.

■ **Example 2.9**

Let the complex number z be:

```
z = 1 + 2 i;
```

(a) The real and imaginary parts of z are given by:

```
realpart = real(z), imagpart = imag(z)
```
realpart =
     1
imagpart =
     2

(b) The complex conjugate is given by `conjugate = conj(z)`

conjugate =
     1.0000 − 2.0000i

and the absolute value of z `absz = abs(z)`

    absz =

        2.2361

(c) The argument of a complex number, that is the phase angle in the complex plane, is given by `arg = angle(z)`

    arg =

        1.1071   ■

There are also functions for transformations between coordinate systems. These functions can operate on vectors and matrices as well, and then the result will be of the same size as the input argument.

Command 11   **COORDINATE TRANSFORMATION**

`[theta,r] = cart2pol(x,y)`	transforms from Cartesian to polar coordinates. The polar coordinates *theta* and *r* are given from the Cartesian *x* and *y*.
`[x,y] = pol2cart(theta,r)`	transforms from polar to Cartesian coordinates. The Cartesian coordinates *x* and *y* are given from the polar *theta* and *r*.
`[alpha,theta,r] = cart2sph(x,y,z)`	transforms from Cartesian to spherical coordinates. The angles *alpha*, *theta* and the length *r* are given from the Cartesian coordinates *x*, *y* and *z*.
`[x,y,z] = sph2cart( alpha,theta,r)`	transforms from spherical to Cartesian coordinates, *x*, *y* and *z* are given from the spherical coordinates *alpha*, *theta* and *r*.

There are also more advanced mathematical functions predefined in MATLAB.

| Command 12 | SPECIAL MATHEMATICAL FUNCTIONS |

`legendre(n,x)`	returns a vector of length $n + 1$ representing the associated Legendre functions of degree n and order 0 to n computed in x. If $x = \mathbf{x}$ is a vector the command returns a matrix, the columns of which are the associated Legendre functions computed for each element of $\mathbf{x}$. The elements of $\mathbf{x}$ must be in the interval $[-1,1]$.
`bessel(n,x)`	gives Bessel functions of the first kind. Both n and x can be vectors but n must increase in steps of one and be in the interval $[0,1000]$. This command calls different routines depending on if $\mathbf{x}$ is complex or not, but these routines can be called directly. Write `help bessel` for more information.
`bessely(n,x)`	gives Bessel functions of second kind with the same arguments as `bessel`.
`gamma(x)`	gives the gamma function, that is for positive x: $$\Gamma(x) = \int_0^\infty t^{x-1} e^{-t} dt$$ To obtain the definition for negative x, type `help gamma`.
`gammainc(x,a)`	gives the incomplete gamma function $$\frac{1}{\Gamma(a)} \int_0^x t^{a-1} e^{-t} dt.$$
`gammaln(x)`	gives the natural logarithm of the gamma function. Avoids overflow and underflow that may occur with `log(gamma(x))`
`beta(x,y)`	gives the beta function, that is $\dfrac{\Gamma(x)\Gamma(y)}{\Gamma(x+y)}$ The argument x must be in the interval $[0,1]$. If the function is called by three arguments the command `betainc` below is used.
`betainc(x,a,b)`	gives the incomplete beta function, defined analogously to the incomplete gamma function.
`betaln(x,y)`	gives the natural logarithm of the beta function.

Command 12	SPECIAL MATHEMATICAL FUNCTIONS (continued)

`expint(x)`	gives $\int_{x}^{\infty} \dfrac{e^{-t}}{t} dt$.
`erf(x)`	gives the error function, that is the integral $\dfrac{2}{\sqrt{\pi}} \int_{0}^{x} e^{-t^2} dt$.
`erfinv(y)`	gives the inverse error function.
`erfc(x)`	gives the complementary error function $1 - \text{erf}(x)$.
`erfcx(x)`	gives the scaled complementary error function. Type `help erfcx` for more information.
`[k,e] = ellipke(m)`	gives complete elliptic integrals of the first and the second kind for $0 < m < 1$.
`[j1,j2,j3] = ellipj(x,m)`	gives the Jacobi elliptic functions.

In addition, you can define your own functions (see Section 2.9). Some of the special mathematical functions are also treated in Section 10.4.

2.5 Counting flops and time-keeping

MATLAB counts the number of arithmetic operations during a session, or parts of a session. This can be useful when we want to compare different algorithms to each other. To obtain an approximate number of floating point operations (flops) the command `flops` is used.

Command 13	FLOPS COUNTER

`flops`	returns an approximate number of floating point operations done since the counter last had the value *0*, which it always has when starting MATLAB. Addition and subtraction counts as one operation if the numbers are real, and two operations if the numbers are complex. Multiplication and division counts as one operation if the numbers are real and six if they are complex. Calls to elementary functions count as one operation if the arguments are real, several if they are complex; the number depends on the function.

Command 13	FLOPS COUNTER (continued)

`flops(0)`	resets the counter to zero.

■ Example 2.10

Counting the number of operations. The following commands:

```
flops(0); x = 10 + 20 + 30*40/50;
numflops = flops
```

give, as expected, the result

numflops =

4 ■

MATLAB can tell you date and time and together with the command `flops` they can be used to analyze the efficiency of an algorithm.

Command 14	TIME AND DATE

`tic`	starts a timer which can be read with the command `toc`.
`toc`	reads the timer, that is displays how long time has passed since it was started. If the timer is not running, `toc` returns no value.
`clock`	returns a row vector with six elements representing date and time in decimal form. The first five elements are integers. The seconds are given with several decimals accuracy. `fix(clock)` rounds the seconds to the nearest integer.
`etime(t1,t2)`	**t1** and **t2** are six element row vectors representing date and time. The command `etime` computes the difference in seconds between **t1** and **t2**.
`cputime`	gives CPU time used by MATLAB in seconds since MATLAB was started.
`date`	returns current date in a string of the form day-month-year.

■ Example 2.11

Timing can be done in the following way:

Save current time by writing

```
t1 = clock
```

Write MATLAB commands and finish with

```
timedifference = etime(t1,clock);
```

to get the time difference, that is the time spent for performing the commands in between. ∎

2.6 Output format

The result is usually displayed on the screen in integer format without decimals or in short floating point format with four decimals.

If all elements in a matrix are integers they are displayed in integer format, but if one or more of the elements are real all elements are displayed in floating point format. An exception is the number *0* which is always written in integer format.

The output format has nothing to do with the accuracy in the computation. MATLAB always performs the computations with full accuracy. For most computers MATLAB uses about 16 decimal places in computations.

The command `format` is used to change the output format. In the Windows and Macintosh versions, the output format can also be controlled through pull-down menus in the command window.

Command 15	NUMERICAL OUTPUT FORMAT
`format defformat`	changes the output format to the format defined by *defformat*, which can be one of the following: `short, long, short e, long e, hex, +, bank, rat`. There are also `compact` and `loose`, which give a more compact, or loose, output format but do not affect the numerical output format.
`more on`	outputs that are longer than the window can display stops when the window is full and waits for a key stroke before further output is displayed. At the bottom of the window MATLAB prints – *more* – to indicate that there are more to be displayed.
`more off`	output is given without considering if the window is big enough or not.
`more(n)`	displays output in *n* lines if the output is longer than *n* lines.

■ **Example 2.12**

Suppose that $p = 1 + 1/3$; and that we first define format and then display
p on the screen, then:

`format short`	gives	*1.3333*	4 decimals
`format long`	gives	*1.33333333333333*	14 decimals
`format short e`	gives	*1.3333e+00*	4 decimals
`format long e`	gives	*1.333333333333333e+00*	15 decimals
`format hex`	gives	*3ff5555555555555*	hexadecimal
`format +`	gives	*+*	positive: +,
			negative: − or zero: 0
`format bank`	gives	*1.33*	dollars and cents
`format rat`	gives	*4/3*	as a rational number ■

It is also possible to reduce the number of blanks that MATLAB uses in the
output, and to direct the output when the line is too long for the window. In this
book, `format compact` is used in the examples to reduce the number of blanks.

2.7 Help commands and demonstrations

Help can always be obtained by using any of the following commands.

Command 16   **HELP COMMANDS**

`help`	MATLAB gives a list of about 20 topics for which general information can be given. These topics are in directories and information about each topic is given by `help dir`, where `dir` is the directory.
`help command`	gives help for the specified `command`.
`help dir`	gives the contents of directory `dir`.
`lookfor text`	searches the first line of all M-files for the string **text**.
`demo`	gives a demonstration of MATLAB's different commands, functions and application areas. The command `demo` runs MATLAB Expo. This displays a menu of different demonstration examples to select. A couple of simple games can also be found.
`expo`	runs MATLAB Expo, see also `demo`.

Command 16	HELP COMMANDS (continued)
`info`	gives information about MATLAB, for example what kind of computers can run MATLAB, how to get more information about the current development and new releases of MATLAB, and so on.
`whatsnew`	gives information about the new commands in the new version.
`subscribe`	gives the opportunity to become a subscribing user of MATLAB.

■ **Example 2.13**

(a) The command `help size` gives:

> *SIZE Matrix dimensions.*
> *D = SIZE(X), for M-by-N matrix X, returns the two-element row vector D = [M, N] containing the number of rows and columns in the matrix.*
>
> *[M,N] = SIZE(X) returns the number of rows and columns in separate output variables.*
> *M = SIZE(X,1) returns just the number of rows.*
> *N = SIZE(X,2) returns just the number of columns.*

Note that MATLAB writes the commands in capital letters in the help text although MATLAB does not accept commands given in capital letters.

(b) To find information about the sine function we type:

> `lookfor sine` which gives:

> | *ACOS* | *Inverse cosine.* |
> |---|---|
> | *ACOSH* | *Inverse hyperbolic cosine.* |
> | *ASIN* | *Inverse sine.* |
> | *ASINH* | *Inverse hyperbolic sine.* |
> | *COS* | *Cosine.* |
> | *COSH* | *Hyperbolic cosine.* |
> | *SIN* | *Sine.* |
> | *SINH* | *Hyperbolic sine.* |
> | *TFFUNC* | *Time and frequency domain versions of a cosine modulated Gaussian pulse.* |
> | *DCT* | *Discrete cosine transform.* |
> | *IDCT* | *Inverse discrete cosine transform.* |
> | *SINEINT (a.k.a. SININT)* | *Numerical Sine Integral* |

■

An excellent way to learn MATLAB commands is to run a couple of demonstration programs with the command `demo`, then examine interesting commands with the command `help` and finally start using the commands.

There are commands that give information about the computer on which you are running MATLAB.

Command 17   **COMPUTER INFORMATION**

`[str,n] = computer`	gives a description of the computer on which MATLAB is running. The string **str** depends on the computer or operative system, for example VAX, Sun, PC, Macintosh and so on, and *n* is the total number of allowed elements in a matrix in the current installation of MATLAB.
`isieee`	returns *1* for computers with IEEE arithmetic, for example IBM PC, Macintosh, and *0* for computers without, for example VAX, Cray.
`version`	returns a string with current MATLAB version number.
`ver`	displays current MATLAB and toolbox version numbers.
`hostid`	returns MATLAB server host identification number.
`getenv(str)`	returns text associated with **str**. Here, **str** is the name of a symbol or an environment variable.
`terminal`	configures MATLAB terminal settings.

■ **Example 2.14**

On a Sun workstation running Solaris 2 the command
`[comp,numb] = computer` returns

> *comp =*
>
>> *SOL2*
>
> *numb =*
>
> *268435455*   ■

2.8 Saving and loading

MATLAB can keep a diary of what is displayed on the screen. This is done by the command `diary`. An exception is graphical output. To print or save graphs, see Section 13.7.

Command 18	DIARY OF A SESSION

`diary filename`	stores the following session in file **filename**.
`diary off`	stops the recording.
`diary on`	starts the recording. Continues on current diary file.
`diary`	stores the following session in file **diary**, but does also work as a switch between `diary on` and `diary off`.

The resulting ASCII file can later be edited and included in documents. However, the values and results saved with the command `diary` cannot usually be read by MATLAB on a later occasion.

To save the variables and their contents so that they can be used in a later session, the commands `save` and `load` should be used. The name of the file, **filename** in the table, is what determines how MATLAB interprets the file. All files that end with **.mat** are interpreted as binary, and all files ending with something else, including **filename.**, are interpreted as ASCII-files.

Command 19	SAVING AND LOADING VARIABLES

`save`	saves all variables on the file **matlab.mat**.
`save filename`	saves all variables on the file **filename.mat**. If one writes **filename.**, with a dot at the end, or if another suffix is added, MATLAB does not add the suffix **.mat**.
`save filename v1 v2...`	saves the variables *v1*, *v2*, and so on on file **filename.mat**.
`save filename v -ascii`	saves the values of variables *v* in readable ASCII-format on the file **filename.mat**. Writes 8 decimals.
`save filename v -ascii  -double`	saves the values of variables *v* in readable ASCII-format in double precision with 16 decimals on the file **filename.**
`load`	loads all variables from the file **matlab.mat**.
`load filename`	If **filename** does not have a suffix, all variables from the file **filename.mat** are loaded to MATLAB. The file is created with `save`. If the file has a suffix but is still binary the option `-mat` should be used.

Command 19 **SAVING AND LOADING VARIABLES (continued)**

> If **filename** contains '.' and a suffix, for example
> **temp.dat**, the data are loaded from the
> corresponding ASCII-file to MATLAB as a matrix
> named **filename** without '.' and suffix. The file is
> either created by `save file var -ascii` or
> directly by using an editor or as an output file from
> another program.

■ **Example 2.15**

Suppose that the ASCII-file **A.dat** is created by an editor or by a program:

```
1       4       5
4       2       9
```

In MATLAB we get the Matrix A by typing:

```
load A.dat, A
```

$A =$

$$
\begin{array}{ccc}
1 & 4 & 5 \\
4 & 2 & 9
\end{array}
$$
■

See also Chapter 15, in which more sophisticated file handling, and how files are used in Fortran and C programs, are discussed.

2.9 Command files and function files

Instead of writing statements of MATLAB commands at the MATLAB prompter you can write them in a text file, created with an editor. These commands are executed by MATLAB when the user writes the file name and its arguments, if any. MATLAB reads the commands from the file instead of the terminal. When the last command in the file read is executed, MATLAB can read commands from the terminal again.

Definition

An M-file is a file of the kind:

filename.m

that is, it must have the suffix **.m**.

An M-file contains a number of consecutive MATLAB commands and it may refer to other M-files. It may even be recursive, that is to say, refer to itself.

There are a number of predefined M-files on MATLAB's 'utility-disk', for example **cond.m**, **demo.m**, **length.m** and **hilb.m**. To see the names of the files one uses the command `what`. Then the M-files defined by the user and stored in the MATLAB directory are listed.

An alternative to `what` is the command `dir`. This command is one of the file commands in MATLAB.

Command 20   SYSTEM COMMANDS

`what`	lists all MATLAB files in a directory or subdirectory.
`dir`	lists all files in a directory or subdirectory. The command can be used with different path names and wildcards.
`ls`	also lists the files but in a different output format.
`pwd`	lists current working directory.
`delete filename`	deletes the file **filename**.
`cd`	changes current directory.
`type filename`	displays the contents of the file **filename**. If no suffix is specified MATLAB reads **filename.m**.
`which filename`	displays the pathname of the function specified by **filename**.
`path`	displays MATLAB's directory search path. If the command is given with arguments the search path is changed. Type `help path` for more information.
`dbtype filename`	displays the contents of the file **filename** with line number. If no suffix is given in **filename** MATLAB uses the suffix **.m**.
`dbtype filename r1:rn`	displays line *r1* to line *rn* in **filename**, with line numbers.
`lasterr`	repeats the last error message.
`!`	The contents of a line starting with an exclamation mark are interpreted as operating system commands. This does not exist in the Macintosh version.
`unix`	executes a UNIX operating system command from MATLAB, similar to `!` Type `help unix` for more information.

It may be a good idea to create a directory named `matlab`, to save one's M-files in. MATLAB looks automatically in this directory and finds the files without the user changing directory.

■ **Example 2.16**

(a) To look at the contents of the file **sec.m**, included in MATLAB, we type:

```
type sec
```

function y = sec(z)

%SEC   Secant.

%   SEC(X) is the secant of the elements of X.

%   Copyright (c) 1984–94 by The MathWorks, Inc.

y = 1./cos(z);

The comments in M-files, that is lines that start with `%`, are used as documentation in MATLAB. Preferably these comments should be informative, and not as in this example confuse **X** and **z**. The operator `./` is defined in Section 3.5.

(b) If `help  sec` is written, the starting comment lines of the file **sec.m** are displayed:

SEC   Secant.

SEC(X) is the secant of the elements of X   ■

This is an example of a **function file**, a user-defined function, that is a special kind of M-file. Apart from the second kind of M-file that we will call a **command file**, a function can have one or several arguments or parameters. These are given with separating commas `,` . In the example `sec`, there is one parameter, that is **z**. The parameters must be surrounded by parentheses `()`.

Functions in MATLAB have strong resemblance to functions in Fortran or C. The function files must have certain properties:

- The first line in a function file must contain the word `function`, command files have no such demand. Therefore M-files without this first line are command files.

- The first line must specify the function name, the input arguments and the output arguments. The input parameters are variables copied from MATLAB's work space to the work space of the function. The first line looks like:

```
function output = name(input)
```

- A function may have zero, one or several input parameters and return values.

A function M-file is called by writing `filename(input arguments)` in MATLAB. It is recommended that `name` is the same as `filename`. The arguments, used when calling, do not need to have the same names as the formal argument in the function file.

The comments coming after the first line are displayed when `help name` is written. A similar convention is used for command files.

Function files and command files are executed just like ordinary MATLAB commands. The statements in the file are executed when the name of the file is written, together with the arguments if there are any.

All M-files are common ASCII files and can be created in a text editor. It might be good to write and test M-files from MATLAB and use the command ! whenever an operative command has to be called, for example when editing the text (see Command 20).

■ Example 2.17

(a) Suppose that a certain matrix is often used. It can be created and then stored according to Section 2.8, and then loaded whenever needed. An alternative way is to create the matrix in an M-file. The following MATLAB command is stored in the file **Thematrix.m**, and creates a matrix that can be used frequently:

```
A = [−9 −3 −16; 13 7 16; 3 3 10];
```

By typing:

`Thematrix`, the matrix A is assigned according to the line above. We show this by typing the command:

```
whos
```

Name	Size	Elements	Bytes	Density	Complex
A	3 by 3	9	72	Full	No

Grand total is 9 elements using 72 bytes

(b) Suppose that the following function is stored in the file **average.m**:

```
function y = average(A)
% The function computes the average of all elements
% of A, the result is scalar.
[m, n] = size(A);
y = sum(sum(A))/m/n;
```

If the matrix from Example (a) is defined, the following command:

```
average_value = average(A) gives as a result
```

average_value =

   2.6667

Another way of writing the function **average** is:

```
function y = average(A)
% The function computes the average of all elements of A,
% the result is scalar.
y = mean(A(:));
```

The commands `sum` and `mean` are defined in Chapter 6, and the colon notation `A(:)` is presented in Section 4.2.

(c) **Startup.m**. is a special user-defined command file. It will run automatically each time you start MATLAB if it is situated in your MATLAB working directory. In it you can define your own predefined constants and settings or, as in this example, make MATLAB greet you as you start a wonderful, new MATLAB session!

```
% My first startup.m
disp('Welcome to MATLAB!')
```

With this command file defined we will see this the next time we start MATLAB:

   < M A T L A B (R) >

   ©Copyright 1984–94 The MathWorks, Inc.

      All Rights Reserved

      Version 4.2c

      December 31 1994

Commands to get started: intro, demo, help help

Commands for more information: help, whatsnew, info, subscribe

Welcome to MATLAB!

>>   ■

More about M-files can be found in Section 12.3.

3 Matrix Operations

Most of the operations in MATLAB can be applied directly to matrices. Apart from the arithmetic operations +, −, *, ^, /, \, discussed in Section 2.4, there is the '-operator for transposition and conjugation, relational operators and logical operators.

Users of the student edition of MATLAB should be aware that the total number of elements in the matrices is limited to 8192 and that the number of either rows or the number of columns of the matrix should be 32 or smaller.

3.1 Addition and subtraction

The sum of two matrices, $\mathbf{A} + \mathbf{B}$, and the difference between two matrices, $\mathbf{A} - \mathbf{B}$, are defined if $\mathbf{A}$ and $\mathbf{B}$ are of equal size. The matrix $\mathbf{A} \pm \mathbf{B}$ has the elements $a_{ij} \pm b_{ij}$. In MATLAB, addition and subtraction can also be performed between an $m \times n$-matrix $\mathbf{A}$ and a scalar, that is a 1×1 matrix s. The matrix $\mathbf{A} + s$ has the same size as $\mathbf{A}$, and the elements are $a_{ij} + s$.

■ **Example 3.1**

Suppose that $\mathbf{A}$ and $\mathbf{B}$ are defined as:

$$\mathbf{A} = \begin{bmatrix} 1 & 2 \\ 3 & 4 \end{bmatrix} \qquad \mathbf{B} = \begin{bmatrix} 5 & 6 \\ 7 & 8 \end{bmatrix}$$

The MATLAB commands

```
Add = A + B, Sub = A - B, Add100 = A + 100
```

give the results:

Add =

6	8
10	12

Sub =

−4	−4
−4	−4

Add100 =

101	102
103	104

■

3.2 Multiplication

Matrix multiplication, that is $C = A\,B$, is defined if the number of columns in **A** is equal to the number of rows in **B**. If this is not the case, MATLAB returns an error message. The only exception is when one of the matrices is 1×1, which MATLAB accepts. The operator for multiplication is * in MATLAB, so that the command is C = A*B.

The element c_{ij} is the **dot product** of the *i*th row in **A** and the *j*th column in **B**. (See Command 21 and Appendix B for definition of dot product.) The matrix **C** has the same number of rows as **A**, and the same number of columns as **B**.

For square matrices the product **BA** is defined as well, but the result is in most cases different from **AB**.

■ **Example 3.2**

(a) Suppose that **A** and **B** are the same as in Example 3.1. The commands
A, B, Multab = A*B, Multba = B*A give the following result displayed on the screen:

A =

1	2
3	4

B =

5	6
7	8

Multab =

19	22
43	50

Multba =

23	34
31	46

(b) Let **x** and **y** be:

$$\mathbf{x} = \begin{bmatrix} 1 & 2 & 3 \end{bmatrix} \qquad \mathbf{y} = \begin{bmatrix} 1 \\ 10 \\ 100 \end{bmatrix}$$

The commands `s = x*y, M = y*x` result in:

s =

    321

M =

1	*2*	*3*
10	*20*	*30*
100	*200*	*300*

   ■

The command `dot(x,y)` gives the **dot product**, also called the **scalar product** or the **inner product**, of two vectors **x** and **y** with equal number of elements. If the dot product is zero the two vectors are **orthogonal**. The dot product of two matrices **A** and **B** is defined if **A** and **B** are of equal size, and is in MATLAB defined columnwise. The result is a row vector where the components are the dot products of the first columns, the second columns and so on. (See also Appendix B.)

Command 21   THE DOT PRODUCT

`dot(x,y)`	gives the dot product of the vectors **x** and **y**.
`dot(A,B)`	gives a row vector of length n where the elements are the dot products of the corresponding columns in **A** and **B**. The matrices **A** and **B** must be of the same size $m \times n$.

For two vectors **x** and **y** with three components each, the command `cross(x,y)` gives the **vector product**, or the **cross product**, that is:

$$\mathbf{x} \times \mathbf{y} = \left[x_2 y_3 - x_3 y_2 \quad x_3 y_1 - x_1 y_3 \quad x_1 y_2 - x_2 y_1 \right]$$

The vector $\mathbf{x} \times \mathbf{y}$ is orthogonal to the vectors **x** and **y**.

The `cross` command can also be applied to $3 \times n$ matrices, then the result is a $3 \times n$ matrix where the ith column is the cross product of the ith columns in **A** and **B**.

Command 22   THE CROSS PRODUCT

`cross(x,y)`	gives the cross product of the vectors **x** and **y**.
`cross(A,B)`	gives a $3 \times n$ matrix where the columns are the cross products of the corresponding columns in **A** and **B**. The matrices **A** and **B** must be of equal size $3 \times n$.

■ Example 3.3

Suppose:

$$\mathbf{x} = \begin{bmatrix} 1 & 0 & 0 \end{bmatrix} \qquad \mathbf{y} = \begin{bmatrix} 0 & 1 & 0 \end{bmatrix}$$

The command `crossprod = cross(x,y)` gives:

crossprod =

0	0	1

which is orthogonal to both **x** and **y**, that is
`scalar1 = dot(x,crossprod), scalar2 = dot(y,crossprod)` give:

scalar1 =

0

scalar2 =

0   ■

The Kronecker tensor product can be used to create large regular block matrices. It is given by the command `kron(A,B)`. If **A** is an $m \times n$ matrix, and **B** is a $k \times r$ matrix the command returns an $m \cdot k \times r \cdot n$ matrix.

Command 23	TENSOR PRODUCT

`kron(A,B)`	gives the Kronecker tensor product of **A** and **B**.

■ Example 3.4

Suppose:

$$A = \begin{bmatrix} 2 & 0 \\ -1 & 1 \end{bmatrix} \qquad B = \begin{bmatrix} 1 & 2 & 3 \\ 1 & 0 & 1 \end{bmatrix}$$

Then the command `K = kron(A,B)` results in:

K=

2	4	6	0	0	0
2	0	2	0	0	0
−1	−2	−3	1	2	3
−1	0	−1	1	0	1

■

3.3 Division

There are two symbols for matrix division in MATLAB, **left division** \ and **right division** /. If **A** is a non-singular square matrix, then A\B and B/A correspond to left and right multiplication of **B** by the inverse of **A**, that is equivalent to the commands inv(A)*B and B*inv(A), respectively. However, MATLAB executes these in another way, which is shown in Example 3.5. The inverse of **A**, inv(A) or $\mathbf{A}^{-1}$, is defined in Section 7.1.

If **A** is a square matrix then X = A\B is the solution $\mathbf{A}^{-1}\mathbf{B}$ of the matrix equations **A X = B**, where **X** is of the same size as **B**. In the special case where **B** = **b** is a column vector, then x = A\b is the solution of the linear system **A x = b**. (See Section 7.2.)

If A is a rectangular $m \times n$ matrix with $m > n$, X = A\B gives the least square solution of the matrix equations **A X = B**. (See also Section 7.7.)

The solution of the matrix equations **X A = B** is **X = B/A** which is the same as **(A'\B')'**, that is right division can be defined by left division. Here, the apostrophe denotes transposition and is explained in Section 3.4.

■ **Example 3.5**

(a) Let **A** and **B** be defined as in Example 3.1. The commands
    A, B, Right = B/A, Left = A\B give:

A =

1	*2*
3	*4*

B =

5	*6*
7	*8*

Right =

−1	*2*
−2	*3*

Left =

−3	*−4*
4	*5*

If instead we type Right = B*inv(A), we get:

Right =

$$\begin{matrix} -1.0000 & 2.0000 \\ -2.0000 & 3.0000 \end{matrix}$$

and `Left = inv(A) * B` gives

Left =

$$\begin{matrix} -3.0000 & -4.0000 \\ 4.0000 & 5.0000 \end{matrix}$$

This is the same as the matrices computed by / and \ respectively, but the floating point format reveals that the computational procedures are different.

(b) Let us now take the following **A** and **b**:

$$\mathbf{A} = \begin{bmatrix} 1 & 3 & 5 \\ 1 & 2 & 4 \\ 0 & 5 & 1 \end{bmatrix} \qquad \mathbf{b} = \begin{bmatrix} 22 \\ 17 \\ 13 \end{bmatrix}$$

The solution of the system **A** x = **b** is typed in MATLAB as `x = A\b`, which gives us:

x =

$$\begin{matrix} 1.0000 \\ 2.0000 \\ 3.0000 \end{matrix}$$

(c) We use the same **A** and **b**. Let us investigate the number of operations to solve the system **A** x = **b**.
The commands `flops(0); x = inv(A)*b; flops` give the result:

ans =

109

and `flops(0); x = A\b; flops` give:

ans =

72

that is fewer operations are required in MATLAB to solve a system with left division than with inversion and multiplication. (For a definition of the command `flops` see Section 2.5.) ∎

3.4 Transposition and conjugation

An important operator is the one for transposition and conjugate transposition, which is written in MATLAB with an apostrophe `'`. In textbooks it is often written with $*$ or H.

If **A** is real then row *1* becomes column *1*, row *2* becomes column *2*, and so on when it is transposed. An $m \times n$ matrix becomes an $n \times m$ matrix. If the matrix is square, the matrix is reflected in the main diagonal.

If the matrix **A** with elements a_{ij} is complex, then the elements are conjugated as well. The matrix **A'** contains $\overline{a}_{ji}$ on entry (i,j).

If only the transposition is desired, a point is typed before the apostrophe `.'`, typing `A.'` means transposing and gives the same result as `conj(A')`. If **A** is real then `A'` is the same as `A.'`.

■ **Example 3.6**

Suppose **A** and **b** are the same as in Example 3.5 (b), `Transp = A'`, `Transpb = b'` then give:

Transp =

1	*1*	*0*
3	*2*	*5*
5	*4*	*1*

Transpb =

22	*17*	*13*

■

3.5 Elementwise arithmetic operations

Arithmetic operations can also be performed element-by-element. Matrices of equal size are required. If the operation is preceded by a point the operation is performed elementwise.

For addition and subtraction there is no difference between elementwise operation and matrix operation. The elementwise operators are:

$$+ \qquad - \qquad .* \qquad ./ \qquad .\backslash \qquad .^{\wedge}$$

Note that `.'` is not in the list. The point has a different meaning in that case. The operator gives only the transpose, as opposed to `'` which gives the conjugate transpose. (See Section 3.4.)

■ **Example 3.7**

Suppose that the following matrices are defined:

$$A = \begin{bmatrix} 1 & 2 \\ -1 & 5 \end{bmatrix} \qquad B = \begin{bmatrix} 7 & 2 \\ 1 & 0 \end{bmatrix} \qquad C = \begin{bmatrix} 1 + 2i & 5 - 2i \\ 3 + i & 1 + 3i \end{bmatrix}$$

(a) `A.*B` gives:

> *ans =*
>
> | | |
> | --- | --- |
> | 7 | 4 |
> | −1 | 0 |

(b) `B./A` gives:

> *ans =*
>
> | | |
> | --- | --- |
> | 7 | 1 |
> | −1 | 0 |

(c) `B.^2` gives:

> *ans =*
>
> | | |
> | --- | --- |
> | 49 | 4 |
> | 1 | 0 |

(d) `A.^B` gives:

> *ans =*
>
> | | |
> | --- | --- |
> | 1 | 4 |
> | −1 | 1 |

(e) The base can be scalar and the exponent a matrix: `2.^[1 2 3 4]` gives:

> *ans =*
>
> | 2 | 4 | 8 | 16 |
> |---|---|---|----|

(f) `C.'` gives:

> *ans =*
>
> | 1.0000 + 2.0000i | 3.0000 + 1.0000i |
> | --- | --- |
> | 5.0000 − 2.0000i | 1.0000 + 3.0000i |

■

3.6 Elementwise functions

The mathematical standard functions which are predefined in MATLAB (see Section 2.4) operate elementwise on matrices. If f is such a function and $\mathbf{A}$ is a matrix with the elements a_{ij} then $f(\mathbf{A})_{ij} = f(a_{ij})$. If the elements are complex then the resulting matrix can also be complex depending on the function. The size of the matrix is not changed.

■ **Example 3.8**

Let $\mathbf{A}, \mathbf{B}$ and $\mathbf{C}$ be

$$\mathbf{A} = \begin{bmatrix} 0 & -3 \\ 5 & 1 \\ 4 & -6 \end{bmatrix} \qquad \mathbf{B} = \begin{bmatrix} \pi & 0 \\ \pi/2 & \pi/4 \end{bmatrix} \qquad \mathbf{C} = \begin{bmatrix} 1+i & -\pi i \\ 0 & 2-i \end{bmatrix}$$

(a) `abs(A)` gives:

> *ans =*
>
> 0   3
>
> 5   1
>
> 4   6

(b) `cos(B)` gives:

> *ans =*
>
> −1.0000   1.0000
>
> 0.0000   0.7071

(c) `sin(abs(C))` gives:

> *ans =*
>
> 0.9878   0.0000
>
> 0   0.7867

■

Elementwise operators and functions are very useful in MATLAB and it is possible to define one's own elementwise functions and store them in M-files (see Section 2.9).

■ **Example 3.9**

The function *sincos(x) = sin(x)cos(x)* is not a standard MATLAB function.

However, you can define your own function *sincos,* and store it in the file **sincos.m:**

```
function y = sincos(x)
y = sin(x).*cos(x);
```

A call to *sincos* would look like:

```
y1 = sincos(pi), y2 = sincos([0 pi/4 pi/2])
```

y1 =

　　　　　1.2246e−16

y2 =

　　　0   0.5000   0.0000

We see that *y1,* which should have been *0,* is a very small number in fact, *eps* is larger. If we call *sincos* with a vector as an argument then the result is a vector since both `sin` and `cos` return vectors. This is very useful when plotting graphs of functions.　　　　　　　　　　　　　　　　　　　　　　　　　■

Applications of M-files can be found in Chapters 12 and 13.

3.7 Powers and functions of matrices

For square matrices, the *p*th power of **A** can be executed with `A^p`. If *p* is a positive integer then the power is defined by a number of matrix multiplications. For *p = 0* we get the identity matrix of the same size as **A**. When *p < 0* then `A^p` is the same as `inv(A)^(-p)`, and is defined if **A**$^{-1}$ exists.

MATLAB expressions like `exp(A)` and `sqrt(A)` are regarded as elementwise operations (see Section 3.6), that is, they apply to the elements one-by-one in **A**.

MATLAB can also treat functions of square matrices, for instance **A**$^{1/2}$ (square root of **A**), or e^A. For instance we have:

$$e^{\mathbf{A}} = I + \mathbf{A} + \frac{\mathbf{A}^2}{2!} + \frac{\mathbf{A}^3}{3!} + \ldots$$

Command 24	MATRIX FUNCTIONS

`expm(A)`	computes e^A using the Pade' approximation and is a built-in function.
`expm1(A)`	computes e^A using an M-file and the same algorithm as the built-in function.
`expm2(A)`	computes e^A using Taylor series.
`expm3(A)`	computes e^A using eigenvalues and eigenvectors.
`logm(A)`	computes the natural logarithm of **A**.
`sqrtm(A)`	computes $\mathbf{A}^{1/2}$. The square root is unique when **A** is symmetric and positive definite.
`funm(A,fcn)`	computes the matrix function of **A** specified in the string **fcn** (see Section 5.4). The string **fcn** could be any of the elementary functions `sin`, `cos`, and so on (see Section 2.4). For example, `expm(A) = funm(A,'exp')`.
`[F,E] = funm(A,fcn)`	computes the matrix function as above but returns both the matrix **F**, the result, and the matrix **E**, an approximation of the residual.
`polyvalm(p,A)`	evaluates a polynomial of the matrix **A**. The vector **p** contains the coefficients of the polynomial (see Section 10.1).

It is important to make a distinction between `expm` and `exp`, `logm` and `log`, and so on.

■ **Example 3.10**

Suppose that:

$$\mathbf{A} = \begin{bmatrix} 1 & 0 \\ 0 & 2 \end{bmatrix}$$

Let us compare `exp` and `expm`:
`Elementwise = exp(A), Operatorwise = expm(A)` give:

Elementwise =
    2.7183   1.0000
    1.0000   7.3891

Operatorwise =
    2.7183   0
       0   7.3891

■

3.8 Relational operators

MATLAB has six relational operators or Boolean operators for comparisons between matrices. It is also possible to compare a matrix with a scalar, then each of the elements of the matrix are compared with the scalar.

The relational operators are:

<	smaller than
<=	smaller than or equal to
>	greater than
>=	greater than or equal to
==	equal to
~=	not equal to

The relational operators compare the corresponding elements and generate a matrix of the same size containing only ones and zeroes. The elements are:

1	if the comparison is **true**
0	if the comparison is **false**

In an expression, arithmetic operators have the highest precedence, relational operators the second highest and logical operators the lowest. Parentheses are used to alter the precedence.

■ Example 3.11

(a) Compare the value of the predefined variable pi   with the rational number that is an approximation of `pi` obtained by the command `rat`.
```
[t,n] = rat(pi), piapprox = t/n;
format long, piapprox, pi, piapprox == pi gives:
```

t =

355

n =

113

piapprox =

3.14159292035398

pi =

3.14159265358979

ans =

    0

(b) Suppose:

$$
\mathbf{A} = \begin{bmatrix} 1 & 2 & 4 \\ 1 & 1 & 1 \\ 2 & 3 & 1 \end{bmatrix}
\qquad
\mathbf{B} = \begin{bmatrix} 2 & 2 & 2 \\ 2 & 2 & 2 \\ 2 & 2 & 2 \end{bmatrix}
$$

Are there any elements in **A** that are greater than in **B**? `Greater = A > B` gives:

Greater =

0	*0*	*1*
0	*0*	*0*
0	*1*	*0*

that is the entries (*1,3*) and (*3,2*) are greater in **A** than in **B**.

(c) Let **A** be as in Example (b). Are there elements in **A** greater than *1*? `Greaterthanone = A > 1` gives:

Greaterthanone =

0	*1*	*1*
0	*0*	*0*
1	*1*	*0*

3.9 Logical operators

There are four logical operators in MATLAB:

`&`	**and**
`|`	**or**
`~`	**not**
`xor`	**exclusive or**

The logical operators have the lowest precedence of the operators. In an expression, both relational and arithmetic operations are performed prior to logical operations.

The operators & and | compare two matrices of equal size. It is also possible to compare a scalar with a matrix, as in the previous section. The logical operators work elementwise. Components that are zero represent the logical value **false** and any other value of the component represents the logical value **true**. The result is a matrix containing ones and zeroes.

Command 25	LOGICAL OPERATORS

`A & B`	returns a matrix with the same size as **A** and **B**, which has ones at entries where both **A** and **B** has elements that are non-zero, and zeroes at entries where any of **A** and **B** is zero.
`A | B`	returns a matrix with the same size as **A** and **B**, which has ones at entries where at least one of **A** and **B** is non-zero, and zeroes at entries where both matrices are zero.
`~A`	returns a matrix with the same size as **A**, which has ones where **A** is zero, and zeroes where **A** is non-zero.
`xor(A,B)`	returns a matrix with the same size as **A** and **B**, which has zeroes where **A** and **B** are either both non-zero or both zero, and ones on entries where either **A** or **B** is non-zero, but not both.

3.10 Logical functions

There are several logical functions in MATLAB. In the definitions of these functions below we assume that **A** is an $m \times n$ matrix and **x** a vector.

In some computations it is important to locate entries with certain properties in a given matrix. For example, in Gaussian elimination with partial pivoting we have to find the largest entry in the column we work in. The MATLAB command `find` can be used for such cases.

Command 26	POSITION

`find(x)`	returns a vector containing the entries for non-zero components in **x**. If all the components are zero then an empty matrix is returned, that is [ ].
`find(A)`	returns a vector containing the entries for non-zero elements in a long vector built of the columns in **A**. The following command is preferable.

Command 26	POSITION (continued)

| `[u,v] = find(A)` | returns the vectors **u** and **v**, containing the entries for non-zero elements in **A**, that is the entries (u_k, v_k) in **A** are non-zero. |
| `[u,v,b] = find(A)` | returns the vectors **u** and **v** containing the entries of the non-zero elements of **A**, and a vector containing the corresponding non-zero elements. The entries (u_k, v_k) in **A** are non-zero and can be found in b_k. |

■ **Example 3.12**

Suppose **x** and **A** are:

$$\mathbf{x} = \begin{bmatrix} 3 & -4 & 0 & 6.1 & 0 \end{bmatrix} \qquad \mathbf{A} = \begin{bmatrix} 1 & 0 \\ 0 & 4 \end{bmatrix} \qquad y = \begin{bmatrix} 1 \\ 0 \\ 0 \\ 4 \end{bmatrix}$$

(a) `ind = find(x)`, `indcol = find(A)` give:

ind =

    1   *2*   *4*

indcol =

    1

    4

that is components 1, 2 and 4 are non-zero in the vector **x**. To obtain `indcol` we could as well have typed:

`find(y)`

(b) The command `find` can be used in combination with the relational operators, this makes the command very useful, for example, `index = find(x > 0.5)` returns:

index =

    1   *4*

If we type `greaterthan = x(index)` we get:

greaterthan =

    3   *6.1*

that is we use the vector **index** to find all elements greater than *0.5* in **x**.

If we just want to know how many elements in **x** are greater than *0.5* we can type: `length(find(x > 0.5))` which for the example above would give:

ans =

    2

(c) To obtain the index of all non-zero elements of **A** we type: `[index1, index2] = find(A)` which gives us:

index1 =

    1

    2

index2 =

    1

    2

that is component *(1,1)* and *(2,2)* are non-zero. ∎

MATLAB has two functions, `any` and `all`, that test logical conditions for matrices and vectors. The result is Boolean, which is either *1* or *0*, **true** or **false**. They are especially useful in if-statements (see Section 12.1).

| Command 27 | LOGICAL FUNCTIONS Part 1 |

`any(x)`	returns a *1* if any of the components in **x** is non-zero, otherwise it returns a *0*.
`any(A)`	operates columnwise on **A** and returns a row vector with ones and zeroes, depending on whether the corresponding column contains non-zero elements or not.
`all(x)`	returns a *1* if all components are non-zero, otherwise a *0* is returned.
`all(A)`	operates columnwise on **A** and returns a row vector with ones and zeroes, depending on whether the corresponding column has all elements non-zero or not.

If one of the functions operates twice on a matrix, for example `any(any(A))` and `all(all(A))` a scalar is returned that is either *1* or *0*.

■ **Example 3.13**

(a) All the components in a real vector **x** are smaller than or equal to 5 if `all(x<=5)` returns the value *1*. If the value *0* is returned at least one component is greater than *5*. All elements of a matrix **A** is smaller or equal to *5* if `all(all(A<=5))` returns the value *1*.

(b) For a real square matrix **A**, **A** is symmetric if `all(all(A==A'))` returns the value *1*.

(c) For a square matrix **A**, **A** is upper triangular if `any(any(tril(A,-1)))` returns the value *0*.

Otherwise there is at least one non-zero element below the diagonal in **A**.

An equivalent command is `all(all(A==triu(A)))` that returns *1* if **A** is upper triangular. ■

The logical functions `isnan`, `isempty` and `finite` are defined in the following table:

Command 28	LOGICAL FUNCTIONS Part 2
`isnan(A)`	returns a matrix with size equal to **A,** having *1* on entries where **A** has 'NaN' and zeroes elsewhere.
`isinf(A)`	returns a matrix with size equal to **A,** having *1* on entries where **A** has 'inf' and zeroes elsewhere.
`isempty(A)`	returns *1* if **A** is an empty matrix, otherwise zero
`isreal(A)`	returns *1* if **A** is a real matrix with no imaginary part, otherwise zero
`finite(A)`	returns a matrix with the same size as **A** with *1* on entries where the elements in **A** are finite and zeroes elsewhere.

There are also logical functions that operates on strings (see Section 5.2).

Creating New Matrices

The basics of matrix definition and assignment are discussed in Section 2.2. It is also possible to create new matrices, for example by typing functions that return a new matrix or by using existing matrices.

4.1 Building new matrices

The **matrix of ones,** whose components all are ones, is created with the `ones` command. The **zero matrix** has all components equal to zero. It is created with `zeros`. The **identity matrix** has ones in the diagonal and zeroes in all other entries. It is created with `eye`. In square matrix operations, the identity matrix of order *n* corresponds to the number *1* in scalar operations.

Command 29	THE MATRIX OF ONES, THE ZERO MATRIX AND THE IDENTITY MATRIX
`ones(n)`	gives an $n \times n$ matrix of ones.
`ones(m,n)`	gives an $m \times n$ matrix of ones.
`ones(size(A))`	gives a matrix of ones of the same size as **A.**
`zeros(n)`	gives an $n \times n$ matrix of zeros.
`zeros(m,n)`	gives an $m \times n$ matrix of zeros.
`zeros(size(A))`	gives a matrix of zeros of the same size as **A.**
`eye(n)`	gives an $n \times n$ identity matrix.
`eye(m,n)`	gives an $m \times n$ identity matrix.
`eye(size(A))`	gives an identity matrix of the same size as **A.**

■ **Example 4.1**

The commands:

```
Onematrix = ones(2,3), Zeromatrix = zeros(size(Onematrix)),
Identity = eye(2), Identity23 = eye(2,3), Identity32 = eye(3,2)
```

give the following result on the screen:

Onematrix =

    1   *1*   *1*

    1   *1*   *1*

Zeromatrix =

$$
\begin{array}{ccc}
0 & 0 & 0 \\
0 & 0 & 0
\end{array}
$$

$Identity =$

$$
\begin{array}{cc}
1 & 0 \\
0 & 1
\end{array}
$$

$Identity23 =$

$$
\begin{array}{ccc}
1 & 0 & 0 \\
0 & 1 & 0
\end{array}
$$

$Identity32 =$

$$
\begin{array}{cc}
1 & 0 \\
0 & 1 \\
0 & 0
\end{array}
$$

■

A **random matrix** is a matrix in which all the components are random numbers. The rand command produces random numbers **uniformly distributed** between 0 and 1. There is also the command randn in MATLAB, which returns **normally distributed** random numbers, with the expected value 0 and variance 1.

Command 30	RANDOM NUMBERS AND MATRICES

rand	gives uniformly distributed random numbers between 0 and 1. Each call gives a new number.
rand+i*rand	gives a complex scalar random number.
rand(n)	gives an $n \times n$ matrix with the components uniformly distributed between 0 and 1.
rand(m,n)	gives an $m \times n$ matrix with the components uniformly distributed between 0 and 1.
randn	gives normally distributed random numbers with expectation value 0 and variance 1.
randn(n)	gives an $n \times n$ matrix with normally distributed random numbers with expected values 0 and variance 1.
randn(m,n)	gives an $m \times n$ matrix with normally distributed random numbers with expected values 0 and variance 1.

The random number generator proceeds as follows. After the process has started, a random number based on the previous random number is produced. To generate a randomizer, the process needs a **seed.** If the same seed is used all the time, the generator produces the same random number sequence. In the first call of a random number generator, MATLAB uses the value *0* as seed, but it is possible to change the value of the seed. Note that the two random number commands, `rand` and `randn`, use different seeds.

Command 31	**RANDOM NUMBER SEED**

`rand('seed')`	returns the current value of the `rand`-seed.
`rand('seed',n)`	sets the seed for `rand` to the integer *n*.
`randn('seed')`	returns the current value of the `randn`-seed.
`randn('seed',n)`	sets the seed for `randn` to the integer n.

■ **Example 4.2**

(a) `aseed = rand('seed'), Random = rand(2,3),...`
     `newseed = rand('seed') return:`

   aseed =

             0

   Random =

       0.2113   0.7599   0.8096

       0.0824   0.0087   0.8474

   newseed =

       55538

(b) Change of the seed, for example `rand('seed',121);` and the generation of a new random matrix, `Newmatrix = rand(2,3)` gives as a result:

   Newmatrix =

       0.7225   0.3871   0.6829

       0.3981   0.6392   0.0672

(c) To avoid starting with the same seed and always getting the same sequence of random numbers, the built-in function `clock` in MATLAB can be used:
    `rand('seed',sum(100*clock));` `rand('seed')` once gave:

$$ans =$$

$$206253$$

The `clock` command is defined in Section 2.5. ■

In MATLAB there are also commands that create new matrices using parts of existing matrices. Suppose **A** is an $m \times n$ matrix, and **x** is a vector with n components. Then the command `diag` produces new matrices as described in Command 32.

Command 32	NEW MATRICES FROM OLD MATRICES, PART 1

`diag(A)`	gives a column vector containing the elements on the main diagonal of **A**. This diagonal always starts in the upper left-hand corner. For square matrices it ends in the lower right-hand corner.
`diag(x)`	gives a square diagonal matrix of order n in which the diagonal is the vector **x** and all other elements are zero.
`diag(A,k)`	gives a column vector containing the elements on the kth diagonal in **A**. If $k = 0$ the main diagonal is referred to, if $k < 0$ it is a diagonal below the main diagonal and if $k > 0$ a diagonal above the main diagonal.
`diag(x,k)`	the result is an $(n + \text{abs}(k)) \times (n + \text{abs}(k))$ matrix with the elements of the vector **x** on the kth diagonal. All other elements are 0. Concerning the parameter k, see the previous command.

■ **Example 4.3**

Suppose:

$$A = \begin{bmatrix} 1 & 2 & 3 & 4 \\ 5 & 6 & 7 & 8 \\ 9 & 10 & 11 & 12 \\ 13 & 14 & 15 & 16 \end{bmatrix} \qquad x = [-5 - 10 - 15]$$

(a) The command `diag_element = diag(A)` gives:

$$diag\_element =$$

$$1$$

$$6$$

$$11$$

$$16$$

(b) `Diag_matrix = diag(diag(A))` returns:

Diag_matrix =

1	*0*	*0*	*0*
0	*6*	*0*	*0*
0	*0*	*11*	*0*
0	*0*	*0*	*16*

(c) The command `Dmatrixx = diag(x)` or `Dmatrixx = diag(x')` gives:

Dmatrixx =

−5	*0*	*0*
0	*−10*	*0*
0	*0*	*−15*

(d) If we type `superdiagelement = diag(A,2)` the output is:

superdiagelement =

3

8

(e) `Newmatrix = diag(diag(A,2))` returns:

Newmatrix =

3	*0*
0	*8*

Note that the size of this matrix is determined by the vector `diag(A,2)`.

(f) `Superdiagonalmatrix = diag(diag(A,2),2)` returns the following matrix:

Superdiagonalmatrix =

0	*0*	*3*	*0*
0	*0*	*0*	*8*
0	*0*	*0*	*0*
0	*0*	*0*	*0*

The second super diagonal of **A** has length 2. Thus the created matrix is of type 4×4 in size. ■

Triangular matrices are created in MATLAB with `triu` and `tril`.

Command 33	NEW MATRICES FROM OLD MATRICES, PART 2

`triu(A)`	gives an upper triangular matrix of the same size as **A**. The elements on and above the main diagonal are the same as in **A**.
`triu(A,k)`	generates a matrix of the same size as **A**, where the elements on and above the kth diagonal are the same as in **A**. Negative numbers of k refer to diagonals below the main diagonal. All other elements are zero. The command `triu(A,0)` is equivalent to `triu(A)`.
`tril(A)`	gives a lower triangular matrix of the same size as **A**. The elements on and below the main diagonal are the same as in **A**.
`tril(A,k)`	generates a matrix of the same size as **A**, where the elements on and below the kth diagonal are the same as in **A**. Negative numbers of k refer to diagonals below the main diagonal. All other elements are zero. The command `tril(A,0)` is equivalent to `tril(A)`.

The following relation is true for every square matrix **A**:

```
A = triu(A) + tril(A) - diag(diag(A))
```

The strictly upper triangular part of **A** is defined as `triu(A,1)` and the strictly lower triangular part of **A** is defined as `tril(A,-1)`. Hence, the following relation is true for every square matrix **A**:

```
A = triu(A,1) + tril(A,-1) + diag(diag(A))
```

Decomposition of matrices in this manner is of importance when systems of linear equations are solved by iterative methods, for example Gauss–Seidel, Jacobi or Successive Over Relaxation (SOR).

■ **Example 4.4**

Suppose:

$$\mathbf{B} = \begin{bmatrix} 9 & 8 & 7 & 6 \\ 1 & 3 & 0 & 7 \\ -4 & 7 & 1 & 9 \end{bmatrix}$$

(a) then `Uppertriangular = triu(B)` returns:

   Uppertriangular =

9	*8*	*7*	*6*
0	*3*	*0*	*7*
0	*0*	*1*	*9*

(b) and `Lowertriangular = tril(B,-1)` results in:

   Lowertriangular =

0	*0*	*0*	*0*
1	*0*	*0*	*0*
-4	*7*	*0*	*0*

■

Suppose **A** is an $m \times n$ matrix and **B** is the resulting matrix.

Command 34	**ROTATING AND RESHAPING MATRICES**

`fliplr(A)`	gives the elements in the rows of **A** in reversed order, that is $b_{ij} = a_{i,n-j+1}$. Here "lr" is short for left-right.
`flipud(A)`	gives the elements of the columns of **A** in reversed order, that is $b_{ij} = a_{m-i+1,j}$. Here "ud" is short for up-down.
`rot90(A)`	gives a *90*-degree rotation of **A** counterclockwise. The element in the upper right-hand corner is placed in the upper left-hand corner. (See also Section 13.5.)
`rot90(A,k)`	gives a $k \times n$-degree rotation of **A** counterclockwise. (See also Section 13.5.)
`reshape(A,mm,nn)`	gives a matrix containing the elements of **A** but in a different shape, that is $mm \times nn$. The command requires that $mm.nn = m.n$. The result can also be obtained by using the colon notation, `B = zeros(mm,nn); B(:) = A` (see Section 4.2).

In MATLAB a matrix or a vector can be extended by new elements, rows or columns. MATLAB changes the size of the matrix automatically.

To build a matrix from old ones is like defining a new matrix. Elements are separated by a blank or a comma and rows are separated by a semicolon or a 'return' (see Section 2.2). In Section 4.2 the opposite procedure, to define submatrices from larger matrices, is covered.

■ Example 4.5

Suppose these matrices are already defined:

$$\mathbf{A} = \begin{bmatrix} 1 & 2 \\ 3 & 4 \end{bmatrix} \quad \mathbf{B} = \begin{bmatrix} 5 & 6 \\ 7 & 8 \end{bmatrix} \quad \mathbf{x} = \begin{bmatrix} 9 & 10 \end{bmatrix} \quad \mathbf{y} = \begin{bmatrix} 11 \\ 12 \end{bmatrix} \quad \mathbf{z} = \begin{bmatrix} 13 & 14 \end{bmatrix}$$

(a) To extend the row vector $\mathbf{x}$ to 1×4 there are several methods. Suppose that we want the new vector to be:

$$\mathbf{xnew} = \begin{bmatrix} 9 & 10 & 0 & 15 \end{bmatrix}$$

The following three methods give us the desired result:

```
1. xnew = x; xnew(3) = 0; xnew(4) = 15;
2. xnew = [x 0 15];
3. temp = [0 15]; xnew = [x temp];
```

(b) To extend $\mathbf{A}$ with a new row, for example the vector $\mathbf{z}$, we have these two alternatives:

```
1. Anew1 = [A; z];
2. Anew1 = [A; [13 14]];
```

In both cases the following is shown on the screen:

Anew1 =

1	*2*
3	*4*
13	*14*

To extend $\mathbf{A}$ with a column, for example $\mathbf{y}$, we have:

```
Anew2 = [A y] or Anew2 = [A [11;12]]
```

both cases give:

Anew2 =

1	*2*	*11*
3	*4*	*12*

To extend with a matrix is similar. By typing `ABvert = [A; B]` and `ABhoriz = [A B]` we obtain:

ABvert =

1	*2*
3	*4*
5	*6*
7	*8*

ABhoriz =

1	*2*	*5*	*6*
3	*4*	*7*	*8*

For **ABvert** the number of columns has to be equal in the two matrices **A** and **B** and for **ABhoriz** the number of rows. ■

4.2 Generation of vectors and submatrices

In MATLAB a colon, `:`, is used to represent a series of values. Colon notation can be used to define a submatrix for instance. Here, the use of colons to define vectors is shown.

Command 35	SEQUENCES OF NUMBERS, PART 1

`i:k`	gives a sequence of numbers from i to k in steps of one, that is $i, i + 1, i + 2, ..., k$. If $i > k$ MATLAB returns an empty matrix, that is [ ]. The numbers i and k do not have to be integers. The last number in the sequence is less than or equal to k.
`i:j:k`	gives a series of values from i to k in steps of j, that is $i, i + j, i + 2j, ..., k$. For $j = 0$ an empty matrix is returned. The numbers i, j and k do not have to be integers. The last number in the sequence is less than or equal to k.

■ **Example 4.6**

(a) If we type `vect = 2:7` or `vect = 2:7.7` MATLAB returns in both cases:

vect =

2	*3*	*4*	*5*	*6*	*7*

(b) Negative step: `vect2 = 6:-1:1` generates:

vect2 =

   6   *5*   *4*   *3*   *2*   *1*

(c) Real numbers: `realvect = 1.2:-0.8:-3.2` results in

realvect =

 1.2000 *0.4000* *−0.4000* *−1.2000* *−2.0000* *−2.8000*

Note that the last number is −2.8.

(d) The command `realvect2 = 0:pi/4:pi` gives:

realvect2 =

 0.0000 *0.7854* *1.5708* *2.3562* *3.1416*

(e) Colon notation can be used to define matrices:
`Mat1 = [2:4 0.1:1:2.1; 1:6]` returns:

Mat1 =

 2.0000 *3.0000* *4.0000* *0.1000* *1.1000* *2.1000*

 1.0000 *2.0000* *3.0000* *4.0000* *5.0000* *6.0000*

(f) Generation of a function table, for example sine:
`a = 0.0; b = 2*pi; n = 10; x = (a:(b − a)/n:b)';`
`y = sin(x); Ftable = [x y]` give as reply:

Ftable =

0	*0*
0.6283	*0.5878*
1.2566	*0.9511*
1.8850	*0.9511*
2.5133	*0.5878*
3.1416	*0.0000*
3.7699	*−0.5878*
4.3982	*−0.9511*
5.0265	*−0.9511*
5.6549	*−0.5878*
6.2832	*−0.0000*

There are also some predefined functions which can be used to generate sequences. It is possible to create linear sequences and logarithmic sequences which can be useful when plotting functions.

Command 36   **SEQUENCES OF NUMBERS, PART 2**

`linspace(a,b)`	returns a vector with *100* equally spaced values in the interval [*a*,*b*].
`linspace(a,b,n)`	returns a vector with *n* elements in the interval [*a*,*b*]. The command works just like the colon notation but gives direct control of the number of elements in the vector.
`logspace(a,b)`	returns a vector with *50* elements whose values are logarithmically distributed in the interval [10^a,10^b]. An exception is if *b=pi*, then the function returns a vector with logarithmically distributed values in the interval [10^a,π].
`logspace(a,b,n)`	returns a vector with *n* elements logarithmically distributed in the interval [10^a,10^b], with the same exception as in the previous command.

The matrix **D** is called a submatrix of **C** if **D** can be obtained from **C** by removing rows and/or columns. The rows and the columns of **C** are also submatrices of **C**. A matrix may have many submatrices.

When a bcolon is used to define a submatrix of the matrix **A** we use the notation shown in Command 37 below.

Command 37   **TO DEFINE A SUBMATRIX**

`A(i,j)`	returns the element at entry (*i,j*) in matrix **A**. (See also Section 2.2.)
`A(:,j)`	returns the *j*th column of **A**.
`A(i,:)`	returns the *i*th row of **A**.
`A(:,j:k)`	returns the submatrix of **A** consisting of the columns *j*, *j+1*,.., *k*.
`A(i:k,:)`	returns the submatrix of **A** consisting of the rows *i*, *i+1*,.., *k*.
`A(i:k,j:l)`	returns the submatrix of **A** consisting of the elements in the rows *i* to *k* and in the columns *j* to *l*.
`A(:,:)`	returns **A** unchanged.

Command 37	TO DEFINE A SUBMATRIX (continued)

`A(:)`	returns **A** as one long column by concatenating the columns of **A** to each other.
`A(j:k)`	returns the elements from *j* to *k* of `A(:)` as a row vector.
`A([j1 j2 ...])`	returns the elements *j1*, *j2*, and so on of `A(:)` as a row vector.
`A(:,[j1 j2 ...])`	returns the columns *j1*, *j2*, and so on of **A**.
`A([i1 i2 ...],:)`	returns the rows *i1*, *i2*, and so on of **A**.
`A([i1 i2 ...],` `[j1 j2 ...])`	returns the submatrix of **A** consisting of the elements in the rows *i1*, *i2*, and so on and the columns *j1*, *j2*, and so on.

■ **Example 4.7**

Suppose that **Ftable** in Example 4.6(f) is defined.

(a) Then the statement `Submatrix = Ftable(2:4,:)` results in the output:

Submatrix =

$$0.6283 \quad 0.5878$$
$$1.2566 \quad 0.9511$$
$$1.8850 \quad 0.9511$$

that is every column from row *2* until *4*.

(b) The colon notation can be used together with relational operators (see Section 3.8). We can sort out the rows in **Ftable** where the element in column *2* has a value greater than *0* by the short command:
`Selected = Ftable(Ftable(:,2) > 0,:)` which produces:

Selected =

$$0.6981 \quad 0.6428$$
$$1.3963 \quad 0.9848$$
$$2.0944 \quad 0.8660$$
$$2.7925 \quad 0.3420$$

■

4.3 Special matrices in MATLAB

The zero matrix, the identity matrix and the matrix of ones are special matrices presented in Section 4.1. In the same section the commands for random matrices can be found.

In addition, MATLAB has commands for generating test matrices. The Hilbert matrix, that is a matrix **H** whose elements are $h_{ij} = 1/(i+j-1)$ is used as a test matrix since it is badly conditioned (see Section 7.6).

Command 38	THE HILBERT MATRIX

`hilb(n)`	gives the Hilbert matrix of size $n \times n$.
`invhilb(n)`	gives the inverse of the Hilbert matrix of size $n \times n$. The elements are integers.

■ Example 4.8

If we type `H = hilb(3), Hinv = invhilb(3)` MATLAB responds with:

$H =$

1.0000	0.5000	0.3333
0.5000	0.3333	0.2500
0.3333	0.2500	0.2000

$Hinv =$

9	−36	30
−36	192	−180
30	−180	180

We see that the Hilbert matrix and its inverse are symmetric matrices (see Appendix B). ■

A Toeplitz matrix is defined by two vectors, a row vector and a column vector. A symmetric Toeplitz matrix is defined by a single vector.

| Command 39 | THE TOEPLITZ MATRIX |

| `toeplitz(k,r)` | gives a non-symmetric Toeplitz matrix which has **k** as first column and **r** as first row. All other elements are defined by the element in the neighboring entry to the left and above. |
| `toeplitz(c)` | gives a symmetric Toeplitz matrix defined by the vector **c**. |

■ **Example 4.9**

Let x = [1 2 3 4]; y = [9 8 7 6]; then...
Toepmatrix1 = toeplitz(x,y), Toepmatrix2 = toeplitz(y,x)
gives:

Column wins diagonal conflict.

Toepmatrix1 =

1	8	7	6
2	1	8	7
3	2	1	8
4	3	2	1

Column wins diagonal conflict.

Toepmatrix2 =

9	2	3	4
8	9	2	3
7	8	9	2
6	7	8	9

■

The other special matrices in MATLAB are given in Command 40 below.

| Command 40 | OTHER SPECIAL MATRICES |

| `compan(p)` | **p** is a vector containing polynomial coefficients (see Section 10.1 for more about polynomials). The result is the companion matrix to this polynomial, that is a matrix whose characteristic polynomial is **p**. |

Command 40	OTHER SPECIAL MATRICES (continued)
gallery(n)	returns $n \times n$ -test matrices known from numerical analysis. For the moment only $n = 3$ and $n = 5$ exist: $n = 3$: ill-conditioned matrix; $n = 5$: interesting eigenvalue problem.
hadamard(k)	returns a Hadamard matrix of order $n = 2^k$. The matrix is defined only when n is divisible by *4*.
hankel(x)	returns a square Hankel matrix defined by the vector **x**. The matrix is symmetric and the elements defined by $h_{ij} = x_{i+j-a}$. The first column is the vector **x**, the elements below the antidiagonal are zero.
hankel(x,y)	returns an $m \times n$ Hankel matrix in which the first column is **x** and the last row is **y**.
magic(n)	gives a magic square of size $n \times n$.
pascal(n)	returns a Pascal matrix of size $n \times n$, that is a symmetric positive definite matrix whose elements come from Pascal's triangle. The elements of the inverse matrix are integers.
pascal(n,k)	gives for $k = 1$ a lower triangular Cholesky factor of the Pascal matrix above. Note that MATLAB normally uses upper triangular Cholesky factors. *For k = 2* a permuted version of the same is given.
rosser	gives the Rosser matrix, a classic and troublesome symmetric eigenvalue problem. The Rosser matrix has size 8×8.
vander(x)	returns a Vandermonde matrix in which the last but one column is the vector **x**. A element, $v_{i,j}$ in the matrix is defined by: $v_{i,j} = x_i^{n-j}$, where n is the length of **x**.
wilkinson(n)	returns the Wilkinson eigenvalue test matrix of size $n \times n$.

■ Example 4.10

A magic square of size $n \times n$ is a matrix with the integers *1, 2, ..., n^2* as elements, with equal row and column sums. To create a magic *3 × 3* square, we type magic(3), which gives as result:

ans =

8	*1*	*6*
3	*5*	*7*
4	*9*	*2*

■

5 Strings

It is possible to operate on characters and strings in MATLAB. Strings can be displayed on the screen and can be used to construct commands which are evaluated or executed within other commands.

5.1 Assignment

A string in MATLAB is defined by apostrophes:

```
nameofvariable = 'text'
```

where `'text'` could be letters, numbers and special characters. This text is stored in a row vector in which each entry represents a character. In reality, the elements contain the internal code of the characters, that is the ASCII code. When the value of a string variable is displayed on the screen the text is shown, not the ASCII numbers. Since strings are stored as vectors, we can refer to any element in them by giving its index.

Matrices of characters are also allowed but have to have the same number of characters in each row.

■ **Example 5.1**

(a) A simple assignment, `name ='John Smith'`, gives the following display on the screen:

> *name =*
>> *John Smith*

(b) If just `'John Smith'` is typed, the variable *ans* is assigned the string:

> *ans =*
>> *John Smith*

(c) Assignment of a character. If **name** from (a) exists then `name(3) = 'a'` gives:

> *name =*
>> *Joan Smith*

(d) To reverse the order of the components for the string **name** from previous examples we type:

```
for i = length(name):-1:1

        eman(i) = name(length(name)+1-i);

end
```

This will give us the string **eman** with the value:

eman =

    htimS naoJ

See Section 12.2 for more about for-loops.

(e) The length of a string: `namelen = size(name)` gives:

namelen =

    1   *10*

(f) The apostrophe character is typed in a string by doubling it:
`whoscat = 'Joan''s cat'` becomes:

whoscat =

    Joan's cat

(g) Strings can be composed just like numerical matrices:
`name1 = 'Joan'; name2 = 'John'; heart = 'is in love with';`
`sentence = [name1 ' ' heart ' ' name2]` give:

sentence =

    Joan is in love with John

(h) It is also possible to use colon notation just like in numerical matrices:
`name = 'Charles Johnson'; firstname = name(1:7)` give:

firstname =

    Charles

(i) `Text1 = 'John'; Text2 = 'Joan'; Couple = [Text1; Text2]`
give:

Couple =

    John

    Joan

5.2 String commands

There are several commands for converting strings to other forms of representation.

| Command 41 | TO CONVERT A STRING |

`abs(str)`	returns a vector with the ASCII codes for the characters in the string **str**.
`setstr(x)`	returns a string composed of the integer vector **x**. The elements in **x** are translated to characters according to the ASCII table, therefore the integers must be in the interval [0, 255] to give a correct result.
`num2str(f)`	converts the scalar *f* into a string representation in floating-point format, consisting of four digits and exponent if required. The command is often used together with `disp, x label` and other output commands.
`num2str(f,k)`	converts the scalar *f* into a string representation in floating-point format, consisting of *k* digits.
`int2str(n)`	converts the integer *n* into a string representation of the integer.
`rats(x,strlen)`	converts the floating point number *x* into a string representation containing the rational approximation of *x*. The integer *strlen* is the number of positions the result is allowed to have, default is 13.
`hex2num(hstr)`	converts the hexadecimal number in the string **hstr** to the corresponding floating point number (IEEE double precision).
`hex2dec(hstr)`	converts the hexadecimal number in the string **hstr** to an integer.
`dec2hex(n)`	converts the integer *n* to the corresponding hexadecimal number. The result is a string.
`sprintf(formatstr,A)`	returns the elements of the matrix **A** in a string of the format defined in the format string **formatstr**, similar to format control in the programming language C. The command performs just like `fprintf` but the result is a string instead of a file. (See Section 15.4, especially Table 15.2).

Command 41	TO CONVERT A STRING (continued)
`[Str,E]=sprintf(...)`	returns the string **str** as above, and a matrix **E**, containing an error message string if an error occurred. If the conversion is correct the empty matrix **E** is returned.
`sscanf(str, formatstr,mn)`	returns a matrix whose elements are read from the string **str** according to the string **formatstr**. The maximum number of elements read is *mn*, but this parameter is optional. Performs like `fscanf`, but operates on a string instead of a file (see Section 15.4).
`[A,nm,E,next] = sscanf(str, formatstr,mn)`	returns a matrix **A** just like `sscanf`, but does also return the number of correct converted elements i *mn*, and the errors in the matrix **E**. The scalar *next* is index to the next element in the case when all the elements are not read.

■ **Example 5.2**

Let these variables be defined: `str = 'ABC'; float = 1.25;`

(a) The command `x = abs(str)` then returns:

> $x =$
>
> >   65   66   67

that is ASCII codes for the characters A, B and C.

(b) If we type `Number = hex2dec(str)`, MATLAB gives:

> *Number =*
>
> > 2748

(c) The line `numstr = num2str(float)` results in:

> *numstr =*
>
> > 1.2500

To show that this in fact is a string, we type `Char = numstr(4)` and MATLAB gives:

> *Char =*
>
> > 5

(d) The command `numinfo = sprintf('The Number = %5.2e',float)` gives:

> *numinfo=*
> *The Number = 1.25e+00*

(e) The command `rational = rats(0.979796)` will give us a string containing the rational approximation of the floating point number *0.979796*:

> *rational =*
> *4995/5098*

The optional number *5* in the command
`littlerat = rats(0.979796,5)` will restrict the string length to be *5*.

> *littlerat =*
> *48/49*

In Section 2.4 the command `rat` is defined. ∎

There are also logical functions that operate on strings and functions to extract substrings. In Command 42 below, let **str** be a string.

Command 42	FUNCTIONS OF STRINGS

`blanks(n)`	returns a string with *n* blanks.
`deblank(str)`	returns the string **str** without trailing blanks.
`lower(str)`	changes all letters in **str** to lower-case letters.
`upper(str)`	changes all letters in **str** to capital letters.
`isstr(x)`	returns a *1* if **x** is a string, otherwise *0*.
`isletter(str (i))`	returns a *1* if the *i*th character in **str** is a letter.
`isspace(str)`	returns a vector of the same size as **str,** whose elements are *1* if the corresponding character in **str** is a blank, tabular or line feed, otherwise *0*.
`strcmp(str1,str2)`	compares **str1** and **str2**. If they are equal, *1* is returned otherwise *0*.
`str2mat(str1,str2, ...)`	creates a string matrix with **str1**, **str2,** and so on. If **str**$_i$ are of different sizes, MATLAB completes the shorter ones with blanks in the end. The function handles at most 11 arguments but **str**$_i$ can also be string matrices.
`findstr(str1,str2)`	returns a vector containing the start positions for the substring **str2** in **str1**.

Command 42	**FUNCTIONS OF STRINGS (continued)**

`strrep(str1, str2,str3)`	returns a modified string **str1** with all existences of **str2** replaced with **str3**.
`strtok(str1,str2)`	returns the part of **str1** that remains when the trailing part after the first appearance of **str2** has been removed. If **str2** is not specified MATLAB uses blanks, that is selects the first sequence in **str1** that does not contain a blank.
`[outstr,rstr] = strtok(str1,str2)`	returns the string **outstr** as above but also the removed part in the string **rstr.**
`lasterr`	returns a string containing the last error message.

■ **Example 5.3**

(a) `name = upper('matlab')` gives:

> *name =*
> *MATLAB*

(b) `fun = strrep('hahaha','a','i')`

> *fun =*
> *hihihi*

(c) Let the string variables

> `greet = 'Welcome', where = 'to Joan''s', party = 'birthday party!'`
> be defined. Then the command `str2mat(greet,where,party)` gives:

> *ans =*
> *Welcome*
> *to Joan's*
> *birthday party!*

(d) It is possible to extract information from a string with the contents separated by commas by using the command `strtok`. We define a string **text** as:

> `text = 'Monday,Tuesday,Wednesday,Thursday,Friday,Saturday,Sunday'`
> `[day,rest] = strtok(text,',')`

> *day =*
> *Monday*
> *rest =*
> *,Tuesday,Wednesday,Thursday,Friday,Saturday,Sunday*

By calling `strtok` with the string **rest** we can find next day and so on:
`[day2,rest] = strtok(rest,',')` gives:

day2 =

  Tuesday

rest =

  ,Wednesday,Thursday,Friday,Saturday,Sunday

Note that the command reads until the second comma, since the first is in the first position of the string and therefore does not separate any part of the string. ■

5.3 Display and input

To display the contents of a numerical matrix or a string vector one can simply type the variable name (see Section 2.2). The result is that both the variable name and the contents are shown.

Another way of displaying the value of a variable is to use the command `disp`. In this case only the contents of the variable are shown on the screen. This can be of special use in string applications.

Command 43	DISPLAY

`disp(A)`	displays the contents of the matrix **A**. If **A** is a string, the text is displayed.

Input from the terminal is received with the `input` command. This also displays text and a prompter. See example in Appendix A, Section A.6. The command `disp` in combination with `int2str` is shown in Example 13.7.

Command 44	INPUT

`input(str)`	displays the text in the string **str** on the screen and waits for an input from the terminal. The read value is returned by `input`.
`input(str,'s')`	prints the text in **str** and returns the input as a string.

■ **Example 5.4**

(a) Read a real number **x**:

  `x = input('Give a number x: ')` results in

Give a number x : 2.0944

x =

    2.0944

(b) Read a matrix **A**.

A semicolon after the command `input` suppresses the printing of the result.
`A = input('Give the matrix A row by row: ');` gives:

Give the matrix A row by row: `[1 2; 3 5]`

(c) It is also possible to use arithmetical expressions and functions:
`A = input('Please give me a matrix: ');` gives:

Please give me a matrix: `rand(4) * hilb(4)`

(d) The `input` command may have more than one argument:

`[m n] = input('Give the size of A: ');`

Give the size of A: `size(A)`

(e) To read a string:

`name = input('What is your last name? ');`

What is your last name?   `'Smith'`

Note that the string in this case must be enclosed by ' '. If the command looks like:

`strname = input('What is your last name? ','s');`

the name can be written directly:

What is your last name?   `Smith`   ■

It is also possible to give a menu of options in MATLAB. A menu is a good method for the user to input choices (see Chapter 12). An explanation of the `menu` command is shown in Command 45.

Command 45   **MENUS**

`menu(titlestr, optstr1,optstr2, ...)`	writes a menu with the title in **titlestr** and with options from **optstr1, optstr2,** and so on, on the screen and waits for an input from the terminal. The `menu` command returns an integer.

Command 45   **MENUS (continued)**

`errordlg(errStr, dlgName)`	creates an error dialog box which displays the string **errStr** in a window named **dlgName**. A button must be pushed to make the window go away.
`warndlg(warn, dlgName)`	creates a warning dialog box which displays the string *warn* in a window named *dlgName*. A key must be pressed to make the window disappear.
`helpdlg(helpStr, dlgName)`	creates a help dialog box which displays the string *helpStr* in a window named *dlgName*. A key must be pressed to make the window disappear.
`questdlg(quest, ... op1,op2,op3)`	creates a question dialog box which displays the string *quest* and buttons marked *op1*, *op2* and *op3*. There can be up to three buttons. A key must be pressed to make the window disappear. Returns the chosen string.

■ **Example 5.5**

To create a simple menu with three choices enter:

```
choice = menu('Choose:','Enter','Wait','Leave')
```

On an Xterminal a window containing the menu in Figure 5.1 is shown.

By clicking the desired option the choice is made. If we choose the Wait-box MATLAB returns:

Figure 5.1 A MATLAB menu.

choice =

    2

since the second option was selected. ■

The menus look different depending on the computer used. If there is no access to graphics, MATLAB gives the options in the command window and waits for an answer from the terminal.

5.4 Evaluation of strings

MATLAB commands can be written and stored as strings. These command strings can be evaluated by the `eval` command.

Command 46	EVALUATION OF STRINGS

`eval(str)`	executes the MATLAB commands contained in **str** and returns the results.
`eval(str1,str2)`	executes the MATLAB commands in **str1**. If the first string is correct it is equal to `eval(str1)`. If there is an error in evaluation of **str1**, the string **str2** will be evaluated, that is giving an error message or something else.

The `eval` command makes MATLAB a flexible programming language. The command is useful, for example, for calls to functions which are not predefined in MATLAB, see Section 12.4.

■ **Example 5.6**

(a) Suppose that the scalars b, k and x are defined. If the string **str1** is defined by: `str1 = 'b.*sin(k.*x)'` then the command
`value = eval(str1)` results in **str1** evaluated with the current values of the variables b, k and x.

If, for example, `b = 3; k = 2; x = 1.2;` then `eval(str1)` gives

value =

    2.0264

It is also possible to give two strings to the `eval` command. Suppose that we have a string

```
str2 = 'disp(''Oops! Maybe the variables b, k and x are
not all defined?'')'
```

defined and that the variables *b*, *k* and *x* are not defined. Since the first string is not possible to evaluate the command `value = eval(str1,str2)` results in

Oops! Maybe the variables b, k and x are not all defined?

value =

> *[]*

Note that the ′ sign has to be repeated twice in a string to become such a sign, otherwise MATLAB interprets it as end of string. The command `disp` is explained in Section 5.3.

(b) String variables can be combined with strings. If we have a variable name `file = 'myfile.mat'` and wish to save the current session to this file, we type `eval(['save ',file])`. This is the same as typing `save myfile.mat`. (The `save` command is defined in Section 2.8.)

(c) MATLAB can also evaluate vector functions. Let **str1** be the same as in (a). If **b**, **k** and **x** are vectors: `b = [1 2 3]; k = [2 2 2]; x = [1.2 1.5 1.2];`

The command `values = eval(str1)` gives:

values =

> *0.6755   0.2822   2.0264*

(d) Let us create a string:

```
fcn = 'input(''Give a function'',''s'')';
```

The `input` command is presented in Section 5.3. Now an optional function can be chosen from the terminal and evaluated.
The command `fplot(eval(fcn),[0,4])` results in the following printed on screen:

Give a function

If we write `sin(x)` MATLAB opens a graphical window and displays the sine function.

Suppose an M-file (see Section 2.9) named **sinx2.m** is defined according to:

```
function y = sinx2(x)

y = sin(x .^ 2);
```

If we write `sinx2` after the text *Give a function* we get a graph of the function $sin\ x^2$:

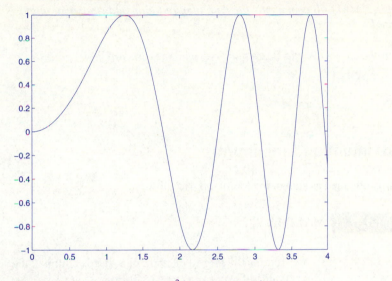

Figure 5.2 The function *sin* x^2 between *0* and *4*.   ■

The strings which are evaluated can also contain MATLAB programming structures, such as `if`, `while`, `for` and others (see Chapter 12).

6 Data Analysis and Statistics

In this chapter, MATLAB commands for data manipulation and statistical analysis are presented.

Throughout the chapter **A** *and* **B** *are matrices and* **x** *is a vector.*

6.1 Maximum and minimum

Maximum is obtained as shown in Command 47 below.

Command 47   MAXIMA

`max(x)`	returns the largest element of **x**. If **x** is complex the value of `max(abs(x))` is returned.
`max(A)`	returns a row vector containing the maxima of the columns in **A**. If **A** is complex, `max(abs(A))` is returned.
`[y,ind] = max(A)`	returns a row vector **y** containing the maxima of the columns in **A** and stores the entries of the largest number in each column in the row vector **ind**.
`max(A,B)`	returns a matrix of the same size as **A** and **B** whose element on entry (i, j) is $\max(a_{ij}, b_{ij})$.

The function `min` returns the **minimum** and is called in the same way as `max`. For complex parameters `min(abs(A))` is returned.

6.2 Sums, products and differences

Different kinds of sums are obtained by the commands `sum` and `cumsum`.

Command 48   SUMS

`sum(x)`	returns the sum of the components in the vector **x**.
`sum(A)`	returns a row vector containing the sums of the columns of **A**.
`cumsum(x)`	returns the cumulative sum of the components in **x**, that is the second element is the sum of the first two components in **x**, and so on.

Command 48	SUMS (continued)

`cumsum(A)`	returns a matrix whose columns are the cumulative sums of the columns of **A**.

■ **Example 6.1**

(a) The trace of a square matrix **A**, that is the sum of the elements of the diagonal, is computed by `sum(diag(A))`.

This is equivalent to `trace(A)` (see Section 7.1).

(b) Examples of ordinary and cumulative sums:
```
A = [1 2 3; 4 5 6; 7 8 9], thesum = sum(A),...
TheCsum = cumsum(A)
```
give:

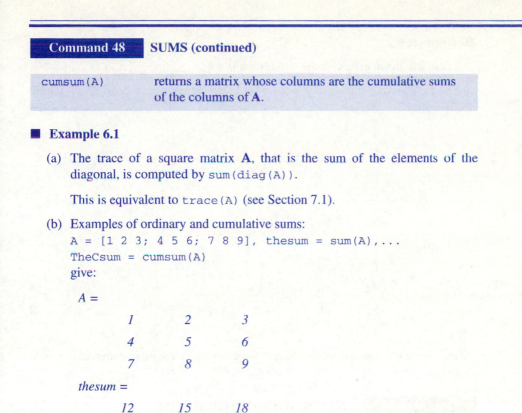

$A =$

1	2	3
4	5	6
7	8	9

thesum =

12	15	18

TheCsum =

1	2	3
5	7	9
12	15	18

■

Products are computed in a similar way.

Command 49	**PRODUCTS**

`prod(x)`	returns the product of the elements in **x**.
`prod(A)`	returns a row vector whose elements are the column products.
`cumprod(x)`	returns a vector with the cumulative product of the element in **x**, that is the second element is the product of the first two components in **x**, and so on.
`cumprod(A)`	returns a matrix in which the columns are the cumulative products of the columns of **A**.

■ **Example 6.2**

Let us use the matrix **A**, defined in Example 6.1.

The commands `A, theprod = prod(A), TheCprod = cumprod(A)` return:

A =

1	*2*	*3*
4	*5*	*6*
7	*8*	*9*

theprod =

28	*80*	*162*

TheCprod =

1	*2*	*3*
4	*10*	*18*
28	*80*	*162*

■

Differences are computed with `diff` and there are also some other commands related to `diff`.

Command 50	DIFFERENCES AND GRADIENT

`diff(x)`	gives for the vector **x** of size *n* a vector of size *n−1* containing differences between adjacent components in **x**. If **x** = [$x_1 x_2 \ldots x_n$], then we have `diff(x)` = [x_2-x_1 x_3-x_2 $\ldots$ x_n-x_{n-1}] .
`diff(A)`	computes the difference of adjacent elements in the columns of **A**: `diff(A) = A(2:m,:) - A(1:m-1,:)`.
`diff(x,k)`	gives the *k*th difference, that is `diff(x,2)` is equivalent to `diff(diff(x))`.
`[dAdx,dAdy] = gradient(A)`	returns the partial derivatives of the matrix **A** in the matrices **dAdx** and **dAdy** which contains *dA/dx* and *dA/dy* on the corresponding entries. Type `help gradient` in MATLAB to get more information.
`del2(A)`	returns the discrete Laplacian, that is a matrix whose elements have the value of the differences between the elements in **A** and the average of its four neighbors.

■ **Example 6.3**

Differences are easily computed and can be used as approximations of derivatives:

```
x = [1 4 9 16 25];
d1 = diff(x), d2 = diff(d1), d3 = diff(d2) give as result:
```

$d1 =$

3	5	7	9

$d2 =$

2	2	2

$d3 =$

0	0

Note that if the computed differences are to be used as approximations of derivatives they must be divided by the distance between the points. ■

6.3 Statistics commands

In the previous section commands operating columnwise on matrices, for example `max`, `min`, `sum`, and `prod` were presented. Here we give a description of commands for statistical analysis of data.

Suppose that **A** is an $m \times n$ matrix, and **x** a vector of the size n.

Command 51	MEAN VALUE, MEDIAN VALUE AND STANDARD DEVIATION

`mean(x)`	gives the arithmetic mean value of the vector **x**.
`mean(A)`	gives a row vector containing the mean values of each of the columns of **A**.
`median(x)`	gives the median value of the elements in the vector **x**.
`median(A)`	gives a row vector containing the median value of each of the columns of **A**.
`std(x)`	gives the standard deviation of the elements in the vector **x**.
`std(A)`	gives a row vector containing the standard deviation of each column of **A**.

■ **Example 6.4**

Let **A** be defined as

$$\mathbf{A} = \begin{bmatrix} 1 & 1 \\ 2 & 2 \\ 3 & 3 \\ 4 & 100 \end{bmatrix}$$

```
average = mean(A), med = median(A), dev = std(A) return
```

average =

    2.5000   26.5000

med =

    2.5000   2.5000

dev =

    1.2910   49.0068   ■

In MATLAB the commands `cov` and `corrcoef` are used to obtain the covariance and the correlation coefficients.

Command 52	COVARIANCE AND CORRELATION
`cov(x)`	returns the variance for the components of the vector **x**.
`cov(A)`	returns the covariance matrix. The elements of the diagonal are the variance for the columns of **A**.
`cov(x,y)`	is equivalent to `cov([x y])`, where **x** and **y** are column vectors.
`corrcoef(A)`	returns the correlation matrix.
`corrcoef(x,y)`	is equivalent to `corrcoef([x y])`, where **x** and **y** are column vectors.

■ **Example 6.5**

Let us define the following vectors:

$$\mathbf{x} = \begin{bmatrix} 1 \\ 1 \\ 1 \end{bmatrix} \qquad \mathbf{y} = \begin{bmatrix} 1 \\ 2 \\ 2 \end{bmatrix} \qquad \mathbf{z} = \begin{bmatrix} 0 \\ -1 \\ 1 \end{bmatrix}$$

(a) We get the variances by `varx = cov(x)`, `vary = cov(y),...`
   `varz = cov(z)`

   varx =

   0

   vary =

   0.3333

   varz =

   1

(b) The covariances:
   `Cvxy = cov(x,y)`, `Cvxz = cov(x,z)`, `Cvyz = cov(y,z)`

   Cvxy =

   0   0

   0   0.3333

   Cvxz =

   0   0

   0   1

   Cvyz =

   0.3333   0

   0   1.0000

(c) The correlation matrices are obtained by:
   `Corrxy = corrcoef(x,y)`, `Corrxz = corrcoef(x,z),...`
   `Corryz = corrcoef(y,z)`

   Warning: Divide by zero

   Corrxy =

   NaN   NaN

   NaN   1

   Warning: Divide by zero

   Corrxz =

   NaN   NaN

   NaN   1

$$Corryz =$$

$$
\begin{matrix}
1 & 0 \\
0 & 1
\end{matrix}
$$

■

6.4 Sorting

With MATLAB it is possible to sort data by using the command `sort`.

Command 53   **SORTING**

`sort(x)`	returns a vector in which the elements of the vector **x** are sorted in ascending order. If the components are complex the absolute values are used, that is `sort(abs(x))`.
`[y,ind] = sort(x)`	in addition to the sorted components of **x** in the vector **y**, the command returns a vector **ind** of entries from **x**, where `y = x(ind)`.
`sort(A)`	returns a matrix where each column of **A** is sorted in ascending order. Note that the rows are changed.
`[B,Ind] = sort(A)`	returns the sorted columns of **A** in matrix **B** and the matrix **Ind** containing the entries used during the sorting. Each column in the matrix **Ind** corresponds to the column **ind** in the vector case above.

■ **Example 6.6**

Suppose **A** is defined by:

$$
\mathbf{A} = \begin{bmatrix} 0 & 4 & 4 \\ 2 & 0 & 2 \\ 4 & 2 & 0 \end{bmatrix}
$$

(a) `[Ascend,Ind] = sort(A)` gives as result:

$$Ascend =$$

$$
\begin{matrix}
0 & 0 & 0 \\
2 & 2 & 2 \\
4 & 4 & 4
\end{matrix}
$$

Ind =

1	*2*	*3*
2	*3*	*2*
3	*1*	*1*

(b) If we want to sort in descending order instead, the following command can be used: Descend = flipud(sort(A)) and gives:

Descend =

4	*4*	*4*
2	*2*	*2*
0	*0*	*0*

The command flipud is defined in Section 4.1.   ■

6.5 Histograms and bar graphs

A set of data can be visualized with histograms and bar graphs using the commands hist, bar, and stairs.

Command 54	HISTOGRAMS AND BAR GRAPHS

hist(x)	plots a histogram with *10* intervals for the data stored in **x**.
hist(x,n)	plots a histogram with n intervals for the data stored in **x**.
hist(x,y)	plots a histogram for the data in **x** with the intervals defined by the vector **y**, a vector with elements in ascending order.
bar(x)	plots a bar graph of the values in **x**.
bar(z,x)	plots a bar graph of the values in **x** in the positions defined in vector **z**. The values in **z** have to be uniformly distributed in ascending order.
bar(x,...,str)	plots a bar graph as above but with the colors and shapes defined by the string **str**. Regarding values of **str**, see Section 13.1.
stairs(x)	plots a stairstep graph, that is a bar graph without internal lines.
stairs(z,x)	plots a bar graph of the data stored in **x** in positions defined by **z**.

Command 54	HISTOGRAMS AND BAR GRAPHS (continued)

`stem(y)`	plots the discrete data stored in **y** as lines emerging from the x-axis terminating at the *y*-value as a circle.
`stem(z,y)`	plots the discrete data stored in **y** as lines emerging from the x-axis in the positions specified by the vector **x** and terminated with a circle at the *y*-value.

The commands `hist`, `bar` and `stairs` can also be used to store data in vectors for further use.

Command 55	DIAGRAMS

`[m,y] = hist(x)`	creates a histogram with *10* uniform intervals between max and min for **x**. The result is a vector **y** with *10* values between *min(x)* and *max(x)* and the vector **m** which contains the number of values in each interval. The histogram can be shown by `bar(y,m)`.
`[m,y] = hist(x,n)`	creates a histogram with n uniform intervals.
`[m,y] = hist(x,y)`	creates a histogram with the intervals defined by the vector **y**.
`[xb,yb] = bar(y)`	creates a bar graph of the values in **y**. `Plot(xb,yb)` displays the bar graph.
`[xb,yb] = bar(x,y)`	creates a bar graph of the values in **y** in positions defined by **x**.
`[xb,yb] = stairs(y)`	creates a stairstep graph of the values in **y**.
`[xb,yb] = stairs(x,y)`	creates a stairstep graph of the values in **y** in positions defined by **x**.

■ **Example 6.7**

Let **x** be defined

```
x = [1 1 3 4 5 1 9 8];
```

(a) Then `hist(x); title('Histogram of x using hist(x)');` give us the graph, Figure 6.1.

The command `title` gives the text above the figure (see Section 13.3).

(b) If we want three intervals we type:

```
hist(x,3); title('Histogram of x using hist(x,3)')
```

which result in the graph, Figure 6.2.

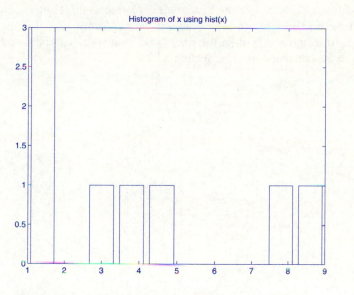

Figure 6.1 Histogram with the standard interval length.

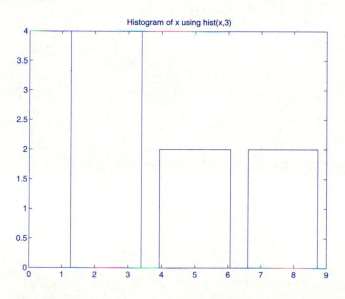

Figure 6.2 Histogram with three intervals.

(c) To draw bar graphs is just as easy: `bar(x);title('bar(x)');` give the graph, Figure 6.3.

(d) If we type `[m,y] = hist(x);` MATLAB creates the vectors **m** and **y**. If we continue with `bar(y,m,'--')` the histogram is plotted again (Figure 6.4). To make it more interesting we have drawn it with a dashed line. It is the string `'--'` that makes `bar` dash the line. Other line styles can be found together with the command `plot` in Section 13.1.

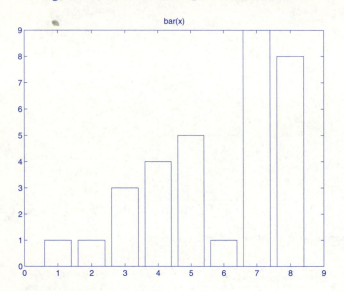

Figure 6.3 Bar graph of x.

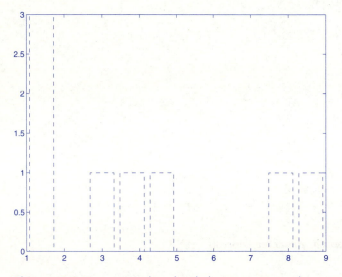

Figure 6.4 Histogram plotted with the `bar` command.

(e) If we still use the vector **x** but use the command `stem` to display the data the result will be `stem(x)` (Figure 6.5).

If we have an additional vector defined by

`x_axis_val=[1.1 1.3 2 2.4 2.5 1.8 3 3.2];`

representing the points of the x-axis, where the data is found. The command `stem(x_axis_val,x,'-.')` results in the graph in Figure 6.6.

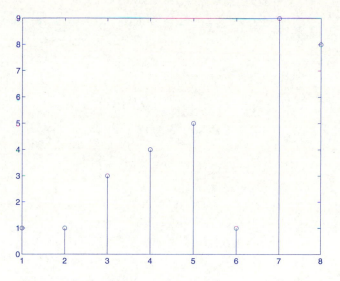

Figure 6.5 The data in **x** plotted with stem.

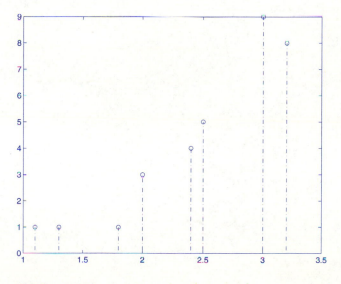

Figure 6.6 The data in **x** plotted against the vector **x_axis_val**.

Note that the elements of the vector **x_axis_val** do not have to be in ascending order. The command `stem` can have a third argument specifying line style and color in the plot just like the command `bar`. ∎

Systems of Linear Equations

Linear systems of equations are probably the most common computational problem. They arise as subproblems in almost all applications. Usually MATLAB solves systems of linear equations by division from the left, with the operator \. Overdetermined systems can also be solved.

Important concepts in the theory of linear systems are determinant, inverse, and rank. First, MATLAB commands for these are discussed, while solving of systems begins in Section 7.2. Some factorizations are presented, followed by definitions of the norm and the condition number. The last section deals with overdetermined and underdetermined systems.

7.1 Determinant, inverse, and rank

The following commands are used to compute the determinant, the inverse, and the rank of a matrix **A**.

> **Command 56** **SOME FUNCTIONS ON MATRICES**

`det(A)`	gives the determinant of the square matrix **A**.
`rank(A)`	gives the rank of **A**, that is the number of linearly independent rows and columns of **A**.
`inv(A)`	gives the inverse of the square matrix **A**. An error message is given if **A** is singular or almost singular.
`pinv(A)`	gives the pseudo-inverse of **A**. The pseudo-inverse is of size $n \times m$ if **A** is an $m \times n$ matrix. For non-singular matrices **A** we have `pinv(A) = inv(A)`.
`trace(A)`	gives the trace of **A**, that is the sum of the diagonal elements.

■ **Example 7.1**

Suppose we have the following matrices:

$$\mathbf{A1} = \begin{bmatrix} 1 & 3 \\ 2 & 4 \end{bmatrix} \qquad \mathbf{A2} = \begin{bmatrix} 1 & 3 \\ 2 & 6 \end{bmatrix} \qquad \mathbf{A3} = \begin{bmatrix} 1 & 3 & 2 \\ 2 & 7 & 6 \end{bmatrix}$$

Let us try the commands `det`, `inv`, `rank`, and a few other commands on these matrices.

(a) `det1 = det(A1), det2 = det(A2), det3 = det(A3)`

det1 =

   –2

det2 =

   0

??? Error using ==> det

Matrix must be square.

The determinant is only defined for square matrices.

(b) The inverse is only defined for square matrices:

   `Inv1 = inv(A1), Inv2 = inv(A2), Inv3 = inv(A3)`

Inv1 =

   –2.0000   1.5000

   1.0000   –0.5000

Warning: Matrix is singular to working precision.

Inv2 =

   Inf   Inf

   Inf   Inf

??? Error using ==> inv

Matrix must be square.

However, the pseudo-inverse is defined for all matrices:

   `Pinv1 = pinv(A1), Pinv2 = pinv(A2), Pinv3 = pinv(A3)`

Pinv1 =

   –2.0000   1.5000

   1.0000   –0.5000

Pinv2 =

   0.0200   0.0400

   0.0600   0.1200

Pinv3 =

   0.9048   –0.3333

   1.0476   –0.3333

   –1.5238   0.6667

Note that the inverse of **A1** is the same as the pseudo-inverse.

(c) The determinant of the inverse of **A**, *det*(**A**$^{-1}$)**,** is the same as $\dfrac{1}{det(A)}$, if the inverse is exists:

```
detinv1 = det(inv(A1))
```

detinv1 =

   −0.5000

(d) The rank of a matrix is the same as the rank of its transpose:

```
rank1 = rank(A1), rank2 = rank(A2), rank3 = rank(A3)
```

rank1 =

      2

rank2 =

      1

rank3 =

      2

```
rankt1 = rank(A1'), rankt2 = rank(A2'), rankt3 = rank(A3')
```

rankt1 =

      2

rankt2 =

      1

rankt3 =

      2

(e) The determinant of a real matrix is the same as the determinant of its transpose:

```
dett1 = det(A1'), dett2 = det(A2'), dett3 = det(A3')
```

dett1 =

       −2

dett2 =

       0

??? Error using ==> det

Matrix must be square. ■

Two linear subspaces associated with linear systems are the **range** and the **null space**. If **A** is an $m \times n$ matrix with rank r, the range of **A** is the linear space spanned by the columns of **A**. The dimension of this space is r, that is the rank of **A**. The columns of **A** are linearly independent if $r = n$. The MATLAB command `orth` gives an othonormal basis in the range of **A**.

The null space of **A** is the space of all vectors **x** for which **A x = 0**. In MATLAB, an orthonormal basis in the null space is obtained with the command `null`.

If we have a set of vectors v_1, v_2, ..., v_n it is possible to check if they are linearly dependent by defining the matrix **B** = [v_1, v_2 ... v_n]. For instance, if the rank of **B** is $n-1$, one of the vectors v_i can be written as a linear combination of the others.

The angle between two vectors, or in general between two subspaces, can be determined by the command `subspace`.

Command 57	RANGE, NULL SPACE, AND ANGLES BETWEEN SUBSPACES
`orth(A)`	gives a matrix whose columns form an orthonormal basis in the range of **A**. The number of columns is equal to the rank of **A**.
`null(A)`	gives a matrix whose columns form an orthonormal basis in the null space of **A**. The number of columns is equal to the dimension of the null space.
`subspace(x,y)`	gives the angle between the column vectors **x** and **y**. The lengths, but not the norms, of the vectors have to be the same.
`subspace(A,B)`	gives the angle between the subspaces spanned by the columns of **A** and **B**. The lengths of the columns have to be the same.

■ Example 7.2

We try the commands `orth`, `null` and `subspace` on the same matrices as in Example figure 7.1:

(a) `Range1 = orth(A1), Range2 = orth(A2), Range3 = orth(A3)`

Range1 =

    0.5760   0.8174

    0.8174 −0.5760

Range2 =

    0.4472

    0.8944

Range3 =

    0.3667   −0.9303

    0.9303   0.3667

(b) `rank1 = rank(orth(A1)), rank2 = rank(orth(A2)),...`
`rank3 = rank(orth(A3))`

    rank1 =

        2

    rank2 =

        1

    rank3 =

        2

The rank of the range of a matrix is of course the same as the rank of the matrix itself.

(c) `nullspace1 = null(A1), nullspace2 = null(A2),...`
`nullspace3 = null(A3)`

    nullspace1 =

        [ ]

    nullspace2 =

      −0.9487

       0.3162

    nullspace3 =

      −0.8729

       0.4364

      −0.2182

The [] indicates that the null space is empty. The null vector is the only vector that results in the null vector when **A** operates on it.

(d) `nullspacet1   =   null(A1'),   nullspacet2   =   null(A2'),...`
`nullspacet3 = null(A3')`

    nullspacet1 =

        [ ]

nullspacet2 =

    −0.8944

    0.4472

nullspacet3 =

    []

(e) `Ranget1 = orth(A1'), range2 = orth(A2'),...Ranget3 = orth(A3')`

Ranget1 =

    0.4046   0.9145

    0.9145 −0.4046

range2 =

    0.3162

    0.9487

Ranget3 =

    0.2197 −0.4357

    0.7508 −0.4958

    0.6229   0.7513

(f) `angle = subspace(null(A2),orth(A2'))` gives

angle =

    1.5708

The angle is $\pi/2$. This implies that the two spaces are orthogonal. Note that the command `subspace` requires columns of equal length.   ■

7.2 Solving linear systems and LU factorization

Linear systems are solved in MATLAB with the operator \, which is a very powerful and intelligent operator. It is often valuable to study the computing process in more detail. There are several commands in MATLAB to do this.

Let **A** be an $n \times n$ matrix, and let **b** and **x** be column vectors with n elements. As an alternative, **B** and **X** can be matrices with n rows and m columns. In MATLAB, the system **A x = b** is solved with the command:

```
x = A\b
```

The more general system **A X** = **B**, that is with multiple right-hand sides, **B** = [**b**$_1$ **b**$_2$ ... **b**$_n$], are solved in the same manner by:

```
X = A\B
```

If **A** is singular, or almost singular, an error message is given.

■ Example 7.3

Let us solve the following system in MATLAB:

$$\begin{cases} 2x_1 + 3x_2 = 7 \\ 4x_1 + x_2 = 9 \end{cases}$$

We form the coefficient matrix **A**, and the right-hand side **b**:

$$A = \begin{bmatrix} 2 & 3 \\ 4 & 1 \end{bmatrix} \qquad b = \begin{bmatrix} 7 \\ 9 \end{bmatrix}$$

The unknown vector **x** = [x_1 x_2]' is sought, and can be obtained by: `x = A\b`

```
x =

    2

    1
```
■

MATLAB uses different methods to solve linear systems, depending on the coefficient matrix **A**. If possible, MATLAB exploits the structure of the matrix. For instance if **A** is positive definite, MATLAB uses Cholesky factorization.

If MATLAB does not find an alternative method, the computations are carried out with Gaussian elimination and partial pivoting, and can be described as an **LU factorization** or **LU decomposition** of **A**. Basically, it holds that **A=L U**, where **U** is an upper triangular matrix and **L** is a lower triangular matrix with a unit diagonal.

However, to guarantee stability in the computations, partial pivoting is used. This means that **L** is usually a permuted lower triangular matrix, that is some rows are interchanged. Thus, **L** might appear to lack structure. These permutations define a **permutation matrix, P.**

A permutation matrix **P** of size $n \times n$ has n unit entries placed in an order where each row and column have all zeros except for exactly one unit entry. The inverse of a permutation matrix is the same as its transpose.

The LU factorization can now be expressed with the non-permuted lower triangular matrix $\mathbf{L}_l$ as:

$$\mathbf{P\,A} = \mathbf{L}_1\,\mathbf{U}$$

that is our permuted matrix $\mathbf{L}$ is given by $\mathbf{L} = \mathbf{P}'\,\mathbf{L}_l$.

In MATLAB the command `lu` makes it possible to obtain $\mathbf{U}$ and either the permuted or the non-permuted lower triangular matrices $\mathbf{L}$. In the latter case the permutation matrix $\mathbf{P}$ is also given.

Command 58	LU DECOMPOSITION

`[L,U] = lu(A)`	gives an upper triangular matrix $\mathbf{U}$, and a permuted lower triangular matrix $\mathbf{L}$, that is $\mathbf{L}$ is the product of a lower triangular matrix with a unit diagonal and a permutation matrix, the inverse of $\mathbf{P}$.
`[L,U,P] = lu(A)`	gives an upper triangular matrix $\mathbf{U}$, a lower triangular matrix $\mathbf{L}$ with a unit diagonal, and a permutation matrix $\mathbf{P}$, so that $\mathbf{L\,U} = \mathbf{P\,A}$.

■ **Example 7.4**

If $\mathbf{A}$ is defined by `A = [1 2 3; 4 5 6; 7 8 0];` and we type `[L,U] = lu(A)` the result is:

$L =$

0.1429	1.0000	0
0.5714	0.5000	1.0000
1.0000	0	0

$U =$

7.0000	8.0000	0
0	0.8571	3.0000
0	0	4.5000

Here the inverse of the permutation matrix is:

$$\mathbf{P}^{-1} = \mathbf{P}' = \begin{bmatrix} 0 & 1 & 0 \\ 0 & 0 & 1 \\ 1 & 0 & 0 \end{bmatrix}$$

Let us perform this Gaussian elimination in detail, and follow what really took place:

$$A = \begin{bmatrix} 1 & 2 & 3 \\ 4 & 5 & 6 \\ 7 & 8 & 0 \end{bmatrix} \quad A1 = \begin{bmatrix} 7 & 8 & 0 \\ 4 & 5 & 6 \\ 1 & 2 & 3 \end{bmatrix} \quad A2 = \begin{bmatrix} 7 & 8 & 0 \\ 0 & 0.4286 & 6 \\ 0 & 0.8571 & 3 \end{bmatrix}$$

$$A3 = \begin{bmatrix} 7 & 8 & 0 \\ 0 & 0.8571 & 3 \\ 0 & 0.4286 & 6 \end{bmatrix} \quad A4 = \begin{bmatrix} 7 & 8 & 0 \\ 0 & 0.8571 & 3 \\ 0 & 0 & 4.5 \end{bmatrix}$$

We start with the matrix **A**. The first pivot element is in position $(1,1)$. By interchanging the first row with the third, we get the largest possible pivot element, that is 7. This is the first permutation, and we get the matrix **A1**. Next the first elimination gives us the matrix **A2**.

The second pivot element is in position $(2,2)$. We switch rows two and three, to get the matrix **A3**, and the elimination gives us **A4**, which is the same as our matrix **U**.

We performed two permutations. First interchange of rows one and three, that is:

$$P1 = \begin{bmatrix} 0 & 0 & 1 \\ 0 & 1 & 0 \\ 1 & 0 & 0 \end{bmatrix}$$

and second interchange of rows two and three, that is:

$$P2 = \begin{bmatrix} 1 & 0 & 0 \\ 0 & 0 & 1 \\ 0 & 1 & 0 \end{bmatrix}$$

The product of **P1** and **P2** forms **P**:

$$P1\ P2 = P = \begin{bmatrix} 0 & 0 & 1 \\ 1 & 0 & 0 \\ 0 & 1 & 0 \end{bmatrix}$$

and its inverse is:

$$P^{-1} = \begin{bmatrix} 0 & 1 & 0 \\ 0 & 0 & 1 \\ 1 & 0 & 0 \end{bmatrix}$$

If we type `[L,U,P] = lu(A)` the result is as expected:

$$L =$$

1.0000	0	0
0.1429	1.0000	0
0.5714	0.5000	1.0000

$$U =$$

7.0000	8.0000	0
0	0.8571	3.0000
0	0	4.5000

$$P =$$

0	0	1
1	0	0
0	1	0

∎

7.3 Row echelon matrices

An alternative method to the LU factorization is to reduce the coefficient matrix **A** to the row echelon form. This is more general since it can be applied to rectangular matrices.

To every $m \times n$ matrix **A** there is a permutation matrix **P**, a lower triangular matrix **L** with unit diagonal, and an $m \times n$ echelon matrix **R** so that $P A = L R$.

A matrix is said to be in **reduced row echelon form** if the following is true:

- Zero rows, if there are any, are placed at the bottom of the matrix.

- The first non-zero element of each row is a *1*. This element is referred to as the leading *1*.

- The leading *1* of every row is placed to the right of the leading *1* of the previous row.

- The rest of the elements of a column with a leading *1* are all zeros.

We can use the command `rref` in MATLAB to analyze the system **A x = b**.

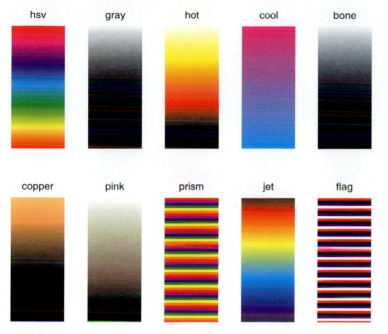

hsv gray hot cool bone

copper pink prism jet flag

Figure C.1 Ten different predefined MATLAB color maps. Defined in Section 13.6. Commands used: `colormap`, `pcolor`, and `subplot`.

Figure C.2 An example of MATLAB as an engineering tool. Computer simulation of airflow around a two-element NACA0012 airfoil for prediction of lift and drag forces. Mach = 0.7. Upper figure: computational grids. Lower figure: pressure distribution. Commands used: `subplot`, `mesh`, `patch`, `axis`, `caxis`, `title`, `surf`, `view(2)`, `colormap`, `shading flat`. In the upper figure we have chosen `'FaceColor' = none` (as defined in Example 14.16(a) in Section 14.2). Grids and computations by Eva Pärt-Enander, Dept Scientific Computing, Uppsala.

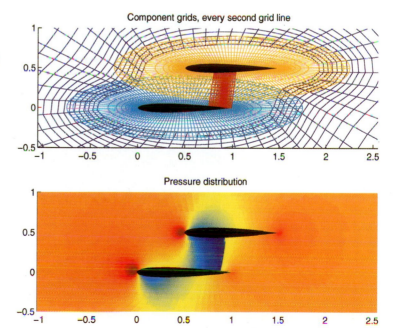

Component grids, every second grid line

Pressure distribution

Figure C.3   A tube surrounding a three-dimensional knot.
Commands used: `surf`, `shading flat`, and `colormap`.

Figure C.4   Zebroid.
Commands used: `surf`,
`shading flat`, and
`colormap`.

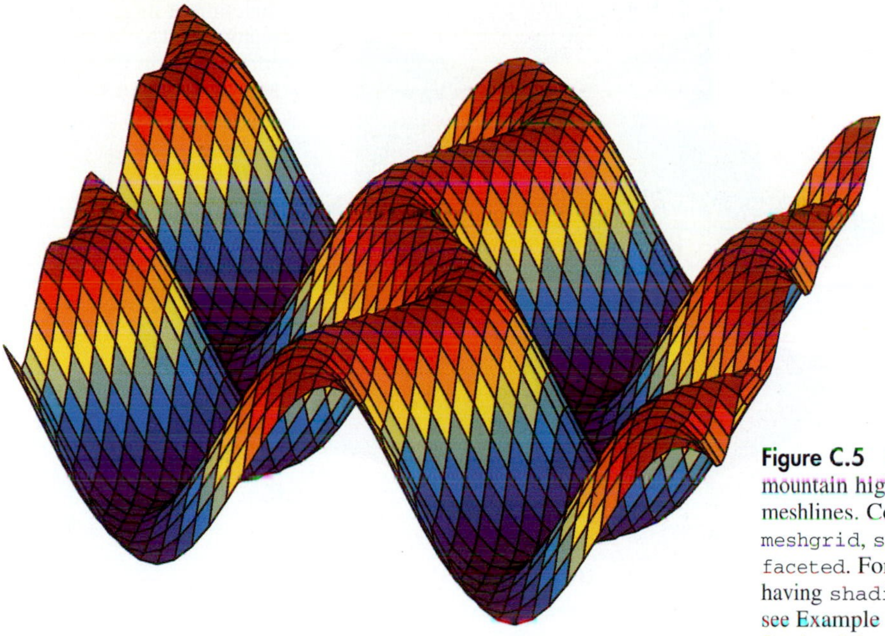

Figure C.5 Cosine mountain highway with meshlines. Commands used: `meshgrid`, `surf`, `shading faceted`. For the case for having `shading interp` see Example 1.1(b) in Section 1.2.

Figure C.6 This is a demonstration of MATLAB graphics being applied to both two- and three-dimensional representations of data. By calling the function `makevase`, the user can specify a two-dimensional line shape, the body-of-revolution corresponding to that line will be plotted using `surfl`.

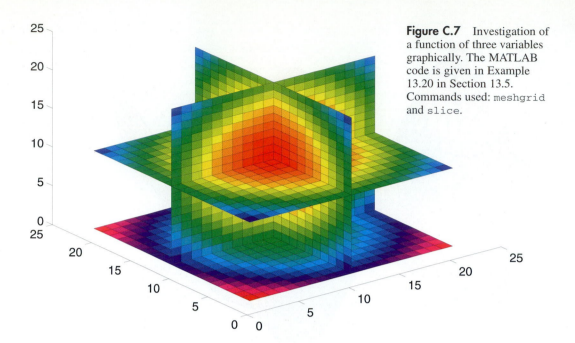

Figure C.7 Investigation of a function of three variables graphically. The MATLAB code is given in Example 13.20 in Section 13.5. Commands used: `meshgrid` and `slice`.

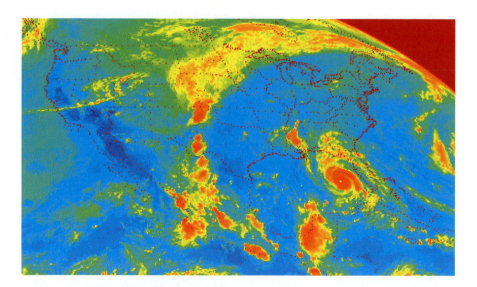

Figure C.8 An example of MATLAB as a vizualization tool when postprocessing data. This is a satellite view of Hurricane Andrew as it crossed Miami on its way towards the Louisiana coast. The image was rendered using the MATLAB `image` function. Data: GOES-7 weather satellite. (Property of The MathWorks Inc.)

Command 59	REDUCED ROW ECHELON FORM

`rref(A)`	gives the reduced row echelon form of **A**, computed by Gauss–Jordan elimination and row pivoting.
`rref(A,tol)`	same as the previous, but uses the tolerance *tol*. The tolerance is used to determine when an element is considered negligible.
`rrefmovie(A)`	computes the reduced row echelon form, and shows step by step how the computations are progressing.

Normally the tolerance used is $tol = max(size(A)) \times eps \times norm(A, inf)$. The command `norm` is defined in Section 7.6.

■ **Example 7.5**

Let

$$A = \begin{bmatrix} 1 & 3 & 3 & 2 \\ 2 & 6 & 9 & 5 \\ -1 & -3 & 3 & 0 \end{bmatrix} \qquad B = \begin{bmatrix} 2 & 1 & 1 \\ 4 & 1 & 0 \\ -2 & 2 & 1 \end{bmatrix}$$

(a) We know that some of the rows of the matrix **A** are linearly dependent if the matrix given by `rref(A)` contains one or more rows of zeros. The same test can be carried out on the columns of **A** by the command `rref(A')`. The commands `Aref = rref(A)`, `Bref = rref(B)` give:

Aref =

1.0000	3.0000	0	1.0000
0	0	1.0000	0.3333
0	0	0	0

Bref =

1	0	0
0	1	0
0	0	1

(b) One way to determine the rank of a matrix **A** is to count the number of non-zero rows in the reduced row echelon form of **A**. In the current example, we see that **A** has rank two, and **B** has rank three. We verify this with the command `rank: rankA = rank(A)`, `rankB = rank(B)` give

$$rankA =$$
$$2$$
$$rankB =$$
$$3$$

■

The command `rref` may be used to investigate a system of linear equations. Let $\mathbf{Ax = b}$ be a linear system of equations, and form the matrix $\mathbf{B} = [\mathbf{A}\ \mathbf{b}]$. The command `C = rref(B)` gives a matrix $\mathbf{C}$ in reduced row echelon form. Then the following holds:

- If $\mathbf{C}$ contains one or more rows with all zeroes, the system contains redundant information. This means that one or more of the equations can be removed.

- If $\mathbf{C}$ contains a row where all elements but the last are zero, that is $(0, 0, \ldots, 0, 1)$, the system contains a contradiction, and no solution exists.

- If the system has a unique solution, it is found in the last column of $\mathbf{C}$.

7.4 Cholesky factorization

If a matrix $\mathbf{A}$ is symmetric and **positive definite**, that is $\mathbf{A} = \mathbf{A}'$ and $\mathbf{x}'\mathbf{Ax} > 0$ for every $\mathbf{x} \neq \mathbf{0}$, then there exists an upper triangular matrix $\mathbf{G}$ with positive diagonal elements such that $\mathbf{G}'\mathbf{G} = \mathbf{A}$.

This special case of LU factorization is called **Cholesky factorization**, and requires only about half as many arithmetic operations as the normal LU factorization. Note that the Cholesky factorization in some textbooks is defined in terms of lower triangular matrices.

Cholesky factorization is used automatically by MATLAB when symmetric positive definite systems are solved with left division, \.

The command `chol` can be used to compute the Cholesky factor of a positive definite matrix $\mathbf{A}$:

Command 60	CHOLESKY FACTORIZATION

`chol(A)`	gives an upper triangular matrix which is the Cholesky factor of $\mathbf{A}$. An error message is given if $\mathbf{A}$ is not positive definite.
`[G,err] = chol(A)`	gives the Cholesky factor $\mathbf{G}$ of the matrix $\mathbf{A}$. No error message is given if $\mathbf{A}$ is not positive definite, instead *err* is set non-zero.

■ **Example 7.6**

(a) `b = [-1 -1 -1]; A = 4*eye(4) + diag(b,-1) + diag(b,1),...`
   `G = chol(A)` give:

   $A =$

4	*−1*	*0*	*0*
−1	*4*	*−1*	*0*
0	*−1*	*4*	*−1*
0	*0*	*−1*	*4*

   $G =$

2.0000	*−0.5000*	*0*	*0*
0	*1.9365*	*−0.5164*	*0*
0	*0*	*1.9322*	*−0.5175*
0	*0*	*0*	*1.9319*

   We check this result by typing `Test = G'*G` and get:

   Test =

4.0000	*−1.0000*	*0*	*0*
−1.0000	*4.0000*	*−1.0000*	*0*
0	*−1.0000*	*4.0000*	*−1.0000*
0	*0*	*−1.0000*	*4.0000*

   Thus we get the matrix **A** back again.

(b) To study the difference in the number of arithmetic operations between the LU and the Cholesky factorizations we type:

   `flops(0), lu(A); flops, flops(0), chol(A); flops`

   and get:

   ans =

   34

   ans =

   30

   However, the difference is more obvious for larger systems.   ■

7.5 QR factorization

A third alternative, in addition to the LU and Cholesky factorizations, is to use **QR factorization** or **QR decomposition**, when linear systems are solved.

Let **A** be an $n \times n$ matrix. Then **A** can be factorized as:

$$\mathbf{A} = \mathbf{Q} \, \mathbf{R}$$

where **Q** is a unitary matrix and **R** is an upper triangular matrix of the same size as **A**. The system **A x = b** can be written as **Q R x = b**, or equivalent:

$$\mathbf{R} \, \mathbf{x} = \mathbf{Q}' \, \mathbf{b}.$$

This is an upper triangular system, and thus easy to solve.

The main advantage of QR factorization in comparison with Gaussian elimination, is a higher numerical stability. However, it is also more expensive in terms of arithmetic operations.

The QR factorization can be obtained in MATLAB with the command `qr`. Note that it is also possible to decompose $m \times n$ matrices. Thus we treat this general case and assume that **A** is an $m \times n$ matrix.

Command 61   **QR FACTORIZATION**

`[Q,R] = qr(A)`	gives an $m \times m$ matrix **Q** whose columns form an orthonormal basis, and an upper triangular $m \times n$ matrix **R**, so that **A = Q R**.
`[Q,R,P] = qr(A)`	gives a matrix **Q**, with orthonormal columns, an upper triangular matrix **R** with diagonal elements decreasing in magnitude, and a permutation matrix **P** so that **A P = Q R**.
`[Q,R] = qr(A,0)`	gives a QR factorization economized in arithmetic operations and storage. If the number of rows is less than the number of columns in the $m \times n$ matrix **A**, then only the first n columns of **Q** are calculated, and thus **Q** is of the same size as **A**. Can also be obtained with a permutation matrix, see above or type `help qr`.
`[Q1,R1] = qrdelete(Q,R,j)`	gives a new QR factorization of the matrix made out of **A** with the *j*th column in the matrix **A** removed. The matrices **Q** and **R** are the QR factors of **A**.

| Command 61 | **QR FACTORIZATION** (continued) |

```
[Q1,R1] =
qrinsert(Q,R,b,j)
```
gives a new QR factorization of the matrix made out of **A** with an extra column **b** inserted before the *j*th column in the matrix **A** where **Q** and **R** are the QR factors of **A**. If $j = n+1$ the new column is the last one.

■ Example 7.7

(a) Let us solve **A** x = **b**, where **A** and **b** are given by:

$$A = \begin{bmatrix} 1 & 2 & 2 \\ 3 & 2 & 2 \\ 1 & 1 & 2 \end{bmatrix} \qquad b = \begin{bmatrix} 7 \\ 9 \\ 5 \end{bmatrix}$$

```
[Q,R] = qr(A), x = R \ Q' * b give:
```

$Q =$

−0.3015	0.9239	−0.2357
−0.9045	−0.3553	−0.2357
−0.3015	0.1421	0.9428

$R =$

−3.3166	−2.7136	−3.0151
0	1.2792	1.4213
0	0	0.9428

$x =$

1.0000

2.0000

1.0000

This is the same as we get by A\b.

(b) Let us compare the number of arithmetic operations required to solve a linear system using the QR factorization and using the left division. To emphasize the difference we apply the methods to a larger system:

```
A = rand(10,10); b = rand(10,1); flops(0)
```

```
x = A\b; lureq = flops
```
lureq =

   1370

```
flops(0), [Q,R] = qr(A); x = R\Q'*b; qrreq = flops
```
qrreq =

   5285

QR factorization can be used to solve overdetermined systems, that is systems with more equations than unknowns (see Section 7.7), and when computing eigenvalues and eigenvectors (see Section 8.2).

One of several ways to compute the QR factorization of a matrix is to apply a series of **Givens rotations**. Givens rotations applied to vectors of length two can be obtained with the command `planerot`. To apply a Givens rotation to a matrix, the colon notation must be used.

Command 62	GIVENS ROTATIONS

`planerot(x)`	gives a Givens rotation in a 2×2 matrix that clears the second element of the two-element vector **x**. The command is used by the MATLAB functions `qrinsert` and `qrdelete`.
`[G,y] = planerot(x)`	gives the Givens rotation as above in **G**, and the result in $\mathbf{y} = \mathbf{G}\,\mathbf{x}$.

■ **Example 7.8**

A Givens rotation can be described as a plane rotation. Let the 2×2 matrix **A** have the vectors **x** and **y** as columns.

$$A = \begin{bmatrix} 1 & 1 \\ -1 & 2 \end{bmatrix} \qquad x = \begin{bmatrix} 1 \\ -1 \end{bmatrix} \qquad y = \begin{bmatrix} 1 \\ 2 \end{bmatrix}$$

If we type `G = planerot(x)`, that is **G** rotates the vector **x** to the x-axis, and let **G** operate on **A** by `Anew = G*A` we obtain as result:

Anew =

   1.4142   −0.7071

      0   2.1213

We see that the vector norms of the columns in **A** and **Anew** are the same by giving the commands:

```
xnorm = norm(x), ynorm = norm(y), xnewnorm = norm(Anew(:,1)), ...
ynewnorm = norm(Anew(:,2))
```

> *xnorm =*
>
>   *1.4142*
>
> *ynorm =*
>
>   *2.2361*
>
> *xnewnorm =*
>
>   *1.4142*
>
> *ynewnorm =*
>
>   *2.2361*

that is the norm (also called length) of each column is unchanged. The command norm is defined in Section 7.6. In Figure 7.1 we see that the rotation is the same for both of the columns in **A**. ∎

To apply Givens rotation on a matrix and in order to reduce the elements in the matrix we have to do some programming. For this, see the example on planerot in Section 12.2.

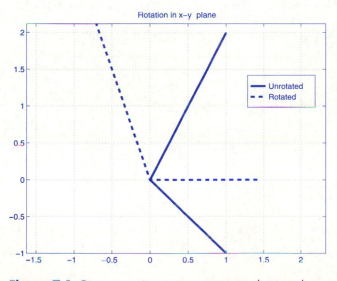

Figure 7.1 Givens rotation on two vectors in the *x–y* plane.

7.6 Norms and condition

A **vector norm** is a scalar, that is a measure of the magnitude or length of a vector, and should not be confused with length as the number of elements in a vector. Various norms can be obtained in MATLAB with the command `norm`.

Command 63	VECTOR NORMS

`norm(x)`	gives $\|\mathbf{x}\|_2 = \sqrt{\sum_k |x_k|^2}$, that is the Euclidean norm.
`norm(x,inf)`	gives $\|\mathbf{x}\|_\infty$, that is the maximum norm, the same as `max(abs(x))`.
`norm(x,1)`	gives $\|\mathbf{x}\|_1$, that is $\sum_k |x_k|$.
`norm(x,p)`	gives $\|\mathbf{x}\|_p$, that is $\sqrt[p]{\sum_k |x_k|^p}$. Thus `norm(x,2) = norm(x)`.
`norm(x,-inf)`	gives the smallest element by absolute value, that is `min(abs(x))`. Note that this is not a vector norm.

■ **Example 7.9**

Let `x = [3 4 5];`

```
norm1 = norm(x,1), norm2 = norm(x,2),...
norminf = norm(x,inf), nonorm = norm(x,-inf) give:
```

norm1 =

   12

norm2 =

   7.0711

norminf =

   5

nonorm =

   3   ■

A **matrix norm** is a measure of the size of a matrix, not to be mixed up with size in the sense of the number of rows and columns. Matrix norms are often used in estimating errors due to perturbations in data or in numerical computations.

The *p*-norms of a square matrix are defined by the vector norms:

$$\|A\|_p = \sup_{x \neq 0} \frac{\|A\,x\|_p}{\|x\|_p}$$

These definitions are not actually used in the computations. Instead the expressions in Command 64 are used. These are equivalent to the definitions above if the matrices are square but they can also be used to compute norms of non-square matrices.

Since the computation of the Euclidean norm is an expensive operation, there is also a command to compute an estimate of the Euclidean norm, `normest`.

Command 64	MATRIX NORMS

`norm(A)`	gives $\|A\|_2$, that is the Euclidean norm, which is the same as the largest singular value of **A**, see Section 8.3.
`norm(A,2)`	gives $\|A\|_2$, the same as `norm(A)`.
`normest(A)`	estimates the Euclidean norm of **A**. The relative error is less than 10^{-6}.
`normest(A,tol)`	estimates the Euclidean norm of **A**. The relative error is less than *tol*.
`norm(A,1)`	gives $\|A\|_1$, that is the largest column sum of **A**. Column sum means the sum of the absolute values of each column element.
`norm(A,inf)`	gives $\|A\|_\infty$, that is the largest row sum of **A**. Row sum means the sum of the absolute values of each row element.
`norm(A,'fro')`	gives $\|A\|_F = \sqrt{\sum_i \sum_j \lvert a_{ij} \rvert^2}$, the Frobenius norm. This can not be obtained by the definition of the matrix *p*-norm above.

■ **Example 7.10**

(a) Let A = [1 1;2 3];

```
norm1 = norm(A,1), norm2 = norm(A,2),...
norminf = norm(A,inf), normf = norm(A,'fro')
```

norm1 =

4

norm2 =

3.8643

norminf =

5

normf =

3.8730

(b) Let us compare the number of arithmetic operations required to compute the Euclidean norm and an estimate of the Euclidean norm of a large matrix.

```
A = rand(1000);
flops(0), norm2 = norm(A), expensive = flops
```

norm2 =

500.1837

expensive =

2.6929e + 09

```
flops(0),normapprox = normest(A), cheaper = flops
```

normapprox =

500.1837

cheaper =

9022008

```
times = expensive/cheaper
```

times =

298.4812

■

Let **A x = b** be a linear system of equations. The **condition number** of a system is a real number greater than or equal to *1*, measuring the sensitivity of the solution **x** with respect to perturbations in the data, that is in **A** and/or **b**. A badly conditioned system has a large condition number. The definition is:

$$\text{cond}(\mathbf{A}) = \|\mathbf{A}\|\|\mathbf{A}^{-1}\|$$

The command `cond(A)` gives the condition number in the Euclidean norm, which can be expressed as the quotient of the largest and the smallest singular value of **A** (see Section 8.3).

Command 65	CONDITION NUMBER

`cond(A)`	gives the condition number of **A** in the Euclidean norm.
`condest(A)`	gives a lower bound estimate in the one-norm of the condition number of the matrix **A**.
`[c,v] = condest(A)`	gives a lower bound estimate of the condition number c, in the one norm of A, and also computes a vector v, where $\|A\,v\| = \|A\| \cdot \|\mathbf{v}\|/c$. For large c this is an approximate null vector.
`[c,v] = condest(A,tr)`	gives c and **v** as above, but also displays information of steps in the calculations. If *tr = 1* information on every step is displayed, and if *tr = -1* the quotient `c/rcond(A)` is displayed.
`rcond(A)`	gives another estimate of the sensitivity of a system defined by the matrix **A**. A badly conditioned matrix **A** gives a number close to *0*, while a well conditioned matrix gives a number close to *1*.

Condition numbers in the other norms must be computed explicitly, for example:

```
cond1(A) = norm(A,1)*norm(inv(A),1),
condinf(A) = norm(A,inf)*norm(inv(A),inf).
```

The condition of a system reveals its sensitivity to perturbations in the data and in the computations.

■ **Example 7.11**

Let us try the Hilbert matrix (see Section 4.3): `bad = cond(hilb(5))` gives:

bad =

>   *4.7661e + 05*

This implies that in the worst case a perturbation on the right-hand side or in the coefficient matrix can be multiplied by the number `bad`, and five decimal places might be lost.   ■

7.7 Overdetermined and underdetermined systems

A linear $m \times n$-system of equations **A x = b** is said to be **overdetermined** if $m > n$, that is if it has more equations than unknowns. These equations are usually inconsistent, and thus the system does not have an exact solution. This is, for instance, a frequent problem when fitting curves to experimental data.

The key is to try to find the vector **x** that minimizes the total error in the m equations. There are several ways to do this, but the most frequently used is to minimize the square of the sum of the errors:

$$ e = \sum_{i=1}^{m} \left(b_i - \sum_{j=1}^{n} a_{i,j} x_j \right)^2 = \| \mathbf{b} - \mathbf{A}\, \mathbf{x} \|_2^2 $$

This is the **method of least squares**, and a **least square solution** can be obtained with either the operator \ or in a special case with the command `nnls`. It is also possible to exploit the sparse matrices discussed in Chapter 9, and here we mention the command `spaugment` which gives a sparse matrix used in the computations.

Command 66	SOLUTIONS BY LEAST SQUARES
`A\b`	gives the solution by the sense of least squares. See also Section 3.3. If **b = B** is a matrix, then the system corresponding to each column in **B** is solved.
`spaugment(A,c)`	gives the square symmetric sparse matrix `T = [c*I A; A' 0]`. The overdetermined system **A x = b** can now be solved by `T\z` where **z** is the vector **b** with trailing zeros. The parameter c can be left out, MATLAB then uses a value according to the setting in `spparms`. Type `help spparms`.

Command 66	SOLUTIONS BY LEAST SQUARES (continued)
nnls(A,b)	gives a solution of the least square problem under the additional constraint that all the components of the solution must be non-negative. Type `help nnls` to get more information.
lscov(A,b,V)	returns the least square solution when the covariance **V** is known. This means that $(b-Ax)'V^{-1}(b-Ax)$ is minimized. Type `help lscov` for more information.

MATLAB usually performs a QR factorization when division from the left is used to solve overdetermined systems. If the system does not have full rank, and lacks a unique least square solution, undetermined values are set to zero. A warning message is then issued.

■ **Example 7.12**

Let:

$$\mathbf{A1} = \begin{bmatrix} 1 & 1 \\ 1 & 2 \\ 1 & 3 \end{bmatrix} \qquad \mathbf{A2} = \begin{bmatrix} 1 & 3 \\ 1 & 3 \\ 1 & 3 \end{bmatrix} \qquad \mathbf{b} = \begin{bmatrix} 2 \\ 0 \\ -1 \end{bmatrix}$$

`fullrank = A1\b, notfullrank = A2\b` gives:

fullrank =

> 3.3333

> −1.5000

Warning: Rank deficient, rank = 1 tol = 3.4613e−15

notfullrank =

> 0

> 0.1111

■

If $n < m$, then the system **A** x=b is underdetermined. Such systems usually have infinite solutions, and MATLAB selects one. No warning message is given.

■ **Example 7.13**

(a) Let:

$$A = \begin{bmatrix} 1 & 1 & 1 \\ 1 & 2 & 3 \end{bmatrix} \qquad b = \begin{bmatrix} 2 \\ 3 \end{bmatrix}$$

```
x = A\b gives:
```

$x =$

   1.5000

   0

   0.5000

The complete solution is:

$$x = \begin{bmatrix} 1.5 - t/2 \\ t \\ 0.5 - t/2 \end{bmatrix} \quad \text{for all values of } t$$

Unfortunately, MATLAB cannot give this general solution.

(b) Let:

$$a = \begin{bmatrix} 1 \\ 2 \\ 3 \end{bmatrix} \qquad b = \begin{bmatrix} 2 \\ -2 \\ 2 \end{bmatrix}$$

We can now study the result of various matrix divisions, **b** divided by **a**.

Division from the left gives:

```
left = a\b
```

left =

   0.2857

or *2/7*, which is the solution of the overdetermined system **a x = b**.

Division from the right gives:

```
Right = b/a
```

Right =

0	0	0.6667
0	0	−0.6667
0	0	0.6667

which is the same as `(a'\b')'`, that is one solution of the underdetermined system **a**′**x**′ = **b**′.

Elementwise division from the left:

```
elementwiseleft = a.\b
```

elementwiseleft =

  2.0000

  −1.0000

  0.6667

which is the same as the elementwise division from the right:

```
elementwiseright = b./a
```

elementwiseright =

  2.0000

  −1.0000

  0.6667

Eigenvalues and Eigenvectors

In MATLAB there are efficient commands for the computation of eigenvalues and eigenvectors. Different subresults and factorizations can also be obtained. This can be useful for instance when teaching linear algebra.

8.1 Computation of eigenvalues and eigenvectors

Let $\mathbf{A}$ be an $n \times n$ matrix. The eigenvalue problem of $\mathbf{A}$ is to find the solution of the system:

$$\mathbf{A}\,\mathbf{x} = \lambda\,\mathbf{x}$$

in which λ is a scalar and $\mathbf{x}$ is a non-zero column vector of length n. The scalar λ is an **eigenvalue** of $\mathbf{A}$, and $\mathbf{x}$ is the corresponding **eigenvector**. Also for real $\mathbf{A}$, the eigenvalues and eigenvectors may be complex. An $n \times n$ matrix has n eigenvalues denoted by $\lambda_1, \lambda_2, ..., \lambda_n$.

In MATLAB there is a command, `eig`, for determining the eigenvalues and the eigenvectors of $\mathbf{A}$. The eigenvectors are normalized, that is the Euclidean norm of each eigenvector is *1* (see Section 7.6).

The command `eig` automatically performs a balancing of $\mathbf{A}$. This means that MATLAB determines a **similarity transformation Q** such that $\tilde{\mathbf{A}} = \mathbf{Q}^{-1}\,\mathbf{A}\,\mathbf{Q}$. The eigenvalue problem of $\tilde{\mathbf{A}}$ usually has a better condition than $\mathbf{A}$. In cases when $\mathbf{A}$ has components of the same size as the machine error, the balancing could be bad for the computational process. The `eig` command with the parameter `nobalance` computes the eigenvalues and eigenvectors without this transformation.

Command 67	EIGENVALUES AND EIGENVECTORS

`eig(A)`	returns a vector containing the eigenvalues of $\mathbf{A}$.
`[X,D] = eig(A)`	returns a diagonal matrix $\mathbf{D}$ with the eigenvalues of $\mathbf{A}$ in its diagonal and a matrix $\mathbf{X}$, whose columns are the corresponding eigenvectors of $\mathbf{A}$ such that $\mathbf{A}\,\mathbf{X} = \mathbf{X}\,\mathbf{D}$. A similarity transformation is performed in order to obtain a matrix with better condition number for the eigenvalues.

Command 67	EIGENVALUES AND EIGENVECTORS (continued)

`[X,D] =` `eig(A,'nobalance')`	determines the eigenvalues and eigenvectors as above, but **A** is not balanced, that is no balancing similarity transformation is performed.
`balance(A)`	gives a balanced matrix.
`[T, B] =` `balance(A)`	gives a diagonal similarity transform **T** and a matrix **B** such that $B = T^{-1} A \, T$. Thus **B** is the balanced matrix of the previous command.

If **A** is real, MATLAB uses the QR factorization in the computations, otherwise the QZ factorization is used.

The **left eigenvectors** are non-zero row vectors **y** that satisfy:

$$y \, A = \lambda \, y.$$

The left eigenvectors can also be computed by `eig` if we use **A′**, since:

$$A' y' = \overline{\lambda} \; y',$$

where the apostrophe is transposition and complex conjugation of the matrix (see Section 3.4), and the overbar denote complex conjugation. The set of eigenvalues of a matrix is called the **spectrum** of the matrix. The **spectral radius**, $\rho(A)$, is defined as `max(abs(eig(A)))`. The product of the eigenvalues of **A** is equal to `det(A)`, and the sum of the eigenvalues is equal to `trace(A)`, that is the sum of the elements on the main diagonal of **A**.

If **X** is a matrix whose columns are the eigenvectors of **A** and the rank of **X** is *n*, then the eigenvectors are linearly independent. If this is not the case, the matrix is called **defective**. If **X′X = I**, then the eigenvectors are orthonormal. This is, for instance, true for symmetric matrices.

■ **Example 8.1**

Let **A** be defined as:

$$A = \begin{bmatrix} -9 & -3 & -16 \\ 13 & 7 & 16 \\ 3 & 3 & 10 \end{bmatrix}$$

(a) The command `[Evect,Evalue] = eig(A)` gives:

  Evect =

0.7071	0.5774	0.5774
−0.7071	0.5774	−0.5774
0.0000	−0.5774	−0.5774

  Evalue =

−6.0000	0	0
0	4.0000	0
0	0	10.0000

The eigenvalues are non-zero and the matrix has full rank, which can be confirmed by `Therank = rank(Evect)`,

  Therank =

  3

We also have `M = Evect'*Evect`

  M =

1.0000	−0.0000	0.8165
−0.0000	1.0000	0.3333
0.8165	0.3333	1.0000

that is the eigenvectors are not orthogonal.

(b) `determinant = prod(diag(Evalue)),...`
`determinant2 = det(A)`

  determinant =

  −240

  determinant2 =

  −240

We see that the determinant is equal to the product of the eigenvalues.

(c) `TheTrace = trace(A), TheTrace2 = sum(diag(Evalue))`

  TheTrace =

  8

  TheTrace2 =

  8

We can see that the trace is equal to the sum of the eigenvalues. ■

If **A** is real, but has complex eigenvalues, these eigenvalues are complex conjugate pairs. If `[X,D]` = `eig(A)`, it is possible to transform **D** to a real block diagonal matrix with the `cdf2rdf` command. Instead of a complex conjugate pair of eigenvalues we obtain a real 2×2 block on the diagonal.

Command 68   **COMPLEX EIGENVALUES IN REAL FORM**

`[Y,E]` = `cdf2rdf(X,D)`   converts a complex diagonal matrix **D** to a real block diagonal matrix **E**. The columns of **Y** are not eigenvectors of **A**.

■ **Example 8.2**

Suppose that **A** is defined as:

$$A = \begin{bmatrix} 0 & 1 & 0 \\ -1 & 0 & 0 \\ 0 & 0 & 3 \end{bmatrix}$$

then `[X,D]` = `eig(A)` returns:

$X =$

0.7071	0.7071	0
0 + 0.7071i	0 − 0.7071i	0
0	0	1.0000

$D =$

0 + 1.0000i	0	0
0	0 − 1.0000i	0
0	0	3.0000

Both **X** and **D** are complex. The command: `[Y,E]` = `cdf2rdf(X,D)` gives the results:

$Y =$

0.7071	0	0
0	0.7071	0
0	0	1.0000

$E =$

0	1	0
−1	0	0
0	0	3

which is the matrix **A** again.

Note: The eigenvalues are the zeros of the characteristic polynomial, $det(\lambda\,\mathbf{I}-\mathbf{A})$, where $\mathbf{I}$ denotes the identity matrix. The `poly` command gives the characteristic polynomial (see Section 10.1). The eigenvalues can then be computed with the `roots` command, but the `eig` command is a far more accurate and efficient method.

The **generalized eigenvalue problem** is to find non-trivial solutions to the system

$$\mathbf{A}\,\mathbf{x} = \lambda\mathbf{B}\,\mathbf{x}$$

where $\mathbf{B}$ also is a square $n \times n$ matrix. The λ-values and the vectors $\mathbf{x}$, which solve the system are called generalized eigenvalues and generalized eigenvectors respectively.

If $\mathbf{B}$ is singular the **QZ algorithm** is used.

Both the standard and the generalized eigenvalue problems can be characterized as special cases of matrix polynomial eigenproblems. These can be solved with the command `polyeig`.

Command 69	GENERALIZED EIGENVALUES AND EIGENVECTORS

`eig(A,B)`	returns a vector containing the generalized eigenvalues, if $\mathbf{A}$ and $\mathbf{B}$ are square matrices.
`[X,D] = eig(A,B)`	returns a diagonal matrix $\mathbf{D}$ with the generalized eigenvalues in the diagonal and a matrix $\mathbf{X}$ whose columns are the corresponding eigenvectors such that $\mathbf{A}\,\mathbf{X} = \mathbf{B}\,\mathbf{X}\,\mathbf{D}$.
`[X,v] = polyeig(A0,A1, ...,Ak)`	gives eigenvalues and eigenvectors to the eigenproblem of degree k $(\mathbf{A}_0 + \lambda\mathbf{A}_1 + \lambda^2\mathbf{A}_2 + \ldots + \lambda^k\mathbf{A}_k)\mathbf{x} = \mathbf{0}$. The vector $\mathbf{v}$, of length nk contains the eigenvalues, and the $n \times nk$ matrix $\mathbf{X}$ has the eigenvectors as its columns. If $\mathbf{A}_0 = \mathbf{A}$, and $\mathbf{A}_1 = -\mathbf{I}$, then it is the standard eigenvalue problem.

To check the condition or sensitivity of the eigenvalues compute the condition number, $cond(\mathbf{X}) = \|\mathbf{X}\|\|\mathbf{X}^{-1}\|$, where $\mathbf{X}$ is the matrix whose columns are eigenvectors of $\mathbf{A}$. A high value of the condition number signals bad condition, that is high sensitivity to perturbations.

To check the condition or sensitivity of the eigenvectors look at the separation of the eigenvalues. Multiple eigenvalues or eigenvalues which are close to each other indicate ill-conditioned problems.

■ **Example 8.3**

Suppose:

$$A = \begin{bmatrix} 3.75 & -0.5 & -0.375 & 0.495 & -1.37 \\ 0.25 & 2.5 & 0.375 & -0.495 & -0.63 \\ 1.25 & -0.5 & 2.875 & 0.495 & -2.12 \\ 0.25 & -0.5 & -0.625 & 2.505 & 0.37 \\ 0.25 & -0.5 & -0.625 & 0.495 & 2.38 \end{bmatrix}$$

The command `[XX,DD] = eig(A)` gives:

XX =

−0.0000	0.0000 − 0.4472i	0.0000 + 0.4472i	−0.4472	0.4472
0.5000	−0.0000 + 0.4472i	−0.0000 − 0.4472i	−0.4472	0.4472
0.5000	0.0000 − 0.4472i	0.0000 + 0.4472i	−0.4472	0.4472
−0.5000	0.0000 − 0.4472i	0.0000 + 0.4472i	−0.4472	0.4472
−0.5000	0.0000 − 0.4472i	0.0000 + 0.4472i	−0.4472	0.4472

Observe that two eigenvectors are non-real, namely column numbers 2 and 3.

DD =

4.0000	0	0	0	0
0	3.0000 + 0.0000i	0	0	0
0	0	3.0000 − 0.0000i	0	0
0	0	0	2.0000	0
0	0	0	0	2.0100

We see that the eigenvalues are *2, 2.01, 3, 3*, and *4*, that is the eigenvector problem is supposed to be ill-conditioned. To get the condition number we type `badmatrix = cond(XX)` which gives:

badmatrix =

1.6388e+08

Compare this number with the condition of the eigenvalues of the matrix in Example 8.2 which is `nicematrix = cond(X)`:

nicematrix =

1.0000

There is a difference!　　　　　　　　　　　　　　　　　　　　■

8.2 Upper Hessenberg form, QR, and QZ factorizations

If only the eigenvalues and eigenvectors themselves are of interest, the methods from the previous section are recommended. However, sometimes it can be of interest to look more closely at the computational process. We define commands for that purpose in this and the next section.

A matrix **H** is an **upper Hessenberg matrix** if all components below the first lower bidiagonal are zero. A symmetric matrix in upper Hessenberg form is therefore tridiagonal. MATLAB can transform a matrix to this form by a similarity transformation.

Command 70	HESSENBERG FORM

`hess(A)`	returns a similarity transformation of **A** into upper Hessenberg form
`[P,H] = hess(A)`	returns the unitary transformation matrix **P** and an upper Hessenberg matrix **H**. These satisfy **A = P H P'** and **P P' = I.**

The **QR algorithm** is a general and efficient numerical method that MATLAB uses to compute all eigenvalues of a matrix, that is when the command `eig` is given. In this method, it is advisable to transform the matrix to a similar upper Hessenberg form.

The QR algorithm is based on the QR factorization. Each $m \times n$ matrix **A** can be written as the product:

$$A = Q R,$$

where **Q** is a unitary $m \times m$ matrix, and **R** is an upper triangular $m \times n$ matrix. If **A** is a square matrix then so is **R**. MATLAB returns the matrices **Q** and **R** when the `qr` command is used (see also Section 7.5).

Command 71	QR FACTORIZATION

`[Q,R] = qr(A)`	gives a unitary $m \times m$ matrix **Q**, and an upper triangular $m \times m$ matrix **R** such that **A = Q R.**
`[Q,R,P] = qr(A)`	produces a unitary $m \times m$ matrix **Q**, whose columns are orthonormal, an upper triangular $m \times n$ matrix **R** with descending diagonal elements and a permutation matrix **P** such that **A P = Q R.**.

If **A** is an upper Hessenberg matrix, then **Q** is also of the same form. This is used in the QR algorithm for which we give a short and incomplete description:

QR Algorithm:

0.   Let $A_0 = A$, $k = 0$.

1.   Find the factorization of A_k: $A_k = Q_k R_k$

2.   Compute the next matrix in the iteration sequence by: $A_{k+1} = R_k Q_k$

        Let $k = k + 1$

3.   Go to 1.

This method, called the unshifted QR method, converges under certain circumstances towards an upper triangular matrix. Since all matrices A_k are **similar** to $A_0 = A$, that is have the same eigenvalues as the original matrix, the diagonal entries of the resulting upper triangular matrix are the eigenvalues of **A**.

If the matrix is transformed first to upper Hessenberg form with zeroes in almost half of the entries, and since this property remains throughout the algorithm, the number of arithmetic operations is reduced considerably. The QR method, as the one built-in in MATLAB, also uses shifts in order to accelerate the convergence.

■   **Example 8.4**

Let us compute the eigenvalues of the matrix

$$A = \begin{bmatrix} -9 & -3 & -16 \\ 13 & 7 & 16 \\ 3 & 3 & 10 \end{bmatrix}$$

which is used in Section 8.1 as well, by executing some steps of the unshifted QR algorithm.

The correct eigenvalues are $\lambda_1 = 10$, $\lambda_2 = 4$ and $\lambda_3 = -6$.
A0 = hess(A); [Q0,R0] = qr(A0); A1 = R0 * Q0 return:

     A1 =

1.7992	*26.8770*	*−12.6126*
2.3625	*4.5085*	*−0.1434*
0	*4.9518*	*1.6923*

We carry out a second step, `[Q1,R1] = qr(A1); A2 = R1 * Q1` and obtain:

$A2 =$

17.607	11.3432	5.0128
−15.3516	−13.6557	−5.8721
0	1.0748	4.0480

In the beginning of the process it is not possible to see what the matrix will converge to but after *10* steps with the algorithm we can see that the components of the lower bidiagonal are small.

`[Q9,R9] = qr(A9); A10 = R9 * Q9` gives:

$A10 =$

10.1297	22.6238	15.3505
−0.0924	−6.161	−5.8036
0	0.0562	4.0319

Note that the upper Hessenberg form is preserved throughout the process. ■

An iterative process like the previous can be written in a short way in MATLAB using the built-in programming language. Examples are shown in Section 12.2.

The **QZ algorithm** is used to compute the **complex eigenpairs** of complex matrices and the generalized eigenvalues, in MATLAB the `qz` command can be called according to Command 72 below.

Command 72   QZ ALGORITHM

`[C,D,Q,Z,V] = qz(A,B)` gives upper triangular matrices **C** and **D** whose diagonal elements are the generalized eigenvalues, and **V** containing the generalized eigenvectors. The matrices **Q** and **Z** are the transformations such that **A = Q, C Z'** and

B = Q' D Z'.

The QZ method is based on the QZ factorization.

8.3 Schur decomposition and singular value decomposition

If **A** is a square matrix, then there is a unitary matrix **U** such that:

$$U^{-1}AU = U'U, AU = T$$

where **T** is upper triangular. This is a similarity transform, so the matrices **A** and **T** have the same eigenvalues and since **T** is a triangular matrix the eigenvalues are located on the diagonal.

If **A** is real and symmetric then **T** has diagonal form, and the columns of **U** are the eigenvectors of **A**.

If **A** is real, but has complex eigenvalues, then **T** is a complex matrix. To avoid complex arithmetic, every pair of complex conjugated eigenvalues can be represented by real *2 × 2* matrices, see Example 8.2 for instance. In that case the matrix **T** is block triangular and real. In MATLAB it is possible to perform a Schur decomposition of a matrix **A** with the `schur` command, which exists in a real and a complex version.

If **A** is real `schur(A)` returns the real Schur form, but if **A** is complex the complex form is returned. The difference is that the real Schur form represents the complex conjugate pairs of eigenvalues as real *2 × 2* blocks in the diagonal, but the complex form returns complex diagonal elements. The function `rsf2csf` converts from real to complex form.

Command 73	**SCHUR DECOMPOSITION**

`schur(A)`	returns the Schur decomposition of **A**, that is the matrix **T** as above.
`[U,T] = schur(A)`	returns the Schur decomposition of **A** and the unitary matrix **U** such that **A = U T U'**.
`[V,S] = rsf2csf(U,T)`	converts matrices **U** and **T** in real Schur form to the matrices **V** and **S** in complex Schur form.

■ **Example 8.5**

Define **A1**, **A2** and **A3** by:

$$A1 = \begin{bmatrix} 2 & 1 \\ 1 & 2 \end{bmatrix} \qquad A2 = \begin{bmatrix} 2 & 1 \\ 0 & 2 \end{bmatrix} \qquad A3 = \begin{bmatrix} 0 & 1 \\ -1 & 0 \end{bmatrix}$$

The commands `Sch1 = schur(A1), Sch2 = schur(A2),...`
`[U,Sch3] = schur(A3)` give:

Sch1 =

1	*0*
0	*3*

Sch2 =

2	*1*
0	*2*

U =

1	*0*
0	*1*

Sch3 =

0	*1*
−1	*0*

We can see that the matrix **Sch3** is not upper triangular due to the complex eigenvalues. To see this we type:

`[V,S] = rsf2csf(U,Sch3)`

V =

0 + 0.7071i	*0.7071*
−0.7071	*0 − 0.7071i*

S =

0 + 1.0000i	*0*
0	*0 − 1.0000i*

that is, the eigenvalues are i and $-i$. ■

MATLAB can also compute the **singular value decomposition**, **SVD**, and the singular values of matrices. These are non-negative numbers. In special cases they are the same as the eigenvalues.

Command 74	**SVD DECOMPOSITION**

`svd(A)`	returns a vector containing the singular values of **A**.
`[U,S,V] = svd(A)`	returns a diagonal matrix **S** and two unitary matrices **U** and **V**, of size $m \times m$ and $n \times n$ respectively. The matrix **S** is of the same size as **A**, that is $m \times n$, containing the singular values of A on the diagonal. The singular values are nonnegative and in descending order. The matrices are such that **A = U S V'** and **U' A V=S**.
`[U,S,V] = svd(A,0)`	returns a more "economic" alternative to the previous command. Only the first n columns of **U** are computed. Here the **S** matrix is $n \times n$.

The pseudo-inverse of **A** is computed by the `pinv(A)` command. MATLAB uses the SVD decomposition to compute the pseudo-inverse (see also Section 7.1).

If s_i are the singular values then $\|\mathbf{A}\|_2 = max\ s_i = s_1$, $\|\mathbf{A}^{-1}\|_2 = (min\ s_i)^{-1} = s_n^{-1}$ and $cond(\mathbf{A}) = s_1/s_n$, where s_n is the smallest singular value. The last expressions are true for nonsingular matrices and also for rectangular matrices of full rank with $m > n$.

■ **Example 8.6**

Let us define these matrices:

$$\mathbf{A} = \begin{bmatrix} 1 & 1 \\ 1 & 2 \\ 1 & 3 \end{bmatrix} \qquad \mathbf{B} = \begin{bmatrix} 1 & -1 & 0 \\ 1 & 2 & 0 \\ 1 & 3 & 0 \end{bmatrix}$$

(a) We compute the singular value decomposition by:

```
[Ua,Sa,Va] = svd(A),  [Ub,Sb,Vb] = svd(B)
```

Ua =

    0.3231   −0.8538   0.4082

    0.5475   −0.1832   −0.8165

    0.7719   0.4873   0.4082

Sa =

4.0791	0
0	0.6005
0	0

Va =

0.4027	−0.9153
0.9153	0.4027

Ub =

−0.1641	0.9668	0.1961
0.5653	0.2551	−0.7845
0.8084	0.0178	0.5883

Sb =

3.9116	0	0
0	1.3036	0
0	0	0

Vb =

0.3092	0.9510	0
0.9510	−0.3092	0
0	0	1.0000

We can see that both **A** and **B** have two non-zero singular values, that is they have rank 2.

(b) The inverses of these matrices cannot be computed, but the pseudo-inverses are obtained by `Pseudoa = pinv(A)`, `Pseudob = pinv(B)`

Pseudoa =

1.3333	0.3333	−0.6667
−0.5000	0	0.5000

Pseudob =

0.6923	0.2308	0.0769
−0.2692	0.0769	0.1923
0	0	0

(c) The norm and the condition number are given by . . .

```
norma = norm(A),
normb = norm(B),...
conda = cond(A), condb = cond(B)
```

norma =
      4.0791
normb =
      3.9116
conda =
      6.7930
Condition is infinite
condb =
          Inf

We can see that the Euclidean norm is equal to the largest singular value and that the condition number is equal to s_1/s_n. ■

9 Sparse Matrices

There are several problems that give rise to matrices in which most of the elements are zero. These matrices are called sparse. One example is numerical solution of ordinary or partial differential equations. To save memory and computing time MATLAB has special commands where the sparsity of the matrices is considered.

9.1 Why sparse matrices?

A sparse matrix has most of the entries equal to zero. This can be used with advantage in computations and in storing the matrix. If we ask MATLAB to treat a matrix as sparse, only the m non-zero entries are stored in an $m \times 3$ matrix. The first column contains the row indices, the second the column indices and the third contains the non-zero elements. The zero entries are not stored. If we suppose that a floating point number requires 8 bytes to be stored, and the indices 4 bytes each, the whole matrix requires $16 * m$ bytes in memory.

■ **Example 9.1**

```
A = eye(1000);
```

is a 1000×1000 identity matrix, that requires about 8 Mb memory. If we use the command

```
B = speye(1000);
```

it is represented by a 1000×3 matrix instead, each row gives a row index, a column index and the element itself. Now only about 16 kb memory is required to store the 1000×1000 identity matrix, that is only about 0.2% of the memory for the full matrix. The same can be done for more general matrices as well.   ■

The computation with sparse matrices is faster since MATLAB only has to operate on the non-zero elements; this is the second great advantage with sparse matrices.

■ **Example 9.2**

Suppose that **A** and **B** are defined as in Example 9.1.

Then the operation `2*A` requires 1 million flops, but the operation `2*B` requires only 2000 flops.   ■

We have to use special commands to get sparse matrices since MATLAB does not create sparse matrices automatically. These commands are presented in the following section. All arithmetic and logical operations from previous chapters can be applied to sparse matrices.

9.2 To create and convert sparse matrices

To create a sparse matrix in MATLAB the command `sparse` is used.

Command 75	CREATING SPARSE MATRICES

`sparse(A)`	returns the matrix **A** in sparse form by removing all non-zero elements. If **A** is already sparse, **A** itself is returned.
`sparse(m,n)`	gives a zero matrix of size $m \times n$ in sparse representation.
`sparse(u,v,a)`	gives a sparse matrix defined by the vectors **u**, **v** and **a** of the same length, where **u** and **v** are integer vectors and **a** is a real or complex vector. The entry (u_i, v_i) has the value a_i. If an element in **a** is zero it is excluded.
	The matrix gets the size $max(u) \times max(v)$.
`sparse(u,v,a,m,n)`	gives a sparse $m \times n$ matrix in which the entry (u_i, v_i) has the value a_i. The vectors **u**, **v** and **a** must be of the same length.
`sparse(u,v,a,m,` `n,nzmax)`	returns a sparse $m \times n$ matrix in which the entry (u_i, v_i) has the value a_i. There is also memory allocated for *nzmax* non-zero elements, and the value of *nzmax* must be at least the length of the vectors.
`find(x)`	returns the indices of the non-zero components of the vector **x**. If **x** = **X** is a matrix, the columns of **X** are considered as one long vector.
`[u,v] = find(A)`	returns the indices of the non-zero elements of the matrix **A**.
`[u,v,s] = find(A)`	returns the indices of the non-zero elements of the matrix **A**, with the values of the elements in the vector **s** and the corresponding indices in **u** and **v**, that is the vectors **u**, **v** and **s** can be used as parameters to the command `sparse`.
`spconvert(D)`	converts a matrix with three columns to a sparse matrix. The first column of **D** contains the row indices, the second column the column indices and the last column the elements.

Furthermore, a sparse matrix can be converted to a full matrix by using the command `full`.

Command 76	CONVERTING TO A FULL MATRIX

`full(S)`	returns the full matrix defined by the sparse matrix **S**.

■ **Example 9.3**

(a) We create a 5×5 identity matrix:

```
A = eye(5);
```

The matrix **A** can be converted to a sparse matrix **B** by

```
B = sparse(A)
```

B =

(1,1)	*1*
(2,2)	*1*
(3,3)	*1*
(4,4)	*1*
(5,5)	*1*

(b) Suppose that these commands are given in MATLAB:

```
ind1 = [1 2 3 3 4 2];
ind2 = [1 2 1 4 5 3];
number = [0 1 2 3 0 5];
```

In this case we have row vectors but column vectors can also be used. The command `Smatrix = sparse(ind1,ind2,number)` results in:

Smatrix =

(3,1)	*2*
(2,2)	*1*
(2,3)	*5*
(3,4)	*3*

The two zero elements are excluded. To convert the matrix to a full matrix we type: `Fullmatrix = full(Smatrix)` which gives:

Fullmatrix =

0	0	0	0	0
0	1	5	0	0
2	0	0	3	0
0	0	0	0	0

Note that the size of the sparse matrix, and consequently the size of the full matrix, is defined by the largest element in **ind1** and **ind2** respectively, even if the corresponding value was zero and excluded in the displayed sparse matrix. If we type the command whos we will get:

Name	Size	Elements	Bytes	Density	Complex
Fullmatrix	4 by 5	20	160	Full	No
Smatrix	4 by 5	4	68	0.2000	No
ind1	1 by 6	6	48	Full	No
ind2	1 by 6	6	48	Full	No
number	1 by 6	6	48	Full	No

We can see that the sizes of the two matrices are the same but the sparse matrix requires fewer bytes.

(c) The find command is useful when dealing with sparse matrices. The command returns the same result independent of the form of the matrix, sparse or full. The three vectors that are returned can be used directly to recreate the matrix in sparse form. Let **Smatrix** be defined as in Example (b). The commands

```
[ind1,ind2,number] = find(Smatrix);
Smaller = sparse(ind1,ind2,number) give as result:
```

Smaller =

(3,1)	2
(2,2)	1
(2,3)	5
(3,4)	3

This is not the same matrix as **Smatrix** which the following command shows:

```
Fullsmall = full(Smaller)
```

Fullsmall =

$$\begin{matrix} 0 & 0 & 0 & 0 \\ 0 & 1 & 5 & 0 \\ 2 & 0 & 0 & 3 \end{matrix}$$

Compare with Example (b). ■

9.3 Sparse matrix operations

The operations and functions for full matrices in MATLAB can also be applied on sparse matrices. Whether the result is sparse or full depends on the operator or function and the operands according to the following:

- Functions which have a matrix as argument and returns a scalar or a vector of given size always return a full matrix, for example the command `size`.

- Functions which have a scalar or vector as argument and return a matrix as result also always return a full matrix, for example the command `eye`. There exist special commands for obtaining a sparse matrix, for example the command `speye`.

- Other functions with one argument return in general a result of the same form as the argument, for example `diag`.

- Operations or functions that require two arguments return, if the two arguments are full matrices, the result in the full form. In case the two arguments are of different form the result is full if the sparsity is not conserved by the command.

- The uniting of two matrices, `[A B]`, results in a full matrix if at least one of **A** or **B** is full.

- Colon notation in the right-hand side of an expression is considered as an operation with one argument and follows the rules for such operations.

- Colon notation in the left-hand side of an expression does not change the form of the matrix.

■ **Example 9.4**

Suppose that we have:

```
A = eye(5); B = sparse(A); h = [1; 2; 0; 4; 5];
```

that is one full 5×5 identity matrix and the corresponding sparse matrix.

(a) `C = 5*B` gives as a result:

$C =$

(1,1)	5
(2,2)	5
(3,3)	5
(4,4)	5
(5,5)	5

which is a sparse matrix.

(b) `D = A + B` gives:

$D =$

$$
\begin{matrix}
2 & 0 & 0 & 0 & 0 \\
0 & 2 & 0 & 0 & 0 \\
0 & 0 & 2 & 0 & 0 \\
0 & 0 & 0 & 2 & 0 \\
0 & 0 & 0 & 0 & 2
\end{matrix}
$$

which is a full matrix.

(c) `x = B\h` gives:

$x =$

$$
\begin{matrix}
1 \\
2 \\
0 \\
4 \\
5
\end{matrix}
$$

which is a full vector. ■

There is a number of commands that handle the non-zero elements.

Command 77   **NON-ZERO ELEMENTS OF A MATRIX**

`nnz(A)`   gives the number of non-zero elements in the matrix **A**. The command works both for full and sparse matrices.

Command 77   NON-ZERO ELEMENTS OF A MATRIX (continued)

`spy(A)`	displays the structure of the sparse matrix **A**. The `spy` command can also be used on full matrices. In that case only zero elements are displayed.
`spy(A,cstr,size)`	displays the structure as above but in colors defined by **cstr**, see Table 13.1, and size according to *size*.
`nonzeros(A)`	gives the non-zero elements in **A** ordered columnwise.
`spones(A)`	returns a matrix with the non-zero elements of **A** replaced with ones.
`spalloc(m,n,nzmax)`	returns an $m \times n$ sparse zero matrix with allocated memory for *nzmax* non-zero elements. This reduces the need for large and time-consuming rearrangement of memory and the addition of elements to a matrix is done with considerably more speed.
`nzmax(A)`	gives the memory allocated for the non-zero elements of **A**. Does not have to be the same as `nnz(A)`, see `sparse` or `spalloc`.
`issparse(A)`	returns *1* if **A** is stored in sparse form, otherwise *0*.
`spfun(fcn,A)`	evaluates the function **fcn** for all non-zero elements of **A**. Works even if the function is not defined for sparse matrices.
`sprank(A)`	returns the structural rank of the sparse matrix **A**. For all matrices `sprank(A)` $\geq$ `rank(A)`.

■ **Example 9.5**

We define a sparse bi diagonal matrix with the following command:

```
A = sparse(diag(ones(5,1),1)) + sparse(diag(ones(5,1),-1));
```

Now we create a larger matrix with the command:

```
Big = kron(A,A)
```

What does **Big** look like? The Kronecker product gives a larger matrix with the structure defined by the arguments. We know it is sparse, and in sparse form, since both arguments are sparse.

To see the structure we type `spy(Big)`, and we get Figure 9.1.

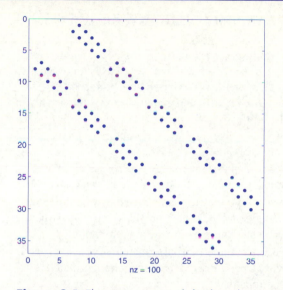

Figure 9.1 The spy command displays the structure of a matrix.

We can see that **Big** is block bidiagonal.   ■

9.4 Special cases of sparse matrices

There are four elementary sparse matrices in MATLAB, **identity matrix**, **random matrices**, **symmetric random matrices** and **diagonal matrices**.

Command 78	SPARSE IDENTITY MATRICES

speye(n)	returns a sparse identity matrix of size $n \times n$.
speye(m,n)	returns a sparse identity matrix of size $m \times n$.

The command speye(A) gives the same result as sparse(eye(A)), but without the step involving storage of a full matrix.

Command 79	SPARSE RANDOM MATRICES

sprandn(A)	gives a sparse random matrix with the same structure as **A**. The random numbers are normally distributed.

Command 79	SPARSE RANDOM MATRICES (continued)
`sprandn(m,n,dens)`	gives a sparse normally distributed random matrix of size $m \times n$ of which a part *dens* is non-zero, that is there are *dens**m*n non-zero elements. $0 \leq dens \leq 1$. The parameter *dens* is the density of the non-zero elements.
`sprandn(m,n, dens,rc)`	gives a sparse random $m \times n$ matrix with the condition number *1/rc*. If *rc* = **rc** is a vector of size $l \leq \min(m, n)$ the matrix gets rc_i as its *l* first singular values. All other singular values are zero.
`sprandsym(S)`	gives a symmetric sparse matrix whose lower triangle and main diagonal have the same structure as **S**. The numbers are normally distributed.
`sprandsym(n,dens)`	gives a symmetric sparse matrix of size $n \times n$ and with density *dens*. The number are normally distributed.
`sprandsym(n, dens,rc)`	gives a symmetric sparse matrix of size $n \times n$ with the condition number *1/rc*. The numbers are symmetrically distributed around *0*, but not normally distributed. If *rc* = **rc** is a vector, the matrix has the eigenvalues rc_i, that is if **rc** is a positive vector then the matrix is positive definite.
`sprandsym(n,dens, rc,k)`	gives a positive definite matrix. If *k* = *1* the matrix is generated by random Jacobi rotation of a positive definite matrix. The condition number is exactly *1/rc*. If *k* = *2* the matrix is created by shifted sums of outer products. The condition number is approximately *1/rc*.
`sprandsym(S, dens,rc,3)`	gives a sparse matrix with the same structure as **S** and the approximate condition number *1/rc*. The parameter *dens* is ignored, but has to be there so the function identifies the two last arguments correctly.

■ **Example 9.6**

(a) Suppose that the following matrix is defined:

$$\mathbf{A} = \begin{bmatrix} 0 & 1 & 0 & 0 \\ 1 & 0 & 0 & 0 \\ 0 & 1 & 0 & 0 \\ 0 & 0 & 1 & 0 \end{bmatrix}$$

We can get a random matrix by typing `Random = sprandn(A)`

Random =

(2,1)	1.1650
(1,2)	0.6268
(3,2)	0.0751
(4,3)	0.3516

with the random numbers at the same positions as the non-zero elements of **A**.

(b) If **A** is the same as in (a) and we type:

`B = sprandsym(A)` we obtain:

B =

(2,1)	−0.7012
(1,2)	−0.7012
(3,2)	1.2460
(2,3)	1.2460
(4,3)	−0.6390
(3,4)	−0.6390

that is the lower triangle and the main diagonal of **A** are used creating a symmetric matrix, with random numbers at the non-zero entries.　■

With the `spdiags` command, diagonals can be selected and diagonal and band matrices created. Suppose that **A** is an $m \times n$ matrix which has non-zero elements in p diagonals, and that **B** is a matrix of size $min(m, n) \times p$, whose columns are diagonals of **A**. The vector **d** has length p, and integer components that define the non-zero diagonals of **A** according to:

$d_i < 0$　a lower diagonal, in relation to the main diagonal. As an example, $d_i = -1$ refer to the first lower diagonal

$d_i = 0$　the main diagonal

$d_i > 0$　an upper diagonal, in relation to the main diagonal.

Command 80	DIAGONALS AND SPARSE MATRICES
`[B,d] = spdiags(A)`	finds all non-zero diagonals of **A** and stores them as defined above, that is the diagonals are stored in the matrix **B** and the positions of these diagonals in the vector **d**.
`spdiags(A,d)`	gives a matrix with the diagonals defined by the vector **d** of the matrix **A**.
`spdiags(B,d,A)`	gives the matrix **A**, but with diagonals defined by **d** replaced with the columns of **B**.
`A = spdiags(B,d,m,n)`	gives a sparse $m \times n$ matrix defined by the diagonals stored in **B** in positions defined by **d**.

■ **Example 9.7**

Now we want to make a typical iteration matrix with a band of non-zero diagonals. We let the first lower and upper diagonals consist of ones and the main diagonal of negative twos. With the `spdiags` command we can type:

```
Ones = ones(n,1);
D2 = spdiags([Ones -2*Ones Ones], [-1 0 1], n, n);
```

First we define a vector of ones. Then we create a sparse $n \times n$ matrix, with the first lower diagonal, that is with number *−1*, consists of ones, diagonal *0*, that is the main diagonal consists of *−2*, and diagonal number *1* consists of ones. For *n = 4* the matrix looks like:

```
D2
```

D2 =

(1,1)	*−2*
(2,1)	*1*
(1,2)	*1*
(2,2)	*−2*
(3,2)	*1*
(2,3)	*1*
(3,3)	*−2*
(4,3)	*1*
(3,4)	*1*
(4,4)	*−2*

■

9.5 Linear systems with sparse matrices

In many applications the sparse structure is kept, but the sparsity can decrease as a result of fill-ins during the computations, for example in LU decomposition. This leads to an increase of floating-point operations and memory storage. To avoid this there are functions in MATLAB that rearrange the matrices. These are briefly described in Command 81 below. Write `help` for each command to obtain more information.

Command 81	PERMUTATIONS
`colmmd(A)`	returns a permutation vector which gives the column minimum degree ordering of **A**.
`symmmd(A)`	returns a symmetric minimum degree ordering.
`symrcm(A)`	gives the inverse Cuthill–McKee-transform of **A**. The non-zero elements of **A** are located around the main diagonal.
`colperm(A)`	returns a vector which gives a column permutation of **A**. The columns are ordered in increasing number of non-zero elements. This is sometimes a useful transformation before an LU factorization, when `lu(A(:,j))` is used. If **A** is a symmetric matrix both rows and columns are ordered, which is sometimes useful before a Cholesky factorization, `chol(A(j,j))`.
`randperm(n)`	gives a random permutation of the integers *1,2,...,n*. This can then be used to create a random permutation matrix.
`dmperm(A)`	performs a Dulmage–Mendelsohn-decomposition of the matrix **A**. Write `help dmperm` for more information.

■ **Example 9.8**

We want to create a permutation matrix of order *4*. We type:

```
i = [1 2 3 4]; aa = ones(1,4); perm = randperm(4);
P = sparse(i,perm,aa);
```

Once `perm = randperm(4)` gave:

> *perm =*
>
> *2   1   3   4*

which gave us the permutation matrix:

$$P =$$

(2,1)	1
(1,2)	1
(3,3)	1
(4,4)	1

If the matrix **A** is defined by:

$$A = \begin{bmatrix} 7 & 4 & 3 & 4 \\ 5 & 2 & 4 & 2 \\ 5 & 6 & 3 & 1 \\ 8 & 1 & 1 & 2 \end{bmatrix}$$

then the commands `Rowchange = P * A; Colchange = A * P;` result in:

Rowchange =

$$\begin{matrix} 5 & 2 & 4 & 2 \\ 7 & 4 & 3 & 1 \\ 5 & 6 & 3 & 1 \\ 8 & 1 & 1 & 2 \end{matrix}$$

Colchange =

$$\begin{matrix} 4 & 7 & 3 & 1 \\ 2 & 5 & 4 & 2 \\ 6 & 5 & 3 & 1 \\ 1 & 8 & 1 & 2 \end{matrix}$$

∎

Sparse linear systems can be solved with the left division operator but there are also some special commands.

Command 82	**SPARSE MATRICES AND LINEAR SYSTEMS**

`spparms(keystr,op)`	sets parameters used in algorithms for sparse matrices. Write `help spparms` for more information.
`spaugment(A,c)`	creates a sparse matrix according to `[c*I A; A' 0]` that expresses a least square problem as a quadratic linear system. (See also Section 7.7.)
`symbfact(A)`	performs a symbolic factorization analysis of Cholesky and LU factorizations of sparse matrices. Type `help symbfact` for more information.

Norms of sparse matrices are computed just like norms of ordinary full matrices with one important exception. The Euclidean norm of a sparse matrix cannot be computed directly. If the sparse matrix is small the norm can be computed by `norm(full(A))`, but for large matrices this is not always possible. However, MATLAB can compute an approximation of the Euclidean norm. The condition number has similar restrictions.

Command 83	APPROXIMATION OF EUCLIDEAN NORM AND CONDITION NUMBER FOR SPARSE MATRICES
`normest(A)`	gives an approximation of the Euclidean norm of **A**. Uses tolerance 10^{-6}.
`normest(s,tol)`	as the previous command but uses tolerance *tol* instead of 10^{-6}.
`[nrm,nit] = normest(A)`	gives an approximation of the norm *nrm*, and also the number of iterations *nit* needed to obtain the norm.
`condest(A)`	gives a lower bound estimate in the one-norm of the condition number of the matrix **A**.
`[c,v] = condest(A)`	gives a lower bound estimate of the condition number *c*, in the one norm of **A**, and also computes a vector **v**, where $\|A\mathbf{v}\| = \|A\| \cdot \|\mathbf{v}\|/c$. For large *c* this is an approximate null vector.
`[c,v] = condest(A,tr)`	gives *c* and **v** as above, but also displays information of steps in the calculations. If *tr = 1* information on every step is displayed, and if *tr = −1* the quotient `c/rcond(A)` is displayed.

■ **Example 9.9**

Suppose `Sprs = speye(4); Sprs(4,1) = 19; Sprs(3,2) = 4;` is given. Then `normapprox = normest(Sprs)`

> *normapprox =*
>
> *19.0525*

and `thenormnorm(full(Sprs))`

> *thenorm =*
>
> *19.0525*

To find the difference we type `difference = thenorm - normapprox` which gives:

difference =

    8.5577e–09

Here, and in most of the applications, `normest` is a good approximation of the Euclidean norm. The number of arithmetic operations required is less than for `norm`. (See also Section 7.6.) ∎

With the `etree` command an elimination tree of a square symmetric matrix can be found. The tree is represented by a vector **f** and can be plotted. The element f_i is the column index of the first non-zero entry in row i of the upper triangular Cholesky factor of the matrix. If there are no non-zero elements then $f_i = 0$. The elimination tree is constructed as follows:

Node i is a son of f_i or if $f_i = 0$ then node i is a root node of the tree.

Command 84	**ELIMINATION TREE OF MATRIX**

`etree(A)`	returns the vector **f** of **A**. The command can also have optional arguments, type `help etree` for information.
`etreeplot(A)`	plots the elimination tree defined by the vector **f**.
`treeplot(p,c,d)`	plots a tree of the vector of pointers **p**. The arguments c and d define colors on the nodes and branches. The command is called by `etreeplot`.
`treelayout`	gives a layout of a tree. The command is called by `treeplot`.

■ **Example 9.10**

Let the symmetric sparse matrix **B** be defined.

$$
B = \begin{bmatrix}
5 & 1 & 0 & 0 & 1 & 0 & 0 & 1 \\
1 & 5 & 0 & 0 & 0 & 0 & 1 & 0 \\
0 & 0 & 5 & 0 & 1 & 1 & 1 & 0 \\
0 & 0 & 0 & 5 & 0 & 0 & 1 & 1 \\
1 & 0 & 1 & 0 & 5 & 0 & 0 & 0 \\
0 & 0 & 1 & 0 & 0 & 5 & 1 & 0 \\
0 & 1 & 1 & 1 & 0 & 1 & 5 & 0 \\
1 & 0 & 0 & 1 & 0 & 0 & 0 & 5
\end{bmatrix}
$$

The command `btree = etree(B)` gives:

btree =

   2   *5*   *5*   *7*   *6*   *7*   *8*   *0*

The number 2 first is not so hard to understand. It is the row number of the first non-zero element in the first column in the matrix and the first row of the Cholesky factor will have its first non-zero element in column 2 due to this. But for the number 5 in the second column we must consider what happens when we reduce the elements in the first column. Due to fill-in; the element in row position 5 of column 2 will be non-zero after reduction in **B**. Thus element 2 in the `etree` vector is 5. The structure of the Cholesky factor can be seen by `spy(chol(B))`. The result is given in Figure 9.2.

The elimination tree of this vector is constructed as follows: there is only one row with zero elements in the upper triangular, node 8, so that is our only root. Node number 1 is a child of node number 2. Nodes 2 and 3 are children of node 5 that is a child of node 6. Nodes 4 and 6 are children of node 7 that is a child of node 8, the root.

If we give the command `etreeplot(B)` we get the structure of the tree, as illustrated by Figure 9.3.

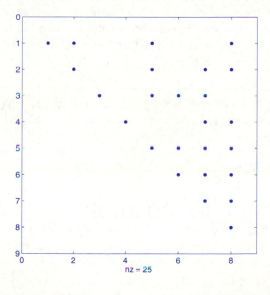

Figure 9.2 Structure of the Cholesky factorization.

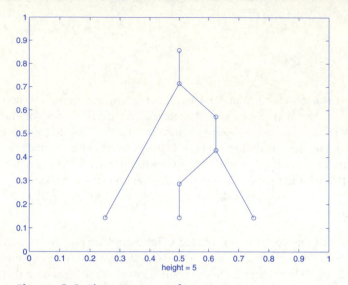

Figure 9.3 Elimination tree of matrix **B**.

The shape of the elimination tree depends on the ordering of the rows and the columns and it is used to analyze the elimination process. ∎

With the `gplot` command it is possible to draw connections between coordinate pairs by using a matrix. To do this, *n* coordinates in an $n \times 2$ matrix are given. Each row of this matrix defines one point. Then an $n \times n$ matrix is created that indicates which points are connected. If point *4* is connected to point *8* the entry *(4,8)* gets the value *1*. Since the matrix can be large, with few non-zero elements it should be created sparse.

This graph can illustrate network problems, for example transport problems. The graph also contains information of dependence between the unknowns in a linear system.

Command 85	NETWORK GRAPHS

`gplot(A,K)`	draws a graph where point k_i is connected with point k_j if entry *(i,j)* in **A** is non-zero. Here **K** is an $n \times 2$ matrix with the coordinates to the points, and **A** is an $n \times n$ matrix indicating the connections.
`gplot(A,K,str)`	draws a graph as the previous command but in color and form defined by **str**. For values of that string, see Table 13.1.

■ **Example 9.11**

Suppose that the following coordinate pairs **K** and connection matrix **A** are defined:

$$K = \begin{bmatrix} 0 & 1 \\ 1 & 0.2 \\ 1.3 & 0.9 \\ 2 & 0 \\ 2 & 1.9 \\ 3 & 2 \\ 4 & 1 \end{bmatrix} \qquad A = \begin{bmatrix} 0 & 1 & 1 & 0 & 1 & 0 & 0 \\ 0 & 0 & 0 & 1 & 0 & 0 & 0 \\ 0 & 0 & 0 & 1 & 0 & 0 & 1 \\ 0 & 0 & 0 & 0 & 0 & 0 & 1 \\ 0 & 0 & 0 & 0 & 0 & 1 & 1 \\ 0 & 0 & 0 & 0 & 0 & 0 & 1 \\ 0 & 0 & 0 & 0 & 0 & 0 & 0 \end{bmatrix}$$

The matrix **A** can be sparse. Then the command `gplot(A,K)` draws Figure 9.4 that illustrates what possible routes there are between point *(0,1)* and point *(4,1)* in a system.

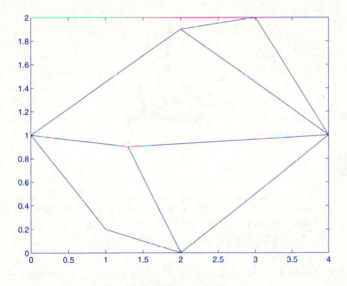

Figure 9.4 An example of the use of `gplot`.

Analysis of Functions, Interpolation, and Curve Fitting

MATLAB has commands for handling polynomials with or without evaluation. There are also powerful commands for analyzing functions, such as finding zeros and minima. MATLAB does also provide several commands and functions for interpolation and curve fitting of data sets.

10.1 Polynomials in MATLAB

A **polynomial**, *p(x)*, of degree *n* is in MATLAB stored as a row vector, **p**, of length *n+1*. The components represent the coefficients of the polynomial and are given in descending order of the powers of *x*, that is:

$$\mathbf{p} = [a_n\ a_{n-1} \dots a_1\, a_0]$$

is interpreted as:

$$p(x) = a_n x^n + a_{n-1} x^{n-1} + \dots + a_1 x + a_0$$

Let **A** be a square matrix, and let the vectors **p** and **q**, of length *n + 1* and *m + 1*, represent polynomials of degree *n* and *m* respectively. In MATLAB the following commands are used to handle polynomials:

Command 86	POLYNOMIALS
`polyval(p,x)`	evaluates the polynomial **p**. If *x* is a scalar the value of the polynomial in the point *x* is returned. If **x** is a vector or a matrix the polynomial is evaluated for all components of **x**.
`[y,err] = polyval(p,x,E)`	evaluates the polynomial **p** for the vector **x**, as above, and returns the result in **y**, but it does also return the error estimate vector **err,** according to the matrix **E** given from the `polyfit` command. (See `help polyval`, `help polyfit` and Section 10.4.)
`polyvalm(p,A)`	operates on the entire matrix **A** directly, and does not work element-by-element as the previous command, that is it evaluates $\mathbf{p(A)} = p_1 \mathbf{A}^n + p_2 \mathbf{A}^{n-1} + \dots + p_{n+1}\,\mathbf{I}$.
`poly(A)`	returns a vector representing the characteristic polynomial of the matrix **A**. (See also Section 8.1.)
`compan(p)`	returns the companion matrix **A** to the polynomial **p**, that is a matrix whose characteristic polynomial is **p**.

Command 86	**POLYNOMIALS (continued)**
`poly(x)`	returns a vector of length *n+1* representing a polynomial of degree *n*. The roots of that polynomial are given in the vector **x**, of length *n*.
`roots(p)`	returns a vector of length *n* with the roots of the polynomial **p**, that is the solutions of the equation $p(x) = 0$. The expression `poly(roots(p))` = `p` is true. The result may be complex.
`conv(p,q)`	gives the product of the polynomials **p** and **q**, it can also be regarded as the convolution of **p** and **q**.
`[k,r] =` `deconv(p,q)`	divides the polynomial **p** with **q**. The quotient polynomial is represented by **k** and the remainder polynomial by **r**. The operation can also be regarded as the deconvolution of **p** and **q**.
`[u v k] =` `residue(p,q)`	returns a partial fraction of $p(x)/q(x)$: $$\frac{p(x)}{q(x)} = \frac{u(1)}{x - v(1)} + \frac{u(2)}{x - v(2)} + \ldots + \frac{u(j)}{x - v(j)} + k(x)$$ The vectors **p** and **q** represent the coefficients of $p(x)$ and $q(x)$ respectively. The residues are returned in the vector **u**, the pole locations in the vector **v**, and the quotient polynomial in the vector **k**.
`[p q] =` `residue(u,v,x)`	returns two polynomials, **p** and **q**, from a partial fraction **u**, **v** and **x**, as above.
`polyder(p)`	returns a vector of length *n* that represents the derivative of the polynomial whose coefficient are stored in the vector **p**.
`polyder(p,q)`	returns a vector representing the derivative of the polynomial defined by `conv(p,q)`.
`[u,v] =` `polyder(p,q)`	returns two vectors, which in the form **u/v** represent the derivative of the polynomial defined by `deconv(p,q)`.

■ **Example 10.1**

We apply some polynomial commands to the following polynomials:

$$p2(x) = 3x^2 + 2x - 4 \qquad\qquad p3(x) = 2x^3 - 2$$

In MATLAB these polynomials are represented by the following vectors:

```
p2 = [3 2 -4];
p3 = [2 0 0 -2];
```

Let us now suppose that they are defined.

(a) To evaluate the polynomials in $x = 1$ we type:
```
value2 = polyval (p2,1),  ...
value3 = polyval(p3,1)
```
which give:

value2 =

1

value3 =

0

(b) Just as easily we can evaluate the polynomials for a vector or a matrix.
```
x = [1 2 3]';
```
```
values2 = polyval(p2,x),  values3 = polyval(p3,x) result in:
```

values2 =

1

12

29

values3 =

0

14

52

(c) If we multiply two polynomials, a new polynomial is obtained:
```
p5 = conv(p2,p3)
```

p5 =

   6   4   −8   −6   −4   8

(d) The roots of the polynomials are found with the `roots` command
```
roots2 = roots(p2),  roots3 = roots(p3)
```

roots2 =

−1.5352

0.8685

roots3 =

−0.5000 + 0.8660i

−0.5000 − 0.8660i

1.0000

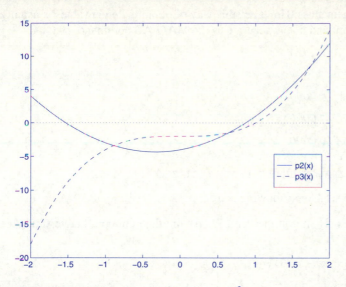

Figure 10.1 The polynomials $p2(x) = 3x^2 + 2x - 4$ and $p3(x) = 2x^3 - 2$.

We show the two polynomials in Figure 10.1.

(e) One Newton–Raphson iteration applied on the polynomial $p(x)$, represented by the vector **p** can be written as:

```
q = polyder(p);
xnext = x - polyval(p,x)/polyval(q,x);
```

(f) The command `roots(poly(A))` returns the eigenvalues of the matrix **A**. Suppose the matrix **A** is defined by:

$$A = \begin{bmatrix} -9 & -3 & -16 \\ 13 & 7 & 16 \\ 3 & 3 & 10 \end{bmatrix}$$

then the command:

```
usedroots = roots(poly(A))
```

usedroots =

10.0000

4.0000

−6.0000

gives the eigenvalues. However, this way of obtaining eigenvalues is usually not as efficient and not as accurate as the MATLAB command `eig(A)`.

```
usedeig = eig(A)
```

usedeig(A) =

$$-6.0000$$
$$4.0000$$
$$10.0000$$

which is the same result only in reversed order.

(g) For all matrices **A** the following is true: `polyvalm(poly(A),A) = 0`

This is the Cayley–Hamilton theorem. We try the theorem on a magic square of order *5*.

```
Magical = magic(5);
almostzero = polyvalm(poly(Magical),Magical)
```

almostzero =

    1.0e–07 *

0.2794	0.3551	0.1723	0.1770	0.2654
0.2765	0.2887	0.2049	0.2142	0.2561
0.1775	0.2468	0.2701	0.3073	0.2375
0.1942	0.2744	0.2759	0.2608	0.2282
0.2082	0.3120	0.2608	0.2515	0.2049

10.2 Zeros of functions

Mathematical functions are represented by M-files in MATLAB (see Section 2.9). The function

$$g(x) = \frac{5x - 6.4}{(x - 1.3)^2 + 0.002} + \frac{9x}{x^3 + 0.03} - \frac{x - 0.4}{(x - 0.92)^2 + 0.005}$$

is available to MATLAB if we type the following M-file stored as **g.m**:

```
function y = g(x)
y = (5.*x-6.4)./((x-1.3).^2+0.002) + (9.*x) ./ ...
(x .^3+0.03) - (x-0.4) ./ ((x-0.92) .^2+0.005);
```

The MATLAB function g has been defined using the elementwise operators . ^ , . /, . ^ , +,- . Consequently, if the function is called by a vector the result is a vector. All MATLAB functions that are described in this chapter require that the mathematical functions are defined in this way.

The function can be plotted using the `plot` command:

```
x = linspace(0,2);              % Creates the x vector
plot(x,g(x));                   % Plots g(x)
grid;                           % Draws grids
title('The g(x) function');     % and title
```

or by using the `fplot` command:

```
fplot('g',[0 2]);                       % Plots the graph
grid; title('The g(x) function'); % Adds grid and title
```

which results in Figure 10.2. Both commands `plot` and `fplot` are defined in Section 13.1.

To find the **zeros** of the function $f(x)$ is equivalent to solving the equation $f(x) = 0$. The zeros of a function of one variable can be found by the MATLAB command `fzero`. For polynomials the `roots` command should be used (see Section 10.1). The algorithm used by `fzero` is iterative, and requires an initial guess not too far from the desired zero.

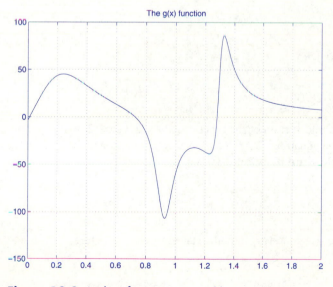

Figure 10.2 A plot of $g(x)$, generated by `fplot`.

Command 87	ZEROS OF FUNCTIONS

`fzero(fcn,x0)`	returns one of the zeros of the function defined by the string **fcn**. The command requires an initial value *x0*. The relative error of the approximation is *eps*.
`fzero(fcn,x0,tol)`	returns one of the zeros of the function defined by the string **fcn**. The command requires an initial value *x0*. The relative error of the approximation is *tol*, defined by the user.
`fzero(fcn,x0,` `tol,pic)`	returns one of the zeros of the function defined by the string **fcn** as the previous command, but does also plot the iteration process if *pic* is non-zero.

The `zerodemo` command gives a demonstration.

■ Example 10.2

(a)   We want to find the zeros of the function **g**, defined at the beginning of this section:

```
x1 = fzero('g',0),...
x2 = fzero('g',.5),...
x3 = fzero('g',2)
```

x1 =

   0.0112

x2 =

   0.7248

x3 =

   1.2805

(b)   To define the intersection of the functions *sin x* and *2x − 2*, that is to find the solution of the equation *sin x = 2x − 2*, we define the function *sinm*, and store it in the M-file **sinm.m** as follows:

```
function s = sinm(x)
s = sin(x)- 2 .* x + 2;
```

Plotting the curve is a good way to find a starting value, therefore:

```
fplot('sinm',[-10,10])
grid on; title('The sin(x)- 2 .* x + 2 function');
```

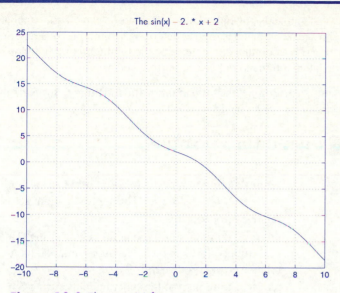

Figure 10.3 The sinm(x) function.

which results in Figure 10.3.

We can see that *2* is an acceptable first guess, and type `xzero = fzero('sinm',2)`

xzero =

      1.4987

which is the solution of the equation *sin x = 2x − 2*. ■

10.3 Minimum and maximum of a function

Optimization is finding the optimal solution, that is finding the maximum or minimum of a function in an interval, with or without constraints. MATLAB uses numerical methods to find the minimum of functions. The algorithms are iterative, that is the process is repeated a number of times. Now, suppose that we want to find a minimum x_{min} of the function f in an interval.

$$f(x_{min}) = min_x f(x)$$

An iterative method needs an initial guess x_0. From this first value x_0, one finds a new value, x_1, which is hopefully closer to x_{min}. How the better approximation x_1 is found depends on which numerical method is used. The iterations continue until an approximation x_i with enough accuracy is found, that is $|x_{min} - x_i|$ is small enough. If there are several local minima `fmin` will find one of them. There is also a special Optimization Toolbox for MATLAB.

Here we mention two commands for optimization that are a part of the standard MATLAB system. The `fmin` command is used to determine a minimum of a function of one variable and the `fmins` command to determine the minimum of a function of several variables. The latter command requires a starting vector.

There is no command to determine the maximum of a function *f*. Instead, the minimum of the function $h = -f$ can be determined.

Command 88　MINIMUM OF A FUNCTION

`fmin(fcn,x1,x2)`	returns a minimum of the function in the string **fcn** in the interval $x1 < x < x2$. The approximation has a relative error less than 10^{-3}.
`fmin(fcn,` `x1,x2,tol)`	returns a minimum of the function in the string **fcn** in the interval $x1 < x < x2$. The approximation has a relative error less than *tol*.
`fmin(fcn,x1,x2,` `tol,movie)`	returns a minimum of the function in the string **fcn** in the interval $x1 < x < x2$. The approximation has a relative error less than *tol* . The different steps of the algorithm are shown during the computation if the parameter *movie* is non-zero.
`fmins(fcn,x0)`	returns a vector containing a minimum of the function **fcn** of several variables. A starting vector **x0** is required. The approximation has a relative error less than 10^{-4}.
`fmins(fcn,x0,tol)`	returns a vector containing a minimum of the function **fcn** of several variables. A starting vector **x0** is required. The approximation has a relative error less than *tol*.
`fmins(fcn,x0,` `tol,movie)`	returns a vector containing a minimum of the function **fcn** of several variables. A starting vector **x0** is required. The approximation has a relative error less than *tol*. The different steps of the algorithm are shown during the computation if the parameter *movie* is non-zero.
`fmins(...,options)`	gives the same as the previous but with some optimization option. Write `help fmins` and `help foptions` for details. As an example, it is possible to determine the number of iterations and the tolerance of the computations of the function to be minimized.

■ **Example 10.3**

(a) We determine the minimum of the cosine function in the interval $[0,2\pi]$.

```
cosmin = fmin('cos',0,2*pi)     % Gives min of cos.
```

cosmin =

  3.1416

which is the expected result.

(b) It is just as simple to determine the minimum of a more advanced function. The function **g** was defined earlier in Section 10.2. We search for minimum of **g** in the interval $[0,2]$.

```
gmin = fmin('g',0,2)
```

gmin =

  1.2277

Note that this is just one local minimum and not necessarily the one that minimizes the function on the interval. If we study Figure 10.2 we see that a smaller interval give us the second minimum, which is smaller than the first:

```
gmin2 = fmin('g',0,1)
```

gmin2 =

  0.9260

(c) The `fmin` command can also be used to find maximum of functions, but first a new function returning −**g** must be written. That function is here stored in the M-file **minusg.m**.

```
function y = minusg(x)

y = - g(x);
```

To find the minimum of this function is equivalent to find the maximum of the **g** function.

```
gmax = fmin('minusg',0,2)
```

gmax =

  0.2433

Here we have several maxima in the interval. It is the first maximum that MATLAB finds, not necessarily the global maximum of the function, that is returned.

(d)   If we want to minimize a multivariable function we use `fmins`.

Suppose that the function is:

$$f(x_1, x_2) = x_1^2 + x_2^2 - 0.5\, x_1 x_2 - \sin x_1$$

We write the M-file **fx1x2.m**:

```
function f = fx1x2(x)

f = x(1) .^ 2 + x(2) .^ 2 -0.5 .* x(1) .* x(2) - sin(x(1));
```

The function `fmins` requires a starting guess, we try (1,0):

```
fx1x2min = fmins('fx1x2',[1,0])
```

fx1x2min =

    0.4744   0.1186

To plot the function we type the following program:

```
x = linspace(-1,1,50);     % Creates x vector.
for i = 1:50
    for j = 1:50
        z(i,j) = f x 1 x 2([x(i) x(j)]);
                            % Computes f x 1 x 2 in each node.
    end
end
meshc(x,x,z);
view(80,10);               % Plots graph with contour lines
                           % and gets a better view.
```

The command `meshc` gives the surface of the function plus contour lines in the *x–y* plane below it. The commands `meshc` and `view` are defined in Section 13.5. The command `linspace` is presented in Section 4.2. The result will be Figure 10.4 where the minimum can be seen.

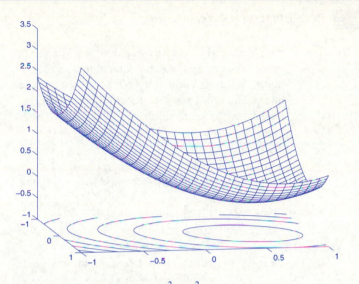

Figure 10.4 The function $x_1^2 + x_2^2 - 0.5\,x_1x_2 - sin\,x_1$ in the interval $[-1,1] \times [-1,1]$. ∎

10.4 Interpolation and curve fitting

If a function is given in a finite number of points it is possible to find approximations in the intermediate points by interpolation. The easiest way is to use the two adjacent points and make a linear interpolation.

There are several functions in MATLAB which perform interpolation of data in different ways:

Command 89   **INTERPOLATION**

`interp1(x,y,xx)`	returns a vector **f**(xx) of the same length as the vector **xx**, where the function **f** is defined by the vectors **y** and **x** such that $y = \mathbf{f}(x)$. The values are computed with linear interpolation. For a correct result the vector **x** must be in descending or ascending order.

Command 89	**INTERPOLATION (continued)**

`interp1(x,Y,xx)`	returns a matrix **F**(xx) corresponding to the vector in the previous command. Each column of the matrix **Y** is a function of **x**, and the values of **xx** are interpolated for each such function. The resulting matrix has the same number of rows as the length of **xx**, and the same number of columns as the matrix **Y**.
`interp1(x, y,xx,metstr)`	performs a one-dimensional interpolation. The string **metstr** defines what method to use, and the possibilities are:
	`'linear'` linear interpolation.
	`'spline'` cubic spline interpolation. Does also accept extrapolation.
	`'cubic'` cubic interpolation, requires equidistant values of **x**.
	For all of the alternatives **x** has to be monotonic.
`interp2(X,Y,Z, Xx,Yy)`	performs a two-dimensional interpolation of the matrices **Xx** and **Yy** on the function Z=**f**(X,Y) that is represented by the matrices **X**, **Y** and **Z**. If any of **X,Y** or **Z** is a vector it is applied in the corresponding rows and columns.
`interp2(x,y,z, xx,yy,metstr)`	performs a two-dimensional interpolation where the string **metstr** defines what method to use according to:
	`'linear'` linear interpolation
	`'cubic'` cubic interpolation
	`'nearest'` interpolation between adjacent points
`griddata(x,y,z, Xx,Yy)`	returns a matrix of the same size as **Xx** and **Yy** that represents a mesh, on which the function $z = f(x,y)$ is interpolated. The vectors **x,y** and **z** contain the x-, y- and z-coordinates of a point in space.
`interp#(...)`	write `help interp3`, ..., `help interp6` for information of remaining interpolation methods. At the moment `interp1 - interp6` are defined.
`interpft(y,n)`	interpolation with the Fast Fourier Transform method, returns a vector of length n, whose components are interpolations of the components of **y**. Requires that the values of **y** are equidistant, and that the result is computed in the same interval as **y**.

■ **Example 10.4**

We make a table of $sin\ x^2$ for *40* values between *0* and 2π.

```
x = linspace(0,2 * pi,40);

y = sin(x . ^2);
```

(a) Now we can compute $sin\ x^2$ for intermediate points using `interp1`, instead of `sin`. The command
`values = interp1(x,y,[0 pi/2 3])` gives:

values =

$$0$$

$$0.6050$$

$$0.3559$$

We compare with the correct results: `correct = sin([0 pi/2 3]'.^ 2)`

correct =

$$0$$

$$0.6243$$

$$0.4121$$

The accuracy could be made better if we used more values in the table.

(b) With spline interpolation we should obtain more accurate results. Suppose the vectors **x** and **y** are defined as above. Then
`better = interp1(x,y,[0 pi/2 3],'spline')` results in:

better =

$$0$$

$$0.6241$$

$$0.4098$$

which is a better approximation.   ■

The command `griddata` creates a function out of a set of arbitrary points in three dimensions.

■ **Example 10.5**

If we generate three vectors with *10* components with values distributed between *0* and *1*.

```
x = rand(10,1); y = rand(10,1); z = rand(10,1);
```

we can interpolate a surface between these points with the command `griddata` if we first create a mesh to compute the surface in.

```
stps = 0:0.03:1;            % A vector with values in [0,1]

[xi,yi] = meshgrid(stps);   % A mesh in [0,1] x [0,1]

zi = griddata(x,y,z,xi,yi); % Interpolates

mesh(xi,yi,zi)              % Plots the surface

hold                       % Holds the picture

plot3(x,y,z,'o')           % Plots the points

hold                       % Releases the picture
```

The command `hold` is described in Section 13.3, the command `meshgrid` in Section 13.4, and the commands `mesh` and `plot3` are found in Section 13.5. The result is shown in Figure 10.5.

Approximation with cubic splines can also be done with the `spline` command. It is possible to obtain the **pp-form** of the cubic spline interpolated vector. The components of the vector are the coefficients of the cubic spline functions. To evaluate the cubic spline functions the `ppval` command is used.

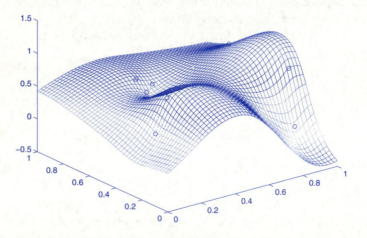

Figure 10.5 Interpolation of *10* random points with `griddata`. The *10* points are marked by small circles.

Command 90	CUBIC SPLINE DATA INTERPOLATION

spline(x,y,xx)	equivalent to interp1(x,y,xx,'spline'), but does only accept vectors as argument.
spline(x,y)	returns the pp-form of the cubic spline interpolating vector that approximates $y = f(x)$. The abbreviation pp stands for "piecewise polynomial" and the components of the returned vector contains, among other things, the coefficients of the computed cubic spline. This can be used with the ppval function.
ppval(pp,xx)	evaluates cubic spline functions. If a cubic spline pp = spline(x,y) is defined then ppval(pp,xx) gives the same result as spline(x,y,xx).

A polynomial can be fitted to data by **least square approximation** (see also Section 7.7) with the polyfit command.

Command 91	POLYNOMIAL CURVE FITTING

polyfit(x,y,n)	returns a vector with the coefficients of the polynomial of degree *n* which is the best least square approximation to the set of data $\{(x_i\ y_i)\}$.
[p,E] = polyfit(x,y,n)	returns a polynomial represented by the vector **p** as above, and a matrix **E**, that are used by the polyval function to estimate errors.

■ **Example 10.6**

Plot the data set $\{(x_i, y_i)\}$ and corresponding polynomial with MATLAB graphics, when

```
x = [-3 -1 0 2 5.5 7];
```

and

```
y = [3.3 4.5 2.0 1.5 2.5 -1.2];
```

The following commands return a picture showing the polynomials of third, fourth and fifth degree approximating the data above:

```
p3 = polyfit(x,y,3);      % Fits the polynomial
p4 = polyfit(x,y,4);      % to the data
p5 = polyfit(x,y,5);      % given in x and y.
```

```
xcurve = -3.5:0.1:7.2;        % Creates x-values.

p3curve = polyval(p3,xcurve); % Computes the polynomial in

p4curve = polyval(p4,xcurve); % these x-values.

p5curve = polyval(p5,xcurve);

plot(xcurve,p3curve,'--',xcurve,p4curve,'-.' ...

,xcurve,p5curve,'-',x,y,'*');

lx = [-1 1.5]; ly = [0,0]; hold on;


plot(lx,ly,'--',lx,ly-1.3,'-.',lx,ly-2.6,'-');

text(2,0,'degree 3');

text(2,-1.3,'degree 4');

text(2,-2.6,'degree 5');
```

The result is shown in Figure 10.6.

As expected, the accuracy is better for polynomials of higher degrees. The polynomial of fifth degree passes all six points, that is it is the **interpolation polynomial** for this particular set of data. For more information on the graphics commands, see Chapter 13.   ■

In MATLAB, the **Legendre functions** are computed for a scalar or a vector with the `legendre` command. The Legendre functions are systems of orthogonal

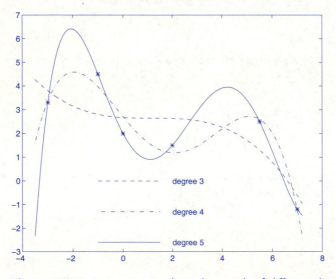

Figure 10.6 Approximation by polynomials of different degrees.

polynomials that form complete orthogonal sets in chosen intervals.The **Legendre polynomials**, that is the Legendre functions of order zero, can be used for curve fitting a given set of data. The **Bessel functions** are classical special functions that, among other things, can be used in mathematical physics.

| Command 92 | THE LEGENDRE AND BESSEL FUNCTIONS |

`legendre(n,x)`	returns a matrix with the values of the associated Legendre functions of degree n and order $m = 0,1,...,n$ computed in **x**. The components of **x** must be in the interval $[-1,1]$. The first row corresponds to $m = 0$ and contains the Legendre polynomial of degree n evaluated in **x.**
`bessel(n,x)`	computes Bessel functions of the first kind. Both n and x may be vectors but n must have the increment 1 and be in the interval $[0,1000]$. Depending on if the components of **x** are complex or not, different functions are called, `besseli`, `besselj`, `besselk` and `bessela`. The functions can also be called directly. Type `help bessel` to get more information.
`bessely(n,x)`	computes Bessel functions of the second kind. Both n and x may be vectors but n must have the increment 1 and be in the interval $[0,1000]$.

10.5 Signal analysis

Here we give a short description of a few of the MATLAB commands for **signal analysis**. More information can be obtained by the `help` and `demo` commands. See also the "Signal Processing Toolbox" and its manual. The commands for complex numbers, Section 2.4, and for convolution, Section 10.1, may also be of interest.

| Command 93 | SIGNAL ANALYSIS |

`fft(x)`	returns a vector containing the discrete Fourier transform of the vector **x**. If the length of the vector is a power of two the Fast Fourier Transform, FFT, is used. Note that the transform is not normalized.
`fft(x,n)`	returns a vector of length n with the discrete Fourier transform of the n first components of **x**. If **x** has $m < n$ components, the last $m + 1,...,n$ elements are supposed to be zero.

Command 93	SIGNAL ANALYSIS (continued)
`fft(A)`	returns a matrix with the discrete Fourier transform of the columns of the matrix **A**.
`ifft(x)`	returns the inverse discrete Fourier transform of **x**, normalized with the factor *1/n*, where *n* is the length of the vector. Can also transform matrices and vectors with a fixed vector length like the `fft` command.
`fft2(A)`	returns a matrix which is the two-dimensional discrete Fourier transform of the matrix **A**. This matrix is not normalized. If **A** = **a** is a vector this command is equal to the `fft(a)` command.
`fft2(A,m,n)`	returns an $m \times n$ matrix, which is the two-dimensional discrete Fourier transform of the corresponding components of the matrix **A**. This matrix is not normalized. If **A** is a smaller matrix the remaining entries are supposed to be zero. If possible MATLAB uses the Fast Fourier Transform, FFT.
`ifft2(A)`	returns a matrix which is the two-dimensional inverse discrete Fourier transform of the matrix **A**, normalized with a factor *1/nm*. The dimensions to be transformed can be changed as for `fft2`.
`fftshift(x)`	returns a vector with the left and right sides of **x** swapped.
`fftshift(A)`	returns a matrix where the first and the third quadrants and the second and the fourth quadrants of **A** are swapped.
`filter(b,a,x)`	returns the data from **x** filtered with the filter described by the vectors **a** and **b**. See `help filter` for more information.

■ **Example 10.7**

We create a "hat function" and its Fourier transform. Our hat function is zero at 0 and 1, and one at 0.5.

The hat function is created with linspace:

```
x = linspace(0,1,100);
y = [linspace(0,1,50) linspace(1,0,50)];
```

We plot this function, illustrated by Figure 10.7, with the command:

```
subplot(1,3,1); plot(x,y); title('A hat function');
```

and the Fourier transform, in the same figure, with:

```
subplot(1,3,2); plot(x,fft(y)); title('The Fourier transform');
```

This Fourier transform is complex valued but only the real part is displayed.
Finally, we make sure that the retransformation gives us our hat function in
return:

```
subplot(1,3,3); plot(x,ifft(fft(y)));
```

```
title('Retransformed hat function');
```

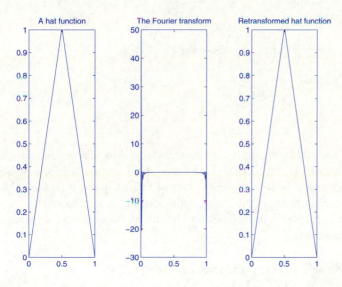

Figure 10.7 The Fourier transform of a hat function.

All plot commands are defined in Chapter 13.

11 Integrals and Differential Equations

Numerical solutions of definite integrals and ordinary differential equations can be computed and plotted with the help of efficient MATLAB commands.

11.1 Integration

In MATLAB we can solve definite integrals of the kind:

$$q = \int_a^b g(x)\,dx$$

numerically.

There are several methods for numerical integration also called numerical quadrature. If we want MATLAB to take care of the whole computation the `quad` command is used. We can also compute the values of the integrand **g** and then let MATLAB compute the integral using the trapezoidal rule and the command `trapz`. This can be useful when there are only discrete points of data and the integrand is not known as an expression.

Command 94	COMPUTATION OF DEFINITE INTEGRALS
`trapz(x,y)`	computes the integral of **y** as a function of **x**. The vectors **x** and **y** have the same length and (x_i, y_i) represents a point on a curve. The spacing between the points does not have to be equidistant and the x-values do not have to be sorted. However, negative intervals and subintervals are considered as negative integrals.
`trapz(y)`	computes the integral of **y** as above, but the x-values are considered to be spaced with distance 1.
`trapz(x,A)`	computes the integral of each column in **A** as a function of **x**, and returns a row vector containing each result of the integrations. The columns of **A** must have the same length as the vector **x**.

Command 94	**COMPUTATION OF DEFINITE INTEGRALS (continued)**

`quad(fcn,a,b)`	returns an approximation of the integral of **g** on the interval [*a,b*]. The string **fcn** contains the name of a MATLAB function, that is a predefined function or an M-file, corresponding to **g**. The function must return a vector when a vector is passed to it. MATLAB performs a recursive adaptive integration with Simpson's rule, the tolerance is 10^{-3}.
`quad(fcn,a,b,tol)`	returns an approximation to the integral of **g** where the relative error is defined by the parameter *tol*. Otherwise the same as above.
`quad(fcn,a,b,` `tol,pic)`	returns an approximation to the integral of **g** where the relative error is defined by the parameter *tol*. If the parameter *pic* is non-zero a picture, displaying which points are evaluated, is shown.
`quad8( ... )`	can be used with the same combinations of parameters and returns the same result as `quad`, but uses a method with a higher order of accuracy. Therefore, when the derivative of the integrand is infinite in some part of the interval, for example for $q = \int_0^1 \sqrt{\sin x} dx$, this command will be better. Both `quad` and `quad8` demand the integrand to be finite in the whole interval.

Type `quaddemo` for a demonstration.

■ **Example 11.1**

Let us compute the following integral with different methods:

$$\int_0^1 e^{-x^2} dx$$

(a) Using the `trapz` command we first have to create a vector with x-values. We try *5* and *10* values:

```
x5 = linspace(0,1,5); x10 = linspace(0,1,10);
```

Then we create the vector **y** as a function of **x**:

```
y5 = exp(-x5 .^ 2); y10 = exp(-x10.^2);
```

Now the integral can be computed:

```
integral5 = trapz(x5,y5), integral10 = trapz(x10,y10) returns:
```
integral5 =

    0.74298409780038

integral10 =

    0.74606686791267

(b) Using the `quad` command, we first have to create the function in an M-file. The file **integrand.m** contains the function and looks like:

```
function y = integrand(x)
y = exp(-x.^2);
```

The integral can be computed, first with standard tolerance and then with the tolerance specified:

```
integralstd = quad('integrand',0,1),
integraltol = quad('integrand',0,1,0.00001) gives as result:
```
integralstd =

    0.74682612052747

integraltol =

    0.74682414517798

(c) Using the `quad8` command: we can use the M-file created in (b), and type:

```
integral8std = quad8('integrand',0,1)
```
integral8std =

    0.74682413281243

This is the most accurate result MATLAB can give.

(d) We want to compute the double integral

$$\int_0^1 \int_0^1 e^{-x^2 - y^2} \, dy \, dx$$

First, an M-file containing the function must be created, **integrand2.m**:

```
function f = integrand2(x,y)
f = exp(-x.^2-y.^2);
```

Then we compute a number of integrals in the *y* direction for fixed *x* values with `quad`:

```
x = linspace(0,1,15)
for i = 1:15
  integral(i) = quad('integrand2',0,1,[],[],x(i));
end;
```

Now we have computed 15 integrals in the *y* direction. The result from these can now be used together with the `trapz` command to obtain the double integral:

```
dintegral = trapz(x,integral)
```
  dintegral =
     0.5575

To get a picture of the area of integration we type:

```
[X,Y] = meshgrid(0:.1:1,0:.1:1);
Z = integrand2(X,Y);
mesh(X,Y,Z); view(30,30)
```

which results in the picture shown in Figure 11.1. The commands `mesh` and `view` are defined in Section 13.5. ■

Indefinite integrals, $\int_a^x f(t)\,dt$, cannot be computed by the commands above.

The MATLAB Symbolic Math Toolbox and the Student Edition of MATLAB provides commands for treating such integrals.

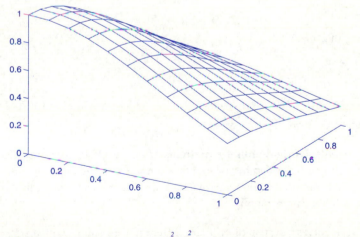

Figure 11.1 The function $e^{-x^2-y^2}$ in the interval $[0,1] \times [0,1]$.

11.2 Ordinary differential equations

Let us now study systems of ordinary differential equations, ODEs, of the first order with the initial values known. We have two unknown functions, $x_1(t)$ and $x_2(t)$, in our examples, and the derivative is denoted by

$$\frac{dx_i}{dt} = x_i'$$

In many applications the independent variable t is the time.

$$\begin{cases} x_1' = f_1(x_1, x_2, t) \\ x_2' = f_2(x_1, x_2, t) \\ x_1(t_0) = x_{1,0} \\ x_2(t_0) = x_{2,0} \end{cases}$$

ODEs of higher order can be expressed as systems of ODEs of the first order. For instance, if we have

$$\begin{cases} x' = f(x, x', t) \\ x(t_0) = x_0 \\ x'(t_0) = xp_0 \end{cases}$$

we can substitute $x_2 = x'$, and $x_1 = x$. Then we get:

$$\begin{cases} x'_1 = x_2 \\ x'_2 = f(x_1, x_2, t) \\ x_1(t_0) = x_0 \\ x_2(t_0) = xp_0 \end{cases}$$

which is a system of ODEs of the first order.

MATLAB uses **Runge–Kutta–Fehlberg methods** to solve ODE problems. The solution is computed in a finite number of points where the spacing depends on the solution. Fewer points are used in intervals where the solution is smooth and more points where the solution varies rapidly.

The function `ode23` solves a system of ordinary differential equations with an order of accuracy (2,3), and the function `ode45` uses a Runge–Kutta–Fehlberg method with an order of accuracy (4,5). Note that in this case, **x'** has the meaning of the derivative of **x**, not the conjugate of **x**.

Command 95	RUNGE–KUTTA–FEHLBERG METHODS

`[t,X] =` `ode23(str,t0,tt,x0)`	computes the solution of the ODE, or the system of ODEs, given by the string **str**. The solution is given in the vector **t**, containing the *t*-values, and the matrix **X** with columns containing the solutions at these points. If the problem is scalar the result is returned in the vector **x**. Solutions are computed from time *t0* to *tt*, and **x0** = **x**(*t0*) are the initial values. The system is determined using the function defined in the M-file **str**, which is required to have two parameters, the scalar *a* and the vector **x**, and to return the vector **x'**. For a scalar ODE, *x* and *x'* are scalars. The approximation has a relative error of 10^{-3}, at most.

`[t,X] =`
`ode23(str,t0,tt,`
`x0,tol,pic)`
	as above but with the addition that the relative error is specified in *tol*. If *pic* is non-zero the results of each step are shown during computation.

`ode23p(...)`	performs like `ode23`, with the addition that a plot of each iteration is produced. (For further information, see `help ode23p`.)
`[t,X] =` `ode45(str,t0,tt,x0)`	see `ode23`. Uses a more accurate method. The approximation has a relative error of 10^{-6}, at most.

`[t,X] =`
`ode45(str,t0,tt,`
`x0,tol,pic)`
	see `ode23`. Uses a more accurate method. The approximation has a relative error of tol at most.

Try the command `odedemo` for an introduction.

■ **Example 11.2**

(a) To solve the following ODE:

$$\begin{cases} x' = -x^2 \\ x(0) = 1 \end{cases}$$

we create the function **xprim1**, stored in the M-file **xprim1.m**:

```
function xprim = xprim1(t,x)
xprim = -x.^2;
```

Then we call MATLAB's ODE solver:

```
[t,x] = ode23('xprim1',0,1,1);
```

Finally, we plot the solution:

```
plot(t,x,'-',t,x,'o');
xlabel('time t0 = 0,tt = 1'); ylabel('x values x(0) = 1');
```

and get Figure 11.2. MATLAB has computed the solution at the point marked with circles. The `plot` command is presented in Section 13.1.

(b) The procedure to solve the following ODE is equivalent:

$$\begin{cases} x' = x^2 \\ x(0) = 1 \end{cases}$$

First we create the function *xprim2*, stored in the M-file **xprim2.m**:

```
function xprim = xprim2(t,x)
xprim = x.^2;
```

Then we call the ODE solver and plot the result:

```
[t,x] = ode23('xprim2',0,0.95,1);
plot(t,x,'o',t,x,'-');
xlabel('time t0 = 0,tt = 0.95'); ylabel('x values x(0) = 1');
```

and obtain Figure 11.3.

Note that the points where MATLAB computes the solution are denser in the area with high derivative.

(c) To solve

$$\begin{cases} x' = x^2 \\ x(0) = -1 \end{cases}$$

the same function as in (b) above can be used. We only have to change the initial data:

```
[t,x] = ode23('xprim2',0,1,-1);
plot(t,x); xlabel('time t0 = 0,tt = 1');
ylabel('x values x(0) = -1');
```

this gives Figure 11.4.

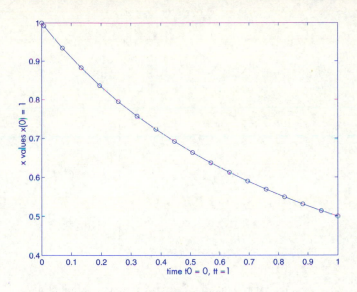

Figure 11.2 The solution of the ODE defined by the function **xprim1**.

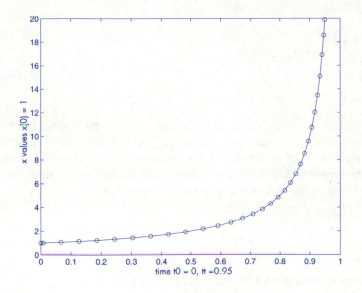

Figure 11.3 The solution of the ODE defined by the function **xprim2**.

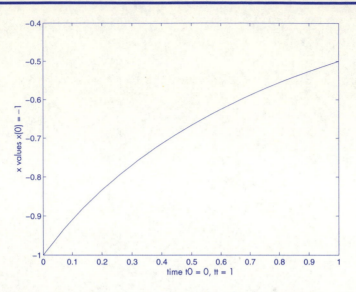

Figure 11.4 The solution to the ODE defined by **xprim2**, with new initial data.

The uppermost curve is x_9.

(d) To solve the following system:

$$\begin{cases} x_1' = x_1 - 0.1 x_1 x_2 + 0.01t \\ x_2' = -x_2 + 0.02 x_1 x_2 + 0.04t \\ x_1(0) = 30 \\ x_2(0) = 20 \end{cases}$$

This system can be regarded as a simplified prey predator model. The prey is represented by x_1 and the predators by x_2. A large supply of prey increases the amount of predators and few predators increases the amount of prey. Moreover, both populations are considered to increase in time. We create the function **xprim3**, stored in the M-file **xprim3.m**:

```
funtion xprim = xprim3(t,x)

xprim(1) = x(1) - 0.1*x(1)*x(2) + 0.01*t;
xprim(2) = -x(2) + 0.02*x(1)×x(2) + 0.04*t;
```

then we make a call to the ODE-solver and plot the result:

```
[t,X] = ode23('xprim3',0,20,[30;20]);
plot(t,X); xlabel('time t0 = 0,tt = 20');
ylabel(' x values x1(0) = 30, x2(0) = 20');
```

which is shown in Figure 11.5.

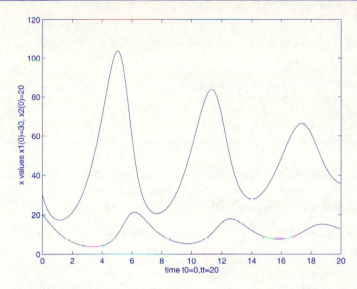

Figure 11.5 The solution to the ODE defined by the function **xprim3**.

It is also possible to plot x_1 as a function of x_2 in MATLAB.
`plot(X(:,2),X(:,1))` displays the phase-plane plot shown in Figure 11.6.

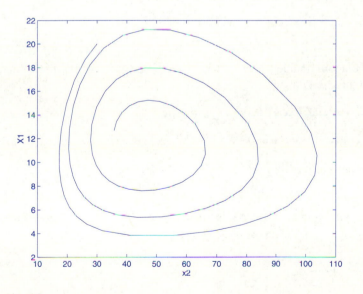

Figure 11.6 The solution of x^1 to ODE defined by *xprim3* as a function of x^2. ∎

■ **Example 11.3**

MATLAB can also solve **boundary value problems** of ODEs of the kind:

$$
\begin{cases}
y'' = f(x, y) & a < x < b \\
y(a) = y_a \\
y(b) = y_b
\end{cases}
$$

numerically by substituting the differential equation by a **difference approximation.** To do this, the interval is divided into a number of smaller intervals and the solution is computed only in *(N–1)* uniformly distributed *x*-values with a distance $h = \dfrac{(b-a)}{N}$ from each other. We approximate y'' by a finite difference according to $\dfrac{y(x_{i+1}) - 2y(x_i) + y(x_{i-1})}{h^2}$.

Here is a simple example. Suppose that $f(x, y) = sin(10x)y$, $N = 4$, $[a,b] = [0,1]$, $y_a = 0$ and $y_b = 4$. Then we have a boundary value problem that looks like

$$
\begin{cases}
y_0 - 2y_1 + y_2 = h^2 sin(10x_1)y_1 \\
y_1 - 2y_2 + y_3 = h^2 sin(10x_2)y_2 \\
y_2 - 2y_3 + y_4 = h^2 sin(10x_3)y_3
\end{cases}
$$

where y_i is the approximation of $y(x_i)$ with $y_0 = y_a$ and $y_4 = y_b$. We have three equations and three unknowns:

$$
\begin{cases}
y_1(-2 - h^2 sin(10x_1)) + y_2 & = -y_0 = 0 \\
y_1 + y_2(-2 - h^2 sin(10x_2)) + y_3 & = 0 \\
y_2 + y_3(-2 - h^2 sin(10x_3)) & = -y_4 = -4
\end{cases}
$$

or, if we write the system in matrix form with the values of x_i, h, y_0 and y_4 substituted:

$$
\begin{bmatrix}
-2 - 0.25^2 sin 2.5 & 1 & 0 \\
1 & -2 - 0.25^2 sin 5 & 1 \\
0 & 1 & -2 - 0.25^2 sin 7.5
\end{bmatrix}
\begin{bmatrix}
y_1 \\ y_2 \\ y_3
\end{bmatrix}
=
\begin{bmatrix}
0 \\ 0 \\ -4
\end{bmatrix}
$$

This system can be solved by left division (see Section 7.2).

Now, here is a demonstration of how to solve the problem with $N = 100$. First, we must create the coefficient matrix of the system.

```
x = linspace(0,1);          % x vector and h.
h = 1/100;                  % Creates right-
a2 = ones(1,2*99);          % hand side
b = zeros(100,1);% Creates right-   % b and upper and
b(100) = -4;                % lower
                            % diagonals of A.

for i = 1:100
    a1(i) = -2 - 10*h*h*sin(10*x(i));   % A's main diagonal.
    u(i) = i; v(i) = i;     % The vectors u and v
                            % describe the
                            % position
end;                        % of the elements of A.

for i = 1:99
    u(i + 100) = i; v(i+100) = i + 1;
    u(i + 199) = i + 1; v(i+199) = i;
end;

a = [a1 a2];                % Puts all elements of
A = sparse(u,v,a);          % A into a long vector.
                            % Creates the sparse
                            % matrix A.
```

Now we can find **y** and study it by:

```
y = A\b;                    % Here the solution is
                            % computed.

plot(x,y); title('y(x) that solves y'''' = sin(10x)*y');
```

The resulting plot is shown in Figure 11.7. The command `sparse` for creating sparse matrices is described in Section 4.2, the `for`-loop in Section 12.2, and the `plot` and `title` commands in Chapter 13. ■

Solutions of ordinary differential equations can in special cases be received in a symbolic form, that is as a formula, by using the Symbolic Math Toolbox.

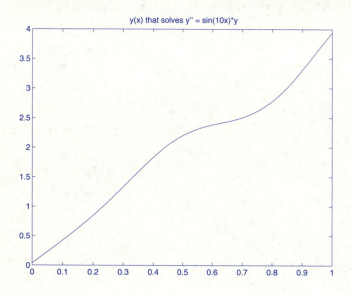

Figure 11.7 The solution of the boundary value problem.

Programming in MATLAB

MATLAB contains several commands to control the execution of MATLAB statements, such as conditional statements, loops, and commands supporting user interaction. In this chapter we describe these facilities. MATLAB can be seen as a high level programming language, enabling the user to solve matrix and other problems. Users who are acquainted with other programming languages, such as Pascal, C++, or FORTRAN have an advantage, but we feel confident that the material can be understood by all readers.

12.1 Conditional statements

Decisions in MATLAB are made with `if`. The basic form of an if statement is:

> `if` *logical expression*
>   *statements*
> `end`

Note that a space is required between `if` and *logical expression*. The *statements* refer to one single command or several commands separated by commas, semicolons, or 'returns'. These commands are only executed if the logical expression is **true**. A logical expression can be a scalar, a vector or a matrix, and a logical expression is **true** if all its elements are non-zero.

An `if` statement can be written in a single line:

> `if` *logical expression, statements,* `end`

However, the former formulation is usually preferable, making the MATLAB program more structured and easy to read.

■ Example 12.1

Suppose an $\mu \times \nu$ matrix **A** is defined. The following statements remove the first column of **A** if all the elements of the first column are zero:

```
if  A(:, 1) == 0
    A = A(1:m, 2:n)
end
```

or written in a single row:

```
if  A(:, 1) == 0, A = A(1:m, 2:n), end
```
■

The `if` statement can be used in more complex contexts in combination with `elseif` and `else`. There are many structures possible:

```
if   logical expression
     statements 1
else
     statements 2
end
```

The commands of *statements 1* are executed if the *logical expression* is **true**, and the commands of *statements 2* if it is **false**.

Consider the following if statement

```
if   logical expression 1
     statements 1
elseif logical expression 2
     statements 2
end
```

The *statements 1* are executed if *logical expression 1* is **true**, while the *statements 2* are executed if *logical expression 1* is **false** and *logical expression 2* is **true**.

Note that `elseif` must be written as a single word, since it is interpreted differently if written `else if`. The command `elseif` does not require an extra `end`, as the command `else if` does.

Another example of how `if` statements can be nested:

```
if   logical expression 1
     statements 1
elseif logical expression 2
     statements 2
else
     statements 3
end
```

and an even more complex construction:

```
if    logical expression 1
    statements 1
    if  logical expression 2
        statements 2
    else
        statements 3
    end
else
    statements 4
end
```

■ **Example 12.2**

(a) Solve the system **A x = b** if **A** is non-singular, otherwise determine the reduced row echelon form of the enlarged matrix [**A b**]. (Hint: a matrix is non-singular if it is square and has full rank.)

```
s = size(A)
if  (s(1) == s(2)) & (rank(A) == s(1))
    x = A\b
else
    rref([A b])
end
```

(b) If the determinant of the matrix **A** is zero, compute how many eigenvalues are zero:

```
if det(A) == 0
    length(find(eig(A) == 0))
end
```
■

12.2 Loops

MATLAB has two commands, **for** and **while**, for repeated execution of statements. These add the flexibility to execute statements once or several times under logical control.

The command `for` is like `do` or `for` commands in most programming languages, repeating a statement or group of statements a predefined number of times. An `end` finishes the group of statements.

The general syntax of a `for`-loop is:

> for *variable = expression*
>> *statements*
> end

Just like the `if` statement, a `for` statement can be written in a single line:

> for *variable = expression, statements*, end

A blank is required between `for` and *variable*. Here, *variable* is the name of the loop variable. The expression assigns an initial value, an incremental value, and a final value of the loop variable. The incremental value can be negative or left out. If left out, the loop variable is increased by *1* in each iteration. Usually, the colon notation is used to define the *expression*, for instance `i:j:k` or `i:j` (see Section 4.2).

The columns of the expression are stored in the loop variable one by one. Thus it is possible to have a matrix as the expression. For instance, the following statement:

> for v = A, ... , end

is equivalent to:

> for j = 1:n, v = A(:,j); ... , end

When the expression is written with colon notation, the columns are scalars, for example, in the MATLAB statement `for v = i:j:k`

Loops can be nested:

> for *variable I = expression A*
>> *statements 1*
>> for *variable II = expression B*
>>> *statements 2*
>> end
>> *statements 3*
> end

■ **Example 12.3**

(a) The following matrix with three non-zero diagonals:

$$
A = \begin{bmatrix} 5 & 1 & 0 & 0 & 0 \\ 1 & 5 & 1 & 0 & 0 \\ 0 & 1 & 5 & 1 & 0 \\ 0 & 0 & 1 & 5 & 1 \\ 0 & 0 & 0 & 1 & 5 \end{bmatrix}
$$

can be created using the command `for` repeatedly, which looks much like it would in an ordinary programming language:

```
A=[];
for k = 1:5
    for j = 1:5
        if k == j
            A(k,k) = 5;
        elseif abs(k-j) == 1
            A(k,j) = 1;
        else
            A(k,j) = 0;
        end
    end
end
```

The semicolon is vital here. If we write these assignments without the semicolon, the matrix **A** is written on the screen *25* times, every time an element of **A** is assigned a value.

This is also an example of how inefficient careless use of `for`-loops can be. The following commands accomplish the same thing, but are much more efficient:

```
A = zeros(5);
for k = 1:4
    A(k,k) = 5;
    A(k,k+1) = 1;
    A(k+1,k) = 1;
end
A(5,5) = 5;
```

This matrix can be obtained in an even more compact and efficient way, yet much clearer, using the command `diag`:

```
A = diag(5*ones(5,1)) + diag(ones(4,1),1) + ...
diag(ones(4,1),-1);
```

It should be added that a large matrix with this type of structure should be created as a sparse matrix (see Chapter 9).

(b) Let us generate a table of the function $y = f(x) = 1 + 1/x$ evaluated in the interval $[-2, -0.75]$ in steps of 0.25. Store the x- and y-values in the vectors **r** and **s**:

```
r = [ ]; s = [ ];
for x = -2.0:0.25:-0.75
    y = 1 + 1/x;
    r = [r x];
    s = [s y];
end
```

Again this table could, and probably should, be generated without using a `for`-loop. To display the result as a table, we type:

```
[r; s]'
```

ans =

−2.0000	0.5000
−1.7500	0.4286
−1.5000	0.3333
−1.2500	0.2000
−1.0000	0
−0.7500	−0.3333

(c) The MATLAB command `sum(A)` gives a row vector containing the sum of elements of the columns of the matrix **A**. A similar result can be obtained with the following `for`-loop:

```
for v = A
    sum(v)
end
```

(d) Let us store the following MATLAB commands in the file **qrmethod.m**:

```
% The matrix A, the integers m and n, should be defined prior
% to calling this file.
% The QR-method is applied after transformation to upper
% Hessenberg.
% Stop after n steps.
% Display the result every mth step.
A = hess(A);
for i = 1:n
    [Q,R] = qr(A);
    A = R*Q;
    nd = norm(diag(A,-1));
    if rem(i,m) == 0
        A,i,nd
    end
end
```

The following commands now perform the unshifted QR-method (see Section 8.2) with *30* iterations, presenting the result every *15*th iteration:

```
A0 = [-9 -3 -16; 13 7 16; 3 3 10]; m = 15; n = 30;
format long; A = A0; qrmethod
```

$A =$

9.98997467074379	22.62301237506361	15.53274662438001
0.00708686385759	−5.98568512552926	5.77401643542404
0	0.00741470005235	3.99571045478546

$i =$
15
$nd =$
0.01025677416162

$A =$

10.00000471624664	22.62743993744967	15.51339551121121
−0.00000333488655	−6.00001449452641	−5.77348898879411
0	0.00001693654612	4.00000977827978

$i =$
30
$nd =$
1.726175143943680e−05

(e) In Section 7.5 the command `planerot` is defined. This algorithm uses that command to return a matrix that zeroes all elements below the main diagonal of any matrix of size $\mu \times \nu$ given as an input argument.

```
function y = givens(AA)

    % AA of size m x n will be reduced to an upper triangular
    % matrix if we multiply with Giv, the matrix that this
    % function returns. That is, this function can be used to
    % QR-factorize AA according to Q = Giv´ and R = Giv * AA
    % so that Q * R = AA.

    [m,n] = size(AA);
    Giv = eye(m);
    for j = 1:n
      for i = j:m
        for k = (i+1):m
            GG = eye(m);
            g = planerot([AA(j,j) AA(k,j)]');% Find 2 x 2 matrix.
            GG(j,j) = g(1,1); GG(k,j) = g(2,1);% Place correctly
            GG(j,k) = g(1,2); GG(k,k) = g(2,2); % in m x m matrix.
            Giv = GG*Giv;
            AA = GG*AA; % <- To see the step-by-step reduction
                        % of AA remove this semicolon.
        end
      end
    end
    y = Giv;
end function
```

The algorithm zeroes one element below the main diagonal for each step of the inner loop by making a 2×2 matrix out of two elements in **AA**. The resulting matrix can be used to create a QR-factorization, that is if we type Giv = givens(AA); where **AA** is a matrix defined as:

$$AA = \begin{bmatrix} 1 & 2 & 3 & 1 & 2 & 3 \\ 4 & 4 & 1 & 2 & 2 & 1 \\ 7 & 6 & 3 & 2 & 1 & 1 \\ 1 & 2 & 1 & 0 & 0 & 2 \end{bmatrix}$$

and then give the commands Q = Giv', R = Giv * AA the result will be:

Q =

0.1222	0.6630	0.6674	0.3162
0.4887	0.1842	−0.5721	0.6325
0.8552	−0.2947	0.2860	−0.3162
0.1222	0.6630	−0.3814	−0.6325

R =

8.1854	7.5745	3.5429	2.8099	2.0769	1.9547
0.0000	1.6208	1.9523	0.4420	1.3997	3.2047
−0.0000	−0.0000	1.9069	0.0953	0.4767	0.9535
0.0000	0.0000	0.0000	0.9487	1.5811	0.0000

If we give the command A = Q*R we will have the original matrix back:

A=

1.0000	2.0000	3.0000	1.0000	2.0000	3.0000
4.0000	4.0000	1.0000	2.0000	2.0000	1.0000
7.0000	6.0000	3.0000	2.0000	1.0000	1.0000
1.0000	2.0000	1.0000	0	0	2.0000

(f) The following program builds a snowflake by using two for-loops and the complex plane. The algorithm is known as Helge von Koch's and is an example of a fractal. The program contains some graphical commands that are defined in Chapter 13 but the comments explain shortly what happens. The algorithm divides each side of the current geometry in three equal parts. The first and the last part are sides to the new geometry.

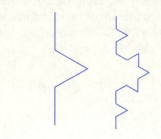

Figure 12.1 Two iterations on a line with the von Koch algorithm.

Between these are two more sides with the same length added. (See also Figure 12.1.)

If we let the iteration go on forever almost every part of a plane would be covered, in fact the fractal has dimension 1.2619, a little more than just one but not quite two.

```
% File: Koch.m
% This program plots Helge von Koch's snowflake, a fractal.
clear;             % Deletes old variables.
                   % Vector new defines a triangle in the
                   % complex plane. That is the start geometry.

new = [0.5 + (sqrt(3)/2)*i,-0.5 + (sqrt(3)/2)*i,0,0.5 + ...
      (sqrt(3)/2)*i];

plot(new);         % Plots the triangle and
pause(0.5);        % waits 0.5 seconds.

for k = 1:5;       % Iterates five times:
  old = new;       % Vector old is the previous iteration
  [m,n] = size(old);
  n = n-1;         % There are n-1 sides in the figure
                   % defined by old.

  for j = 0:n-1; % For each side:
                 % Define 4 new points (one is "old").
    diff = (old(j+2) - old(j+1))/3;
    new(4*j+1) = old(j+1);
    new(4*j+2) = old(j+1) + diff;
    new(4*j+3) = new(4*j+2) + diff*((1-sqrt(3)*i)/2);
    new(4*j+4) = old(j+1) + 2*diff;
  end;             % End of inner loop.
```

```
   new(4*n+1) = old(n+1);    % Last element of vector new
                             % is same as last element in old.
   plot(new);                % Plots the new figure
   Pause(0.5);               % and waits 0.5 seconds.
end;                         % End of outer loop.

% The last line makes the plot more 'neat' by removing
% the axis and making them equal.

axis off; axis square;
end function
```

Running this program will result in a figure that gradually becomes more complex. In Figure 12.2 we see the final plot.

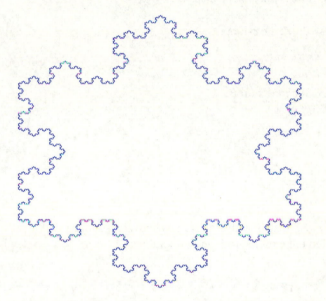

Figure 12.2 Helge von Koch's fractal after 5 iterations. The original geometry was a triangle.

The command `while` repeats statements as long as a logical expression is true. The construction is terminated with an `end`, just like the `for`-statement. We use the term `while`-loop to denote the whole `while` statement, that is

> `while`, *statements*, `end`.

The general `while`-loop has the form

> `while` *logical expression*
>
>   *statements*
>
> `end`

and a single line `while`-loop looks like:

> `while` *logical expression*, *statements*, `end`

While-loops can be nested like `for`-loops:

> `while` *logical expression A*
>
>   *statements 1*
>
>   `while` *logical expression B*
>
>   *statements 2*
>
>   `end`
>
>   *statements 3*
>
> `end`

■ Example 12.4

(a) Build a random 2×2 matrix with eigenvalues between -1 and 1. This can be carried out with the following iterations:

```
A = rand(2);
while max(abs(eig(A))) >= 1
    A = rand(2);
end
```

The result may be the following matrix

$$\mathbf{A} = \begin{bmatrix} 0.4845 & 0.0726 \\ 0.5965 & 0.2831 \end{bmatrix}$$

with eigenvalues $\lambda_1 = 0.6149$ and $\lambda_2 = 0.1527$. The result may of course vary (see Section 4.1 on the command `rand`).

A variable can be added to count the number of iterations:

```
A = rand(2); niter = 1;
while max(abs(eig(A))) >= 1
    A = rand(2); niter = niter + 1;
end
```

(b) The Maclaurin series of the function $ln(1 + x)$ is

$$ln(1 + x) = \sum_{k=1}^{\infty} \frac{(-1)^{k+1} x^k}{k}$$

Estimate $ln(1 + x)$, with $x = 0.5$ by adding terms until the next term to be added is smaller than the built-in variable *eps*. Count the number of terms. This can be carried out in the following way:

```
lnsum = 0; x = 0.5; k = 1;
while abs((x^k)/k)>= eps
    lnsum = lnsum + ((-1)^(k+1))*((x^k)/k);
    k = k + 1;
end
lnsum, k - 1
```

which gives the result:

lnsum =
    0.4055
ans =
        47

We verify this result with:

```
ln = log(1.5)
```
ln =
    0.4055

■

Sometimes it is useful to quit a loop prior to its natural termination. This can be accomplished with the command `break`. If `break` is applied to an inner loop of nested loops, only the inner loop is terminated, and the outer loop or loops continue.

The use of `break` should be avoided, since a program using the command `break` is usually difficult to understand and maintain. Such a program can always be rewritten without `break`.

■ **Example 12.5**

Determine the machine epsilon through iterations.

(a) For-loop with the command `break`:

```
macheps = 1;
for i = 1:1000
    macheps = macheps/2;
    if macheps + 1 <= 1
        break
    end
end
macheps = macheps*2
```

The result on a Sun Sparc station is:

macheps =
    2.2204e–16

(b) `While`-loop without `break`.

```
macheps = 1;
while 1 + macheps > 1
    macheps = macheps/2;
end
macheps = macheps*2
```

■

12.3 More about M-files

We introduced M-files in Section 2.9. In this section we cover some additional aspects of M-files.

MATLAB can handle recursive functions. Such a function makes a call to itself but with some criterion changed so the program does not enter an eternal loop.

■ **Example 12.6**

We have the following M-file named **sqpulse.m** defined:

```
function f = sqpulse(n,x)

% Recursive function for the sum
% 1/2 + 2/pi cos(x pi) + ... +
% 2 sin(n pi/2)cos(n x pi)
% For n --> inf this will be equal to a square pulse.

if (n == 1)
    f = 1/2 + 2/pi*cos(x*pi); % stop criterion.
else
    f = 2*sin(n*pi/2)/n/pi*cos(n*x*pi) + sqpulse(n-1,x);
end

end function
```

This function will return, if *n* is large enough, the value *1* for $\xi = [-0.5, 0.5]$ and for *x* that can be made a part of that set by adding an even number, that is
$x = -1.75$ will give `sqpulse(n,x)` = 1 since $-1.75 + 2$ equals *0.25*. For all other numbers the function **sqpulse** is zero (see Figure 12.3).

If *n* is chosen too small the square pulse will be sinusoidal due to the cosine functions that our square pulse is built of.

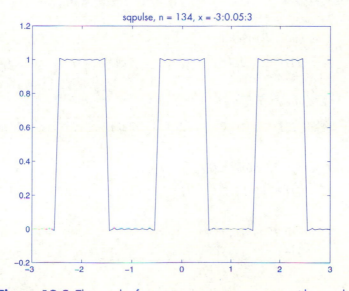

Figure 12.3 The result of `plot(x,sqpulse(n,x))` with x and n as in the title.

Multidimensional arrays are not built into MATLAB but one can create own functions to handle this.

■ Example 12.7

This example demonstrates how one can map a four-dimensional vector to a single vector. Create the following M-file:

```
function position = fourindex(d,i,j,k,l)
position = (i+(j-1)*d(1) + (k-1)*d(1)*d(2)+...
(l-1)*d(1)*d(3)*d(2));
```

The function can be used like this:

```
d = [2 3 2 3];
A = zeros(size(1:(2*2*3*3)))

for ii = 1:2;
    for jj = 1:3;
        for kk = 1:2;
            for ll = 1:3;
                A(fourindex(d,ii,jj,kk,ll)) =
                ii*1000 + jj*100 + kk*10 + ll;
end;end;end;end
A

A =

Columns 1 through 6

    1111    2111    1211    2211    1311    2311

Columns 7 through 12

    1121    2121    1221    2221    1321    2321

Columns 13 through 18

    1112    2112    1212    2212    1312    2312

Columns 19 through 24

    1122    2122    1222    2222    1322    2322
```

Columns 25 through 30

| *1113* | *2113* | *1213* | *2213* | *1313* | *2313* |

Columns 31 through 36

| *1123* | *2123* | *1223* | *2223* | *1323* | *2323* |

The elements of the vector are defined so that *1221* is positioned in *[1,2,2,1]* in the four-dimensional array.

To get one element out of **A** we type:

```
aa = A(fourindex([2 3 2 3], 2, 2, 2, 2))
```

    aa =

        2222   ■

Comments have been added to many M-files already. They are written after a percentage sign `%`:

```
% Comment.
```

It's good practice to always add comments to programs, enabling future understanding of what the programs do, and preferably how they do it.

The command `lookfor` (see Section 2.7) browses the first comment line of all M-files for a specified text. Thus it can be a good idea to include keywords in the first comment line.

■ Example 12.8

```
% Solution of assignment 7: Systems of equations.
% T.P. 950505
A = [1 2;0 3];
b = [9;8];
x = A\b          % Solves the system A x = b.
```
■

Making comments can be useful in debugging. By adding a `%` in front of a command, it is turned into a comment and thus ignored. By applying this to key commands, a bug might be located. (See also Section 12.5.)

The command `echo` toggles between echoing or not echoing the commands as they are executed from a command file. When the echo is turned on, all commands and comments are echoed to the screen, which is also very useful in the process of killing bugs. The command `echo` can also be given explicitly as `echo on` and `echo off`.

Function files are not affected by the above. Instead the following holds for function files:

Command 96 ECHO FROM FUNCTION FILES

`echo fname on`	turns on the echo of the function **fname.m**
`echo fname off`	turns off the echo of **fname.m**
`echo fname`	toggles the echo between on and off in the function **fname.m**.
`echo on all`	turns on the echo of all functions.
`echo off all`	turns off the echo of all functions.

A function can have zero, one, or several arguments, and the same function can also be called with a varied number of arguments. For instance, the function `triu(A)` returns an upper triangular matrix, while `triu(A,1)` returns a strictly upper triangular matrix.

Command 97 NUMBER OF ARGUMENTS

`nargin`	is a variable containing the number of arguments the function was called with.
`nargout`	is a variable containing the number of return arguments the function was called with.

■ **Example 12.9**

A variable number of arguments can be used to define default values, that is values to use if nothing else is specified. The function random stored in the function **random.m** generates an $\mu \times \nu$ matrix with random values of normal distribution. If the expectation value ν is not specified then $\nu = 0$ is used.

```
function A = random(m,n,v)
% Returns a matrix of size m x n
% with variance 0 and expectation v.
% If v is not specified, use v = 0.
if nargin == 2, v = 0; end
A = randn(m,n) + v;
```

The calls `A = random(2,2,4); B = random(2,2);`

give the elements of **A** the expectation value *4*, and the elements of **B** the expectation value *0*. ■

A function can also have an optional return argument. For instance `bar(x,y)` plots the elements of the vector **y** at the locations of vector **x** while `[xx,yy] = bar(x,y)` does not plot anything but returns the vectors **xx** and **yy** such that the command `plot(xx,yy)` will give the same graph as `bar(x,y)`.

■ **Example 12.10**

We have the M-file **ngon.m** written below. It computes the roots of $\chi^v = 1$ as default but as an optional input argument the complex number z can be defined and then the roots of $\chi^v = \zeta$ is computed. These roots define an n-gon in the complex plane. If we do not give any output arguments the figure will be plotted. If we give one output argument we get a complex vector that defines the corners of the polygon in the complex plane. If we give two output arguments, two real vectors that define the polygon in a plane are returned.

```
function [aa,bb] = ngon(n,z)
                  % The n roots of c^n = z are the corners
                  % of an n-gon in the complex plane.
if nargin ==1

    z = 1 % Default z = 1.end
k = 1:n;          % The roots are c = re+i*im, k = 1:n
re = abs(z) * cos((angle(z) + (k-1) *2*pi)/n);
im = abs(z) * sin((angle(z) + (k-1) * 2 * pi)/n);
xx = [re re(1)]; yy = [im im(1)];
                  % If nargout == 0 plot n-gon in a shade of
if nargout == 0   % blue depending on the phase angle of z.
    patch(xx,yy,[0 abs(angle(z)/pi) 1])
    axis('equal')
elseif nargout == 1% If nargout == 1 return complex vector
    aa = xx+yy*i;  % such that plot(cc) draws the outlines
                  % of the polygons in the complex plane.
else
    aa = xx;      % If nargout == 2 return real xx and yy
    bb = yy;      % vectors such that plot(xx,yy) draws the
```

```
end                    % outline of the polygon.
end function
```

The command `angle` is introduced in Section 2.4 and `patch` in Section 14.2. To see what **ngon** does let us give the following commands:

```
subplot(2,2,1); ngon(5);
```

The upper left corner will be plotted by **ngon.** The equation solved is $\chi^v = 1$:

```
subplot(2,2,2); cv = ngon(5,i); plot(cv); axis('equal')
```

The upper right corner is the complex plane with the solutions to $\chi^v = \iota$ as corners of the polygon:

```
subplot(2,2,3); [rv1,rv2] = ngon(5,-1);
plot(rv1,rv2); axis('equal')
```

The lower left corner is a polygon with the solutions to $\chi^v = -1$ equal to rv1 + i*rv2:

```
subplot(2,2,4); ngon(5,-i);
```

The lower right corner shows a polygon whose corners are the solutions of $\chi^v = -\iota$.

The polygons are shown in Figure 12.4. We have manipulated the axes a little for a better visualization of the complex plane. This was done by using graphical objects which are described in Chapter 14. To find the definitions of `subplot` and `plot` see Chapter 13.

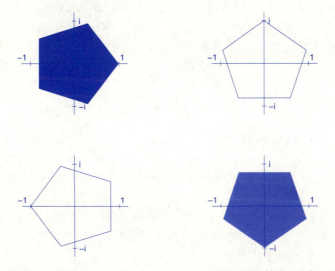

Figure 12.4 Pentagons created with the user-defined function **ngon**.

All variables in function files are local. Thus, a variable in a function file with the same name as a variable in the MATLAB workspace is a completely different variable, stored at a different memory location. Like all rules, this rule has an exception, that is global variables can be used in MATLAB.

A global variable is accessible in all function files where it is declared global. It is possible to see which variables are declared global with the commands who or whos. To clear global variables, see Section 2.3. Other commands controlling M-files are shown in Command 98 below.

Command 98	CONTROL OF M-FILES

pause	pauses the execution of an M-file. The execution is resumed as soon as an arbitrary key is pressed (see Example 13.15 (c)).
pause(n)	pauses the execution during *n* seconds before resuming the execution. The pause command can for instance be useful when a lot of graphics is to be presented.
pause off	instructs MATLAB to skip subsequent pauses.
pause on	instructs MATLAB to take pauses when a pause is given.
break	terminates for and while loops. If this command is given in a nested loop, only the innermost loop is terminated (see Section 12.2).
return	terminates an M-file. MATLAB immediately returns to the place where the function was called.
error(str)	terminates the execution of an M-file and writes both an error message and the string **str** on the screen.
global	declares variables as global. Global variables can be accessed in function files without being included in the parameter list. The command global is followed by a list of variables separated by spaces. Variables declared as global remain global until the complete workspace is cleared, or the command clear global is used.
keyboard	calls the keyboard as if it was a command file. When given inside an M-file, the execution is paused, and commands can be given in the MATLAB command window. The prompt is now $K >>$ to indicate this special status. This is a way to check or change variables when an M-file is executed, and all MATLAB commands are allowed. The execution of the M-file is resumed as soon as the keyword return is written. If keyboard is called in a function file, the workspace of this function and its global variables is accessible. The command keyboard is useful when debugging.

12.4 Functions as parameters to other functions

In most high-level languages, like Pascal or FORTRAN, it is possible to write a general function **F** by including another function **f** as a parameter. This can also be done in MATLAB, by including a string **f** containing the expression describing the function or a name of a function. Inside **F**, the function **f** can be evaluated using `eval` or `feval`.

The command `eval` (see Section 5.4) evaluates a MATLAB-expression given as a string. This string can for instance contain mathematical expressions:

        a = eval('sin(2*pi)') or x = 2*pi; b = eval('sin(x)').

The variables used in the string **f** must have the same names as the variables in **F** if `eval` is used.

The command `feval` evaluates functions, either built-in functions like `sin`, or functions stored as M-files. A call to `feval` can look like this:

        a = feval('sin',2*pi).

Command 99	EVALUATING FUNCTIONS

`feval(fcn,x1,` `...,xn)`	evaluates the function given by the string **fcn**. The parameters *x1 ... xn* are passed to the function in the order of appearance.
`[y1,y2,...] =` `feval(fcn,x1,...,xn)`	is the same as the previous, but now returns multiple variables.

Suppose a function **fcn** is written with the elementwise operators, that is +, -, .*, ./, .\, .^. Then the command `feval(fcn,x)` returns a vector if **x** is a vector, and there is no problem passing a vector valued function as parameter to **F** as `feval` is used in **F**. If the command `eval` is used inside **F**, and is applied directly to vectors, the elementwise operators must be used in the parameter string function **f**.

■ Example 12.11

We now want to write a MATLAB function returning a table of *f(x)*, with *x* in the interval [*a*,*b*], in steps of *k*. We assume that the function **f** is defined with elementwise operators.

(a) With `feval`:

      Input arguments: A string with the name of a function, limits *a* and *b*, and the step length *k*.

Output arguments: A matrix with two columns, the *x*-values and *f(x)* for these values.

The following function is stored in the file **Functab1.m**.

```
function Y = Functab1(f,a,b,k)
% Evaluates a scalar function in [a,b]
% at the values x(j) = a + j*k.
% The result is a table containing
% x-values and f(x) for those x-values.

x = a:k:b;
z = feval(f,x);
Y = [x; z]';
```

(b) With `eval`.

The same result can be obtained by using a command string as input argument to the function. This command string is evaluated with the command `eval` (see Section 5.4).

Input arguments: A command string containing an expression defining the function, limits *a* and *b*, and the step length *k*.

Output arguments: A matrix with two columns, the *x*-values and *f(x)* for these values.

The following function is stored on the file **functab2.m**.

```
function Y = Functab2(f,a,b,k)
% Evaluates a scalar function in [a,b]
% at the values x(j) = a + j*k.
% The result is a table containing
% x-values and f(x) for those x-values.

x = a:k:b;
z = eval(f);    % f must be a function of x
Y = [x; z]';
```

Suppose we want a table of the function `oneplusx(x)` = 1 + *x* for *x* in [*-1, 1*]. The function **oneplusx** is stored in the file **oneplusx.m**. The following are examples of how the functions **Funktab1** and **Funktab2** can be called to generate such a table. They all give the same result.

```
Tab = Funktab1('oneplusx',-1,1,0.25)
```

Tab =

−1.0000	*0*
−0.7500	*0.2500*
−0.5000	*0.5000*
−0.2500	*0.7500*
0	*1.0000*
0.2500	*1.2500*
0.5000	*1.5000*
0.7500	*1.7500*
1.0000	*2.0000*

■

```
Tab = Funktab2('oneplusx(x)',-1,1,0.25);
Tab = Funktab2('1+x',-1,1,0.25);
```

■

12.5 Debugging

There are commands in MATLAB that can be useful when debugging M-files, that is looking for errors in them. These commands can be used to set and clear breakpoints, execute M-files line by line, and check variables in different workspaces. The debug commands all start with the letters db, and we have already encountered dbtype, which produces a program list with line numbers.

The commands to set, clear, and list all breakpoints are given in Command 100 below.

Command 100	BREAKPOINTS

`dbstop in fname`	places a breakpoint at the first executable line in the M-file **fname**.
`dbstop at r in fname`	places a breakpoint at line r in the M-file **fname**. If r is not an executable line, the execution is stopped at the first executable line after r.
`dbstop if v`	the execution is stopped when the condition v is met. The condition v can be either `error` if an error occurs, or `naninf/infnan` if a NaN or inf occurs.

Command 100	BREAKPOINTS (continued)

`dbclear at r in fname`	removes the breakpoint at line *r* in the file **fname**.
`dbclear all in fname`	removes all breakpoints in the file **fname**.
`dbclear all`	removes all breakpoints in all M-files.
`dbclear in fname`	removes the breakpoint at the first executable line in the file **fname**.
`dbclear if v`	removes the breakpoint at line *v* set with `dbstop if v`.
`dbstatus fname`	produces a list of all breakpoints in the file **fname**.

These commands, together with the commands listed below, give us good tools to follow and control the execution of M-files.

Command 101	CONTROL OF THE EXECUTION

`dbstep`	executes the next line of the M-file.
`dbstep n`	executes the next *n* lines and then stops.
`dbstep in`	stops the execution at the first executable line in the next function called.
`dbcont`	executes all lines until the next breakpoint or the end of the file is reached.
`dbquit`	quits the debugging mode.

To start debugging, a function with a breakpoint is called. MATLAB now enters the debugging mode, which is indicated by a K in the MATLAB-prompt: K >>. The most important difference is that we now can access the local variables of the function, but not the variables in the MATLAB workspace. We illustrate this with the function **Factab.m** that produces a table of the factorials *1!,...,n!*.

■ **Example 12.12**

First we list the function **Factab.m** with line numbers:

```
dbtype Factab
1 function Tab = Factab(n)
2 % Generates a table of 1!,...,n!
3 numbers = 1:n;
4 facts = [];
5 for i =numbers
```

```
6    facts = [facts factorial(i)];
7 end
8 Tab = [numbers' facts];
```

This function calls the function **factorial**, which is also listed:

```
dbtype factorial
1 function f = factorial(n)
2 if (n == 0)
3    f = 1;
4 else
5    f = prod(1:n);
6 end
```

To start debugging, we set a breakpoint at the first executable line of the function and then make a call to it. Notice the letter K that appears in the prompt.

```
dbstop in Factab        % Sets a breakpoint in Factab.
Table = Factab(5);      % Calls Factab to debug it.
3 numbers = 1:n;
K >> dbstep             % Execute one line.
4 facts = [];
K >> numbers            % Returns the variable numbers.
numbers =
    1    2    3    4    5
K >> numbers = [numbers 6]
                        % Enlarges the vector numbers with a 6.
numbers =
    1    2    3    4    5    6
K >> dbstop 8           % Breakpoint at line 8.
K >> dbcont             % Continues to the next
breakpoint.
8 Tab = [numbers' facts'];
K >> dbquit             % Quits the debugging.
>> dbstatus Factab      % Lists all breakpoints.
Breakpoints for Factab are on lines 3, 8.                    ■
```

A function which is calling another function is referred to as a nested function call. MATLAB uses a stack to keep track of workspaces and variables in the functions, and the following commands can be used to switch between workspaces of the nested functions.

Command 102	CHANGE WORKSPACE

dbstep in	steps into the function if the next executable line is a function call.
dbup	switches to the workspace of the calling function, allowing its variables to be examined.
dbdown	switches back down to the workspace of the called function.
dbstack	shows the stack of nested function calls.

■ Example 12.13

We again use the function **Factab** (see Example 12.12). We start by placing breakpoints in both **Factab** and **factorial**:

```
dbstop Factab        % Sets a breakpoint in Factab.
dbstop factorial     % Sets a breakpoint in factorial.
Factab(3);           % Calls Factab.

3 numbers = 1:n;
K >> dbcont          % Steps to next breakpoint.
2 if (n ==0)

K >> dbstack         % We are now in factorial.
In /home/matlab/VER42/mfiler/K12/factorial.m at line 2
In /home/matlab/VER42/mfiler/K12/Factab.m at line 5

K >> who             % Shows the current variables.
Your variables are:
f    n

K >> dbup            % Switches to the calling workspace.
In workspace belonging to /home/matlab/VER42/mfiler/K12/Factab.m.
```

```
K >> Who              % Which variables are now current?
```
Your variables are:
facts   i   n   Tab   numbers

```
K >> dbdown           % Back to the workspace of the
                      % function.
```

In workspace belonging to /home/matlab/VER42/mfiler/K12/factorial.m.

```
K >> dbquit           % Quits the debugging.
```

To debug command files, use the command `keyboard`. MATLAB's special debugging commands can only be used to debug function files. ∎

Graphics and Sound

13

MATLAB has a wide range of two- and three-dimensional graphics commands which are flexible and easy to use. Some of them are demonstrated in previous chapters. Histograms and bar graphs are treated in Chapter 6. It is also possible to include sound effects in MATLAB programs. Many graphics commands are shown in the demonstration programs included in MATLAB.

The graphics commands are presented in two chapters. This chapter covers the basic high-level commands, while Chapter 14 focuses on the low-level control of details.

13.1 Two-dimensional graphics

The MATLAB user can easily plot a set of ordered pairs, and one way to do it is to use the `plot` command. This command can be given with different numbers of arguments. The simplest form is just to pass the data to `plot`, but line styles and colors can also be specified by using a string here denoted **str**. The styles and colors allowed in this string are listed in Table 13.1. If the type of line is not specified, a solid line is used.

Command 103	THE PLOT COMMAND
`plot(x,y)`	plots the vector **y** versus the vector **x**. The ordered set of coordinates (x_j, y_j) are drawn, with the horizontal axis as the x-axis, and the vertical axis as the y-axis.
`plot(y)`	plots the ordered set of coordinates (j, y_j). The horizontal axis is the j-axis, and the vertical axis is the y-axis.
`plot(z)`	plots the ordered set of coordinates $(real(z_k), imag(z_k))$. The horizontal axis is the real axis, and the vertical axis is the imaginary axis. Thus, the complex numbers z_k are drawn in the complex plane.
`plot(A)`	plots the columns of **A** versus their indices. For an $m \times n$-matrix **A**, n sets of m pairs, or n curves with m points are plotted. The different curves are drawn in different colors on a color monitor, and with different line types on a black-and-white monitor.

Command 103	THE PLOT COMMAND (continued)
`plot(x,A)`	plots the matrix **A** versus the vector **x**. For an $m \times n$-matrix **A** and a vector **x** of length m, the columns of **A** are plotted versus **x**. If **x** is of length n, the rows of **A** are plotted versus **x**. The vector **x** can be either a row or a column vector.
`plot(A,x)`	plots the vector **x** versus the matrix **A**. For an $m \times n$-matrix **A** and a vector **x** of length m, the vector **x** is plotted versus the columns of **A**. If **x** is of length n, the vector **x** is plotted versus the rows of **A**. The vector **x** can be either a row or column vector.
`plot(A,B)`	plots the columns of **B** versus the columns of **A**. Thus if **A** and **B** are both $m \times n$-matrices, n sets of curves with m coordinates are plotted.
`plot(...,str)`	draws a plot according to the arguments, but using the color and style given by the string **str**. The values allowed in **str** are listed in Table 13.1 below.
`plot(x1,y1,str1, x2,y2,str2,...)`	plots **x1** versus **y1** with color and style according to **str1**, then plots **x2** versus **y2** according to **str2** and so on. Each pair of entries can have any of the forms above, but real and complex data cannot be mixed. If the strings **str1, str2**... are left out, MATLAB chooses the color and style of each plot.

By passing the string **str** as argument to `plot`, the color and style in the plots can be specified. The values allowed, and their meaning, are listed in Table 13.1.

Table 13.1   Point types, line types and colors.

Point types		Line types		Colors			
.	period, dot	–	solid line	y	yellow	c	cyan
*	star	--	dashed line	g	green	w	white
x	the letter x	-.	dash - dotted line	m	magenta	r	red
o	the letter o	:	dotted line	b	blue	k	black
+	plus						

Style and color can be combined. For instance, 'y+' gives a plot drawn with yellow plus signs, and 'b--' a blue dashed line. If several series of data are to be drawn, but no styles are specified, they are given different colors from yellow to black following Table 13.1. On a black-and-white terminal, the series are given different line types.

The size of the symbols, the widths of the lines, and so on, can also be changed (see Section 14.2).

The axes are automatically scaled, using the minima and maxima of the data to be plotted. To manually set the scaling, see the command `axis` in Section 13.3.

■ Example 13.1

   (a) Let us make a plot of the following data:

```
x = [-4 -2 0 1 3 5];
y = [16 4 0 1 9 25];
```

       The command `plot(x,y)` gives Figure 13.1.

   (b) Points can be plotted as easily in MATLAB:

```
x = -pi:0.05:pi;
plot(x,sin(x) .* cos(x),'o') gives us Figure 13.2.
```

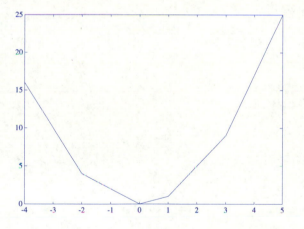

Figure 13.1 The vector **y** plotted versus the vector **x**.

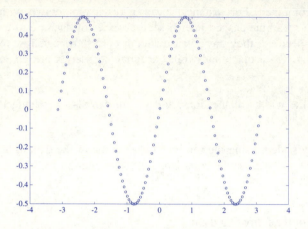

Figure 13.2 The function $sin\,x \cdot cos\,x$ plotted with small circles.

(c) Several functions can be drawn on the same graph:

```
x = 0:0.1:2;
A = [sin(pi*x); 0.5 + 0.5*x];
plot(x,A)  gives us Figure 13.3.
```

(d) The axes can be switched by shifting the arguments. Compare Figure 13.3 with Figure 13.4 given by:

```
x = 0:0.1:2;
A = [sin(pi*x); 0.5+0.5*x];
plot(A,x)
```

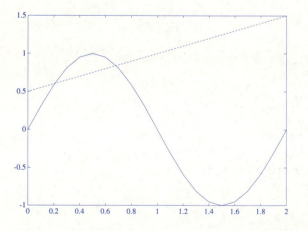

Figure 13.3 The matrix A plotted versus the vector x.

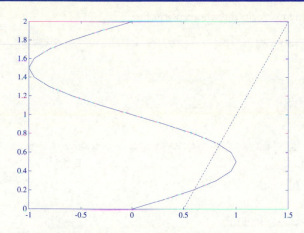

Figure 13.4 The vector **x** plotted versus the matrix **A**.

(e) The command `plot` can also handle complex matrices.

```
r = linspace(0,2);           % Creates a vector r.

theta = linspace(0,10*pi);   % Creates a vector of angles.

[x,y] = pol2cart(theta,r);   % Transforms polar coordinates
z = x + i*y;                 % to a complex vector.
plot(z)                      % Plots z.
```

This gives us Figure 13.5. Notice that complex data also can be plotted with the commands `polar`, `quiver`, `feather`, `compass`, and `rose` (see Section 13.2).

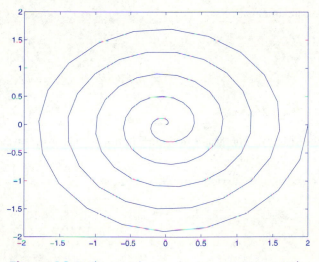

Figure 13.5 The complex vector **z** represents a spiral.

(f) The following commands form the file **expotest.m**:

```
% Prior to execution, the following parameters should be
% set: n,a,b.
% Number of points: n
% Interval: [a,b]

x = [];
e1 = []; e2 = []; e3 = []; e4 = [];      % Clear e1-e4.
for i = 1:n
    xx = a + (b - a)*(i - 1)/(n - 1);
    x(i) = xx;
    e1(i) = exp(-(xx^2));
    e2(i) = xx^2 * exp(-(xx^2));
    e3(i) = xx*exp(-(xx^2));
    e4(i) = exp(-xx);
end
```

However, the following code, with the same result, is much more efficient, easier to read and less prone to entry errors:

```
x = linspace(a,b,n);
e1 = exp(-x .^ 2);
e2 = (x ^ 2) .* exp(-x .^ 2);
e3 = x .* exp(-x .^ 2);
e4 = exp(-x);
```

Now the following statements:

```
n = 50;
a = 0;
b = 3;
expotest
plot(x,e1,x,e2,x,e3,x,e4)
```

give the graph in Figure 13.6(a). The graph in Figure 13.6(b) is the result of the following command:

```
plot(x,e1,'+',x,e2,'*',x,e3,'o',x,e4,'x').
```

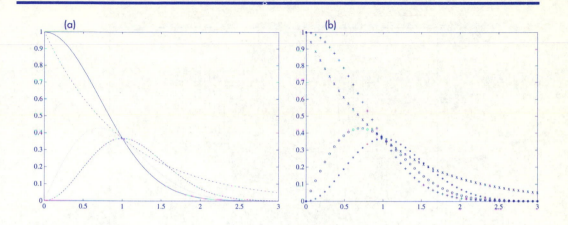

Figure 13.6 Some exponential functions plotted with standard symbols, (a), and user-chosen symbols, (b).

The command `errorbar` can be used in MATLAB to plot data with error bars. This command is used just like the command `plot`, but now error bounds are supplied to each point.

<table>
<tr><td>**Command 104**</td><td>**PLOT WITH ERROR BARS**</td></tr>
</table>

`errorbar(x,y,e, str)`	plots the vector **y** versus the vector **x**, and draws error bars of size e_i symmetrically above and below y_i. The optional string **str** determines the style and the color, see Table 13.1.
`errorbar(x,y,l,u)`	plots the vector **y** versus the vector **x**, and draws error bars of size l_i below and u_i above y_i.

■ **Example 13.2**

We now generate a data series, and suppose that the error bounds are 15%. Then we generate a graph showing the data, and the error bars:

```
x = linspace(0,10,50);    % Creates a series of values.
y = exp(sin(x));          % Creates the data.
delta = 0.15*y;           % Calculates 15% error bounds.

errorbar(x,y,delta);      % Plots the graph with error bars.
```

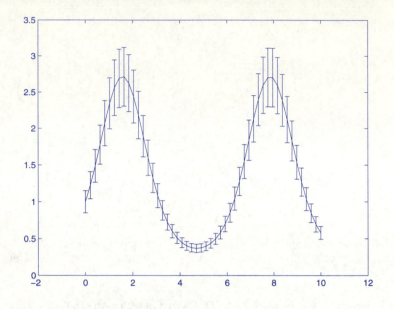

Figure 13.7 The exponential of the sine function with error bars. ∎

These commands give us Figure 13.7.

Comet plots can be drawn with the command `comet`. A comet plot is an animation of the drawing process.

Command 105	COMET PLOT

`comet(x,y)`	draws a comet plot of the vector **y** versus the vector **x**. If only one vector is given, it is plotted versus its indices.
`comet(x,y,l)`	draws a comet plot with a comet tail of length *l*, given as a relative length of the vector **y**. Default is, if no length is given, *l = 0.1*.
`comet`	draws an example of a comet plot.

Standard MATLAB and user-defined functions can be plotted with the command `fplot`.

Command 106	GRAPHS OF FUNCTIONS

`fplot(fkn, lim,str)`	plots the function specified in the string **fcn**. This can be either a standard function, or a user-defined function in the M-file **fcn.m**. The vector **lim** = $[x_{min}\ x_{max}]$ determines the plotting interval. The vector can also include four components, where the third and fourth arguments are limits on the *y*-axis, **lim** = $[x_{min}\ x_{max}\ y_{min}\ y_{max}]$. If the string **str** is passed to `fplot`, the style and color of the plot can be changed according to Table 13.1. Some extra line types are available to `fplot`, type `help fplot` to get more information.
`fplot(fkn, lim,str,tol)`	plots as above, but with a relative error that is less than *tol*.

■ **Example 13.3**

We write the following to plot *sin x²*:

```
fplot('sin(x^2)',[0 10]);
```

and we get Figure 13.8.

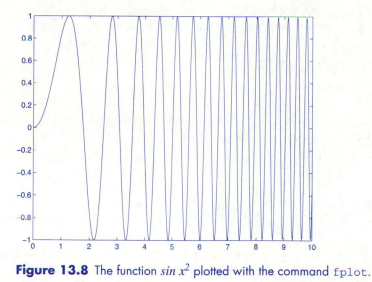

Figure 13.8 The function *sin x²* plotted with the command `fplot`. ■

13.2 Plots in other coordinate systems and in the complex plane

The command `plot` uses Cartesian coordinates. However, it is also possible to use other coordinate systems. A string argument **str** can be passed to all the following commands, specifying the style and color of the plot. Values allowed are listed in Table 13.1.

Command 107	TO PLOT IN OTHER COORDINATE SYSTEMS

`polar(theta,r)`	plots in polar coordinates. The elements of the vector **theta** are the arguments in radians, and the elements of the vector **r** are the distances from the origin.
`semilogx(x,y)`	plots in a semi-logarithmic coordinate system, a log_{10} scale is used for the *x*-axis. This is the same as `plot(log10(x),y)`, but no warning message is given for $log_{10}(0)$.
`semilogy(x,y)`	plots in a semi-logarithmic coordinate system, a log_{10} scale is used for the *y*-axis. This is the same as `plot(x,log10(y))`, but no warning message is given for $log_{10}(0)$.
`loglog(x,y)`	plots in a logarithmic coordinate system. Both axes are scaled with a log_{10} scale. This is the same as `plot(log10(x),log10(y))`, but no warning message is given for $log_{10}(0)$.

■ **Example 13.4**

(a) To draw a graph in a semi-logarithmic coordinate system is as easy as in the normal Cartesian system with the command `plot`.

```
x = linspace(0,7);           % Creates x values.
y = exp(x);                  % Creates y values.

subplot(2,1,1); plot(x,y);      % Draws an ordinary plot.

subplot(2,1,2); semilogy(x,y);  % Draws a semilogarithmic.
```

The command `subplot` allows several small graphs to be drawn in the same graphics window (see Section 13.3). When these commands are executed, we obtain Figure 13.9:

(a)

(b)

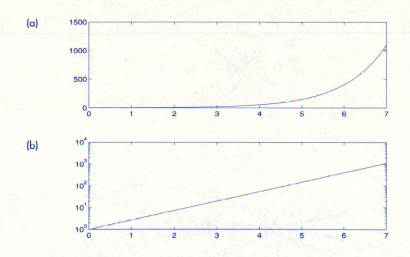

Figure 13.9 The exponential function drawn with normal axes (a) and with logarithmic scale on the *y*-axis (b).

(b) To plot a graph when the coordinates are polar one uses the command `polar`. The function

$$r = e^{cost} - 2\cos 4t + \left(sin \frac{t}{12} \right)^5$$

describes a curve in the complex plane. Here we describe two ways of plotting it.

```
t = linspace(0,22*pi,1100);

r = exp(cos(t)) - 2*cos(4*t) + (sin(t./12)).^5;

subplot(2,1,1)
p = polar(t,r);              % Plot in polar coordinates.

subplot(2,1,2)

[x,y] = pol2cart(t,r);   % Find the cartesian coordinates.

plot(x,y);                   % Plot in x-y plane.
```

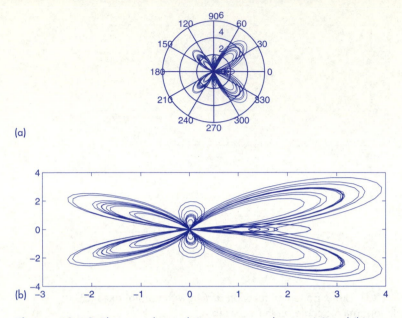

(a)

(b)

Figure 13.10 Plots in polar and Cartesian coordinates, (a) and (b) respectively. ∎

The two different plots can be seen in Figure 13.10 (a) and (b).

Complex numbers can be plotted with the commands `quiver`, `feather`, `compass`, and `rose`. These can also be used for real matrices (see Example 13.13b).

Command 108	COMPLEX PLANE GRAPHICS

`quiver(X,Y)`	draws an arrow for each pair of coordinates given by x_{ij} and y_{ij}. The command `quiver(real(Z),imag(Z))` can be interpreted as a plot of the argument and magnitude of the complex numbers in the matrix **Z.**
`quiver(x,y,dx,dy)`	draws an arrow at the coordinates (x_i,y_i), with argument and magnitude given by (dx_i,dy_i).
`quiver(X,Y,Dx,Dy)`	draws an arrow at the coordinates (x_{ij},y_{ij}), with argument and magnitude given by (dx_{ij},dy_{ij}).
`quiver(X,Y,...,s)`	draws arrows as above, but now scaled with a factor s. If left out, the default value is $s = 1$.
`quiver(X,Y,..,str)`	draws the arrows using the line type **str**, see Table 13.1.

Command 108	COMPLEX PLANE GRAPHICS (continued)

`feather(Z)`	draws arrows showing the magnitudes and arguments of the elements of the complex matrix **Z**, originating from equidistant points on the *x*-axis.
`feather(X,Y)`	is equivalent to `feather(X + Y * i)`.
`feather(Z,str)`	draws the arrows using the line type **str**, see Table 13.1.
`compass(Z)`	draws arrows originating from the origin, showing the magnitudes and arguments of the elements of the complex matrix **Z**.
`compass(X,Y)`	is equivalent to `compass(X + Y * i)`.
`compass(Z,str)`	draws the arrows using the line type **str**, see Table 13.1.
`rose(v)`	draws an argument histogram, that is a circular histogram showing the frequency of the arguments in the vector **v**. *36* intervals are used.
`rose(v,n)`	the same as the above, but now *n* intervals are used.
`rose(v,x)`	draws an argument histogram, using the intervals specified in the vector **x**.

■ **Example 13.5**

Let **Z** be defined as:

$$Z = \begin{bmatrix} 1+i & 2-i & 3-5i \\ -4+3i & 5-5i & i \\ -1-i & 3+3i & -1 \end{bmatrix}$$

The following commands give Figure 13.11 (a)–(d).

```
clf;
subplot(2,2,1); quiver(real(Z),imag(Z));   title('quiver');
subplot(2,2,2); feather(Z);                 title('feather');
subplot(2,2,3); compass(Z);                 title('compass');
subplot(2,2,4); rose(angle(Z(:)));          title('rose');
```

The command `subplot` makes it possible to draw several plots in the same graphics window (see Section 13.3).

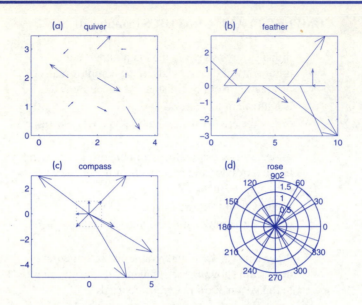

Figure 13.11 Complex numbers represented by graphics.

13.3 Controlling the graphics

The graphics in MATLAB are object orientated. The commands listed in this chapter are used to set and create the necessary objects to draw and change graphics. In this section we discuss a few commands which on a high level change these objects, many by a single command. It is also possible to manipulate the attributes of a single graphics object. This is discussed in detail in Chapter 14, which describes commands for advanced graphics.

MATLAB has two kinds of windows, **command windows** and **graphics windows**. The command window is used when the MATLAB commands are given. A graphics window is the window in which all the graphics are shown.

The hardware determines if it is possible to have graphics windows as well as the command window on the screen simultaneously. There are commands to switch between the windows, to clear the windows, and to hold the current plot.

Command 109	WINDOW COMMANDS

| `figure(gcf)` | shows the current graphics window. The command `figure` can also be used to change active graphics window, and to create new graphics windows (see Section 14.2). |

Command 109	WINDOW COMMANDS (continued)
`clf`	clears the current graphics window. Warning: the window is cleared also if `hold on` is set.
`clg`	is an old command equivalent to `clf`. May be removed in later versions of MATLAB.
`clc`	clears the command window.
`home`	moves the cursor to its 'home', that is the upper left corner of the command window.
`hold on`	holds the current plot, enabling graphics to be added to the current plot.
`hold off`	releases the graphics window, so the next plot will replace the current graphics. This is the default status.
`hold`	toggles between `hold on` and `hold off`.
`ishold`	returns *1* if the current plot is held, otherwise *0*.

The command `subplot` is used to draw several plots in the same graphics window. `subplot` does not draw anything, but defines how the graphics window is to be divided, and in which subwindow the next plot is to be drawn.

Command 110	SUBPLOTS
`subplot(m,n,p)`	splits the graphics window into *m* rows, and *n* columns, and sets subwindow *p* as the current. The subwindows are numbered by row from left to right, top to bottom. This command can in the current version of MATLAB also be written `subplot(mnp)`.
`subplot`	sets the graphics window to the default mode, that is a single window. The same as `subplot(1,1,1)`.

■ **Example 13.6**

(a) Show a matrix with running random numbers in top left corner of the command window:

```
clc                    % Clears the command window.
for i = 1:25
    home               % Sends the cursor "home".
    A = rand(5)        % Creates and prints the matrix.
end
```

(b) The following MATLAB commands plot the function $f(x) = -x \sin x$ in the top left subwindow, its derivative $f'(x) = -x \cos x - \sin x$ in the top right subwindow, an approximative derivative in the bottom left, and the difference between the exact and approximate derivative in the bottom right subwindow.

```
x = linspace(-10,10,1000);         % Creates x-values.
y11 = (-x).*sin(x);                % Generates f-values
y12 = (-x).*cos(x) - sin(x);       % and the derivative.
y21 = diff(y11)./(x(2)-x(1));      % Approximates
                                   % derivative
y22 = (y21 - y12(1:999))./norm(y12);% and its relative
                                   % error.

subplot(2,2,1); plot(x,y11); title('The function')
                % Plots in upper left-hand corner.
subplot(2,2,2); plot(x,y12); title('The derivative')
                % Plots in upper right-hand corner.
subplot(2,2,3); plot(x(1:999),y21);
                % Plots in lower left-hand corner.
title('The approximated derivative')

subplot(2,2,4); plot(x(1:999),y22); title('The relative error
                % Plots in lower right-hand corner.
```

These commands give Figure 13.12 (a)–(d).

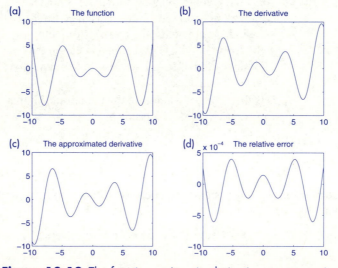

Figure 13.12 The function $x \sin x$, its derivative, an approximate derivative and the relative error of the approximate derivative.

The command `subplot` can also be used for three-dimensional graphics and the subplots can be of different sizes in the same window as the following example shows.

■ **Example 13.7**

This example contains an M-file that computes the Mandelbrot fractal and visualizes it in three different ways. The program takes points in a grid defined by the user in the complex plane and iterates each number c that belongs to the defined grid according to this algorithm:

$$z_0 = 0$$

$$z_{i+1} = z_i^2 + c$$

If z_i is divergent then the current c is not a part of the Mandelbrot set. The number of iterations in each point c of the complex plane is saved in a matrix **mandelbrot** with the same size as the resolution of the complex plane. The algorithm will only iterate *100* times so divergent points will get the value *100*.

```
% Mandelbrot program.
clear;
epsilon = 1e-14;
renum = input('renum: ');   % Reads number of real points.
imnum = input('imnum: ');   % Reads number of imaginary points.
remin = -2; remax = 1; immin = -1.5; immax = 1.5;
                             % Defines which numbers to compute.
reval1 = linspace(remin,remax,renum);
imval1 = linspace(immin,immax,imnum);
                             % Makes vectors of correct size.
[Reval, Imval] = meshgrid(reval1,imval1 );
                             % Constructs grid in imaginary
plane.
Imvalreal = Imval;
Imval = Imval*i;
Cgrid = Reval + Imval;
%--------------------------------------------------
```

```
for reind = 1:renum
    disp(['reind = ', int2str(reind)]);
                        % Lets the user know the loop status.
    for imind = 1:imnum
        c = Cgrid( reind, imind );
                    % Iteration loop z(i+1) = (z(i))^2 + c.
                    % Initiations.
        numc = 0;
        zold = 0.0 + i*0.0;
        z    = zold^2 + c; % z(0) = c.
        while ( abs(z) <= 2 ) & ...
              ( abs( z-zold) >= epsilon ) & ...
              ( numc < 100 )
            numc = numc + 1;
            zold = z;
            z = zold^2 + c;    % New z!
        end
        Mandelbrot(reind,imind) = numc;
        % Let the matrix mandelbrot have the number
        % of iterations for the point Cgrid(n,m) in
        % position Mandelbrot(n,m).
    end
end
% Graphics, displays the matrix mandelbrot in three
% different ways:
clf;                    % Clears the figure.
whitebg('k');           % Sets background black.
subplot(2,2,1);         % Upper left corner
mesh( reval1, imval1, Mandelbrot );% Plots mesh grid
axis([-2 1 -1.5 1.5 0 100])% Change axis limits.
```

```
subplot(2,2,2);                    % Upper right corner
contour( reval1, imval1, Mandelbrot, 100  );

grid;                              % Plots contour plot grid;
                                   % Adds grid.

subplot(2,1,2);                    % Lower figure (only one)!
surf(Reval,Imvalreal,Mandelbrot ) ;
                                   % Surface plot of Mandelbrot
view(2);                           % Viewpoint directly above.

shading flat;                      % Each cell has only one color.
colormap(flipud(jet));             % Colour map defined
inverse jet. colorbar; axis([-2 1 -1.5 1.5]);
                                   % Show colorbar. Change axis.
```

This program results in Figure 13.13.

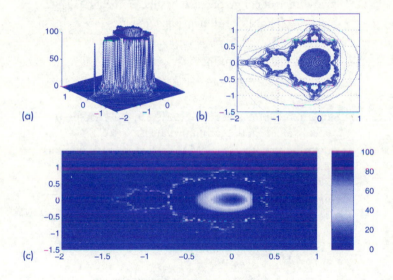

(a)

(b)

(c)

Figure 13.13 The Mandelbrot fractal visualized in three different ways: (a) subplot: a mesh plot; (b) subplot: a contour plot; (c) subplot: a surface plot viewed from directly above.

Graphics can be placed almost anywhere in the graphics windows, with more control than allowed by `subplot`, see Chapter 14.

The axes of each plot are usually automatically scaled to fit all the points in the window. Thus the corners of the plot are defined by:

$$(min(\mathbf{x}), min(\mathbf{y})), (max(\mathbf{x}), min(\mathbf{y})), (min(\mathbf{x}), max(\mathbf{y})), (max(\mathbf{x}), max(\mathbf{y})).$$

Sometimes it can be hard to see some of the points, since they might coincide with the axes due to the scaling. Fortunately, the command `axis` in MATLAB can be used to change the scaling.

It is also possible to use the mouse to change the scaling. This is possible by the command `zoom`.

| Command 111 | AXES, SCALING, AND ZOOMING |

`axis`	returns the limits of the current plot to a row vector. For two-dimensional graphics, it has the elements: $[x_{min}\ x_{max}\ y_{min}\ y_{max}]$. For three-dimensional graphics (see Section 13.5), it is $[x_{min}\ x_{max}\ y_{min}\ y_{max}\ z_{min}\ z_{max}]$.
`axis(v)`	sets the scales according to the vector $\mathbf{v}$, making $x_{min} = v_1$, $x_{max} = v_2$, $y_{min} = v_3$, $y_{max} = v_4$. For three-dimensional graphics also $z_{min} = v_5$ and $z_{max} = v_6$ are set. For logarithmic plots, discussed earlier in this chapter, use the actual values, not logarithmic values.
`axis(axis)`	locks the scaling. Keeps MATLAB from changing the scale when plots are added to existing plots. See the command `hold`, in Section 13.3.
`axis(str)`	gives different results depending on the string **str**:
	`'auto'` resets the scaling to MATLAB's automatic scaling.
	`'equal'` sets the same scale to both the x- and the y axes.
	`'ij'` flips the y-axis, so that positive y is down, and negative is up.
	`'xy'` resets the y-axis, making positive y up.
	`'image'` resizes the graphics window, to make the pixels have the same height as width, adapting to the computer.
	`'square'` resizes the graphics window to make the window square.

| Command 111 | AXES, SCALING, AND ZOOMING (continued) |

	`'normal'` resets the graphics window to standard size.
	`'off'` tells MATLAB not to show the axes or the scale.
	`'on'` tells MATLAB to show the axis and the scale again.
	This command can also be given in the form `axis normal`, and so on.
`grid on`	draws a grid in the graphics window.
`grid off`	removes the grid from the graphics window.
`grid`	toggles between `grid on` and `grid off`.
`zoom on`	enables the user to zoom in on two-dimensional graphics by clicking the left mouse button in the graphics window. The right mouse button can be used to zoom out. It is also possible to select an area by "click and drag". The scale is adjusted to make the selected area fill the graphics window.
`zoom off`	disables the zoom.
`zoom out`	resets the full scale.
`zoom`	toggles between `zoom on` and `zoom off`.

The axes and the grid can be controlled in more detail (see Chapter 14). Closely related to the command `axis` are the commands `caxis` and `saxis`, setting the scales for the colors and sounds, respectively (see Sections 13.6 and 13.8).

As described in Section 2.3, commands can be considered to be functions with string arguments. Hence, `axis('square')` can also be written as `axis square`, and `grid off` is equivalent to `grid('off')`.

■ **Example 13.8**

(a) Let us define a set of values representing the unit circle:

```
t = 0:0.2:2*pi + 0.2;     % A parameter for the angle.
x = sin(t);               % x-values.
y = cos(t);               % y-values.
```

The following command gives us Figure 13.14:

```
plot(x,y,'-')
```

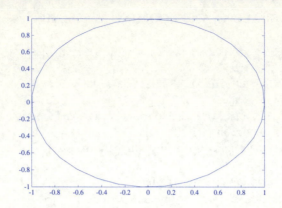

Figure 13.14 A circle might look oval if the scales are not adjusted.

(b) The axes can be rescaled to make the circles look like circles. We also draw a grid this time.

```
axis('square');          % Adjusts the scale.
grid on                  % Draws a grid.
```

These commands give us the plot on the left of Figure 13.15. The plot on the right of the same figure is obtained with:

```
axis('normal');          % Resets the axes.
grid off;                % Turns off the grid.
axis([-2 2 -3 3])        % Changes the axes, scaling.
```

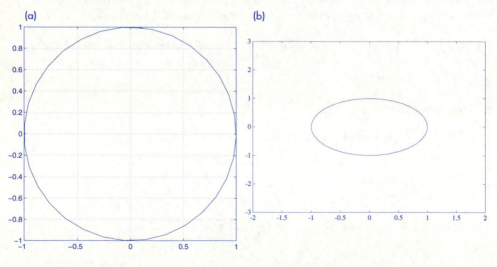

Figure 13.15 In plot (a), the axes are set square, and in plot (b) the scale is set manually.

There are several commands to write text in a graphics window. The commands `title`, `x-`, `y-`, `zlabel` write standard text items. The command `text` can be used to write text anywhere in the graphics window. All these commands are applied to the current `subplot`, and should usually be given after the graphics is drawn in the window. To change fonts and other properties, see Section 14.2.

Command 112	TEXT IN GRAPHICS WINDOWS

`title(txt)`	writes the string **txt** as a title centered in the top of the graphics window.
`xlabel(txt)`	writes the string **txt** as a label centered below the *x*-axis.
`ylabel(txt)`	writes the string **txt** as a label centered beside the *y*-axis.
`zlabel(txt)`	writes the string **txt** as a label centered beside the *z*-axis.
`text(x,y,txt)`	writes the string **txt** in the graphics window at position (x, y). The coordinates x and y are given in the same scale in which the plot is drawn. For **x** and **y** vectors, the string **txt** is written at positions (x_i, y_i). If **txt** is a vector of strings, that is a matrix of characters, with the same number of rows as **x** and **y**, the string on the ith row is written at position (x_i, y_i) in the graphics window.
`text(x,y,txt,'sc')`	writes the string **txt** at position (x, y) in the graphics window. The coordinates are given with $(0.0, 0.0)$ as the lower left-hand corner, and $(1.0, 1.0)$ as the top right-hand corner.
`gtext(txt)`	lets the user place the string **txt** in the graphics window. A cross is moved in the graphics window, with the arrow keys or a mouse. When the cross is at the desired location, the user presses any key, or any button on the mouse, and the string is written to the window.
`legend(st1,st2,...)`	writes a legend in the current plot with the specified strings **st1**, **st2** and so on as labels. The legend can be moved by pressing the left mouse button on the legend and dragging it to another position.
`legend(l1,st1,l2,st2,l3,st3,...)`	writes a legend in the current plot with the strings **st1**, **st2** ... as labels and with the line styles $l1, l2$ ... (See Table 13.1 for valid line styles.)
`legend off`	removes legend from current plot.

The commands converting numbers to strings, that is num2str, int2str, sprintf, and so on (see Section 5.2) can be useful and sometimes even necessary to use together with these text commands.

■ **Example 13.9**

Let us write a simple program that performs a random walk. This can be a simulation of the movement of a particle in air.

The program is stored as **particle.m**:

```
% Random walk. A particle starts at the origin, and is
% moved randomly up to a half unit in either direction
% in every step.

disp('Give the number of steps')  % The number of steps.
n = input('>>>');

x = cumsum(rand(n,1)-0.5);         % Random x-values.
y = cumsum(rand(n,1)-0.5);         % Random y-values.

clf;                               % Clears the
                                   % graphics window.
plot(x,y);                         % Plots the walk.
hold on;                           % Holds the plot.
plot(x(1),y(1),'o',x(n),y(n),'o');% Marks start/
                                   % finish.
axs = axis;                        % Gets min and max.
scale = axs(2)- axs(1);            % Calculates a
                                   % scale.

text(x(1)+scale/30,y(1),'Start'); % Writes text to
                                   % the right
text(x(n)+scale/30,y(n),'Finish');% of Start and
                                   % Finish.
hold off;                          % Resets standard,
                                   % hold off.
xlabel('x');  ylabel('y');   title('Random walk')
```

When this program is run, with the command particle, we get:

Give the number of steps
>>> 100

We now obtain Figure 13.16.

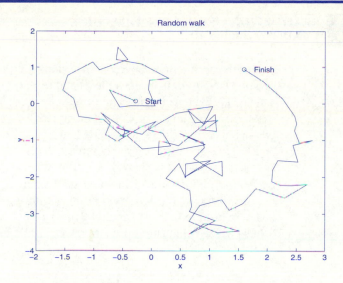

Figure 13.16 Random walk.   ■

The command `ginput` is used to get information from a graphics window. This command places a cursor in the graphics window, and this cursor can be moved by the user, either with the keyboard or with the mouse. By moving it to the desired position, and pressing a key or a mouse button, the coordinates are passed to MATLAB. If the number of coordinates to be read is not specified, MATLAB keeps reading coordinates for each key or mouse button pressed until the key "return" is pressed.

Command 113	**READING DATA FROM THE GRAPHICS WINDOW**

`[x,y] = ginput`	reads coordinates from a graphics window. A cursor which can be positioned with the mouse, or with the arrow keys, is placed in the graphics window, and by pressing a mouse button or any key, the coordinates are sent to MATLAB. These coordinates are stored in the vectors **x** and **y**. The process is terminated with the "return" key.
`[x,y] = ginput(n)`	reads *n* coordinates from the graphics window.
`[x,y,t] = ginput(...)`	also returns a vector **t** with integers specifying which mouse buttons were pressed. The left button returns *1*, the middle button *2*, and the right button returns *3*. If the keyboard was used, the ASCII codes of the keys pressed are returned.

Command 113	**READING DATA FROM THE GRAPHICS WINDOW (continued)**
`[x,y] =` `ginput(...,'s')`	returns the positions as above, but in a coordinate system where *(0,0)* is the lower left-hand corner, and *(1,1)* is the upper right-hand corner.
`waitforbuttonpress`	stops MATLAB until a mouse button or a key is pressed in current figure. If a mouse button is pressed, `waitforbuttonpress` returns *0*, if a key on the keyboard is pressed, *1* is returned.
`rbbox`	draws dashed lines around a rubberband box in the current figure. It can be used together with `waitforbuttonpress` to control dynamic behavior. The command is used in `zoom`.

■ **Example 13.10**

The `ginput` and `waitforbuttonpress` commands provide the MATLAB programmer with tools to create simple interactive programs. The M-file below uses both commands for drawing a picture out of points specified by the user. When the plot is drawn the program waits for the user to click in the figure before deleting it.

```
% M-file for interactive drawing.
n = figure;                % New figure.
disp('To draw a line in the figure:')
disp('Press the left mouse button in the figure for start,')
disp('each bend and stop of the line.
disp ('Press right mouse button')
disp('when finished.')
[x,y,t] = ginput(1);    % Read first mouse button press coord
plot(x,y,'o')           % Marks it with a circle.
xx = x; yy= y;          % Saves coordinates
hold; axis([0 1 0 1]);  % Holds the figure and lock the axis.
while t~= 3              % While not the right button pressed
   [x,y,t] = ginput(1); % reads new coordinates and
   plot(x,y,'o')        % marks it with a circle.
```

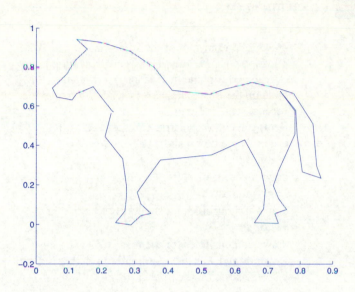

Figure 13.17 A result of the interactive program in Example 13.10.

```
    xx = [xx x];    % Saves coordinates.
    yy = [yy y];
end
clf; line(xx,yy); % Clears the figure and draw a line.
disp('Click on the figure when you are done')
waitforbuttonpress% Wait until button press in figure.
delete(n);         % Remove figure.
```

The commands `figure`, `delete` and `line` are introduced in Section 14.2. Other interactive commands are presented in Section 14.4. Figure 13.17 is a result from the M-file above. ∎

13.4 Generating grids and drawing contour plots

Contour plots in both two and three dimensions can be drawn to a function of two variables, such as $z = \mathbf{f}(x,y)$. The former is done with the command `contour`, and the latter with `contour3`. These commands can only be used on a rectangular grid.

Command 114	**CONTOUR PLOTS**

`contour(Z)`	draws a contour plot of the values in the matrix **Z**. The elements are interpreted as representing levels over the (x,y)-plane. If **Z** is an $m \times n$-matrix, the scale on the horizontal axis is set as *1* to *n* and the vertical scale is set to *1* to *m*. Returns a contour matrix **C** to be used by, for example, the command `clabel`. See also `contourc`.
`contour(Z,n)`	draws contour lines for *n* levels. If not specified, *10* levels are drawn.
`contour(Z,v)`	draws contour lines for the levels specified in the vector **v**.
`contour(x,y,Z)`	draws contour lines for the matrix **Z**, using the vectors **x** and **y** as the coordinates to **Z**, that is **x** and **y** set the scale on the axes.
`contour(x,y,Z,n)`	draws *n* levels, using the vectors **x** and **y** as the scale of the axes.
`contour(x,y,Z,v)`	draws contour lines at the levels specified by the vector **v**, using the vectors **x** and **y** as the scale of the axes.
`contour(...,str)`	draws contour lines using the line types and colors defined by the string **str.** See the `plot` command and Table 13.1 in Section 13.1.
`contourc(...)`	computes the contour matrix **C** for use by `contour` and `clabel` without drawing the contour lines. **C** is a two-row matrix containing the drawing segments for each level curve stored consecutively. Type `help contourc` for more information.
`contour3(x,y,Z,n)`	draws contour lines at *n* levels in three dimensions, that is without projecting the lines to the (x,y)-plane. Returns the contour matrix used by `clabel`.
`clabel(C)`	writes numbers by the contour lines to indicate the levels they represent. The positions are random. The matrix **C** is the contour matrix returned by the commands `contour` or `contour3`.
`clabel(C,v)`	writes numbers indicating the levels specified in the vector **v**. The matrix **C** is the contour matrix returned by the commands `contour` or `contour3`.

| Command 114 | **CONTOUR PLOTS (continued)** |

clabel(C,'manual')   lets the user place numbers indicating the levels at that position. A cursor is placed in the contour plot, and the user moves this cursor either with the mouse, or the arrow keys. Pressing a mouse button or any key, places the number. The process is terminated by pressing the key "return".

If a matrix **Z** is defined and we wish to see a contour plot of it, the command contour(Z) or contour3(Z) can be used.

■ **Example 13.11**

(a) Suppose we have defined a matrix **Z** which describes the surface of the two-dimensional function shown in Figure 13.30. Then the following program gives the plots in Figure 13.18:

```
subplot(2,1,1);       % Upper subplot.
v1 = -4:-1;
v2 = 0:4;
contour(Z,v1,'k-'); % draws solid lines for Z negative.
hold on;
contour(Z,v2,'k--');% draws dashed lines for Z nonnegative.
hold off;
subplot(2,1,2);       % Lower subplot.
C = contour(Z);       % Draws the contour lines.
clabel(C);            % Writes the contour labels.
```

(b) To see what a contour matrix looks like, we construct the contour plot of the same function, using a smaller matrix **Zsmall.** The program only shows two levels, that is, when **Zsmall** takes the values 1 or 2 (see Figure 13.19).

```
v = 1:2;              % Only levels 1 and 2.
C = contour(Zsmall,v);% Constructs the contour matrix C.
clabel(C);            % Writes the contour labels.
size(C)               % Shows the size of C.
C                     % Shows C itself.
```

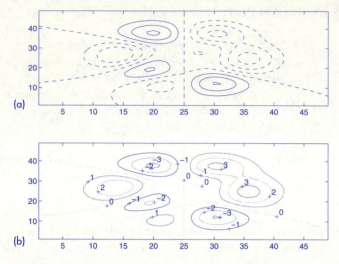

(a)

(b)

Figure 13.18 Contour plots.

The result of the program is:

ans =

   2   28

C =

Columns 1 through 7

1.0000	2.0000	3.0000	3.2808	3.0000	2.0000	1.8245
7.0000	4.2734	4.2466	4.0000	3.8678	3.8063	4.0000

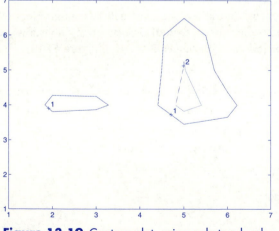

Figure 13.19 Contour plot, using only two levels.

Columns 8 through 14

| 2.0000 | 1.0000 | 6.0000 | 5.6894 | 5.4944 | 5.0000 | 4.5378 |
| 4.2734 | 11.0000 | 4.3756 | 5.0000 | 6.0000 | 6.4866 | 6.0000 |

Columns 15 through 21

| 4.4883 | 4.4046 | 5.0000 | 6.0000 | 6.2220 | 6.0000 | 2.0000 |
| 5.0000 | 4.0000 | 3.4553 | 3.6576 | 4.0000 | 4.3756 | 7.0000 |

Columns 22 through 28

| 5.0000 | 4.9766 | 4.8093 | 5.0000 | 5.3970 | 5.0316 | 5.0000 |
| 5.2546 | 5.0000 | 4.0000 | 3.8255 | 4.0000 | 5.0000 | 5.2546 |

As we can see, there are two level curves for the value *1*, the first one contains seven coordinate pairs and the second has *11* pairs. Contour level *2* is described by seven coordinate pairs.   ∎

However, it might be necessary to compute **Z**. This is accomplished in two steps. First, we define a grid in the domain where we wish to draw the contour lines. The domain is defined by two vectors **x** and **y** with length n and m respectively, for the x- and y-values in the grid. Note that the elements of **x** and **y** do not have to be equidistant. We then form the grid with the command `[U,V]   =   meshgrid(x,y)`. The actual grid is the two matrices **U** and **V**, containing its x- and y coordinates. The matrix **U** consists of the vector **x** copied to m rows, and **V** of the vector **y** copied to n columns. This is shown in Figure 13.20, where the y axis is drawn downwards to emphasize the correspondence between the grid points and the elements of the matrices.

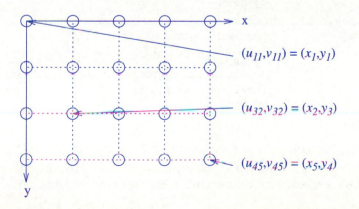

Figure 13.20 A grid with five x values and four y values defines two 4×5 matrices **U** and **V** with elements from the vectors **x** and **y**.

The `meshgrid` command has equivalents for generating cylinder grids and spherical grids.

Command 115   GENERATION OF GRID

`[U,V] =` `meshgrid(x,y)`	gives matrices forming a grid with the x-coordinates and y-coordinates from the vectors **x** and **y**. A vector **x** of length n containing the x-coordinates in ascending order, and a vector **y** of length m in ascending order, are copied m and n times respectively, to form the two $m \times n$-matrices **U** and **V**. These matrices represent the x- and y-coordinates in the whole rectangular domain. The coordinate pairs (u_{ij}, v_{ij}), $i = 1, ..., m$, $j = 1, ..., n$, can be used to calculate $z_{ij} = \mathbf{f}(u_{ij}, v_{ij})$, with the command `z=f(U,V)`. (See Figure 13.20.)
`[U,V,W] =` `meshgrid(x,y,z)`	gives a three-dimensional grid in the same manner, and can be used to evaluate functions of three variables.
`[X,Y,Z] =` `cylinder(r,n)`	returns coordinate matrices like `meshgrid`, but the generated coordinates form the surface of a cylinder or cone. The radii of the cylinder are taken from the vector **r**, containing the radius in n equidistant points along the cylinder axis. If n is not specified, $n = 20$ is used. If neither **r** nor n are specified, $\mathbf{r} = [1\ 1]$ and $n = 20$ are used.
`cylinder(r,n)`	plots the cylinder according to the above instead of returning the coordinates.
`[x,y,z] = sphere(n)`	returns n equally spaced coordinates on a unit sphere in the matrices **X**, **Y**, and **Z**, all $(n + 1) \times (n + 1)$-matrices.
`sphere(n)`	plots the sphere according to the above instead of returning the coordinates.

■ Example 13.12

Suppose we want to define a grid **U**, **V** over the unit square and that we want *5* grid points along the x axis, and *4* grid points along the y axis, just like in Figure 13.20. We first define the vectors **x** and **y**, and then form the grid:

```
x = linspace(0,1,5);        % Defines the x values.
y = linspace(0,1,4);        % Defines the y values.
```

```
[U,V] = meshgrid(x,y)          % Forms the grid.
```

$U =$

0	0.2500	0.5000	0.7500	1.0000
0	0.2500	0.5000	0.7500	1.0000
0	0.2500	0.5000	0.7500	1.0000
0	0.2500	0.5000	0.7500	1.0000

$V =$

0	0	0	0	0	■
0.3333	0.3333	0.3333	0.3333	0.3333	
0.6667	0.6667	0.6667	0.6667	0.6667	
1.0000	1.0000	1.0000	1.0000	1.0000	■

The second step is to evaluate the function $z = \mathbf{f}(x,y)$ over the domain. With the grid defined, this is just $Z=f(U,V)$. This requires the function $\mathbf{f}$ to be defined with elementwise operators, see Section 3.5.

■ Example 13.13

(a) Let us draw contour plots for the following three functions:

$$z_1 = f(x,y) = \sin x \cdot \sin y \qquad x, y \in [0,\pi] \times [0,\pi]$$
$$z_2 = f(x,y) = x - 0.5x^3 + 0.2y^2 + 1 \qquad x, y \in [-3,3] \times [-3,3]$$
$$z_3 = f(x,y) = \sin((x^2 + y^2)^{0.5})/(x^2 + y^2)^{0.5} \quad x, y \in [-8,8] \times [-8,8]$$

The first part of the program generates the grids and evaluates the functions. The final part of the program draws the plots. This is the program **contours.m**:

```
x = 0:0.2:3*pi;             % Generates coordinates.
y = 0:0.25:5*pi;
[XX,YY] = meshgrid(x,y);
Z1 = sin(XX) .* sin(YY);    % Evaluates the function.

x = -3:0.25:3;              % Generates coordinates.
y = x;
[XX,YY] = meshgrid(x,y);
```

```
Z2 = XX - 0.5*XX.^3 + 0.2*YY.^2 + 1;
                          % Evaluates the function.
x = -8:0.5:8;            % Generates coordinates.
y = x;
[XX,YY] = meshgrid(x,y);
r = sqrt(XX.^2 + YY.^2) + eps;
Z3 = sin(r)./r;          % Evaluates the function.
clf

subplot(2,2,1); contour(Z1);
title('sin(x)*sin(y)');
subplot(2,2,2); contour(x,y,Z3);
title('sin(r)/r');
subplot(2,2,3); contour3(Z2,15);
title('x-0.5x^3 + 0.2y^2 + 1');
subplot(2,2,4); contour3(x,y,Z3);
title('sin(r)/r');
```

When we execute this program, we get Figure 13.21 (a)–(d). These functions can also be seen as surface plots in Figure 13.25.

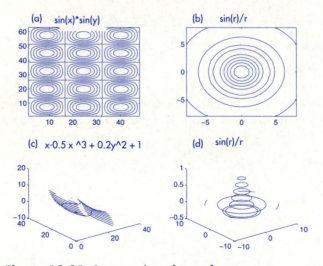

Figure 13.21 Contour plots of some functions.

(b) To get a really revealing plot of a function, we draw contour lines in the same plot as we plot gradients. The gradients can be computed with the command `gradient` (see Section 6.2) and they can be plotted with the command

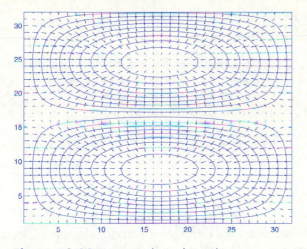

Figure 13.22 Contour plot with gradients.

quiver (see Section 13.2). This interesting plot can be obtained with the following statements:

```
[X,Y] = meshgrid(-pi/2:0.1:pi/2,-pi:0.2:pi);
Z = abs(sin(Y).*cos(X));
[DZDX,DZDY] = gradient(Z,.1,0.2)
contour(Z); hold on; quiver(DZDX,DZDY); hold off;
```

and we get Figure 13.22.   ■

13.5 Three-dimensional graphics

A three-dimensional plot can be drawn with the command plot3. This command is almost the same as plot, but plot3 needs a third vector or matrix argument. Style and color can be specified with a string (see Table 13.1).

Command 116	THREE-DIMENSIONAL GRAPHICS, PART 1

plot3(x,y,z)	plots a graph through the points defined by (x_i, y_i, z_i). The vectors **x**, **y**, and **z** must be of equal length.
plot3(X,Y,Z)	plots graphs for each column of the matrices **X**, **Y**, and **Z**. These matrices must be of equal size. Alternatively, some of the matrices can be vectors of the same length as the columns of the matrices.

Command 116	THREE-DIMENSIONAL GRAPHICS, PART 1 (continued)
`plot3(x,y,z,str)`	plots a graph according to the above, and uses the style and color specified by the string **str**. (See Table 13.1 for allowed values.)
`plot3(x1,y1,z1,str1, x2,y2,z2,str2,...)`	plots the graph (**x1**, **y1**, **z1**) with style and color according to **str1**, and (**x2**, **y2**, **z2**) with style according to **str2**, etc. If **str1**, **str2**, and so on are left out, MATLAB chooses colors and styles.

■ Example 13.14

Inspired by Example 13.9 we now write a program simulating a random walk in three dimensions. The program called **particle3.m** looks like this:

```
n = input('Give the number of steps');% The number of
                                       % steps.
x = cumsum(rand(1,n)-0.5);             % x-values.
y = cumsum(rand(1,n)-0.5);             % y-values.
z = cumsum(rand(1,n)-0.5);             % z-values.

plot3(x,y,z);                          % Plots the walk.
text(x(1),y(1),z(1),'Start');          % Writes Start.
text(x(n),y(n),z(n),'Finish');         % Writes Finish.
```

We get Figure 13.23 when this program is executed.

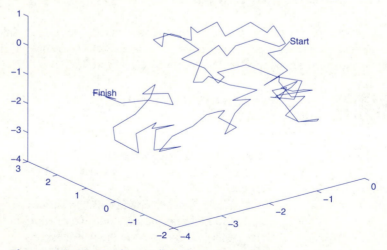

Figure 13.23 *Random walk in three dimensions.*

In the same way as a two-dimensional plot can be animated with the command comet, a three-dimensional plot can be animated with the command comet3.

Command 117   COMET PLOT IN THREE DIMENSIONS

comet3(x,y,z)	draws an animated three-dimensional plot of the function $z=\mathbf{f}(x,y)$, that is a plot with a comet tail between the coordinates (x_i, y_i, z_i).
comet3(x,y,z,p)	gives the same animated plot as above, but the tail is of length p. The length of the tail is given as relative part of the vector **y**, and p is set to *0.1* if not specified.

Text in three-dimensional figures is written with the same commands as for two-dimensional figures, that is title, text, xlabel, ylabel, and zlabel (see Section 13.3).

A surface graph of the function $z = \mathbf{f}(x,y)$ can be obtained in the following way in MATLAB:

1. form the grid as described in Section 13.4;

2. evaluate Z = f(U,V), where the matrices **U** and **V** are the coordinates for the x and y values respectively;

3. draw the surface with one of the surface graphics commands available in MATLAB. Note that the grid does not need to be rectangular, but if not, the grid coordinates must be included in the function call.

The commands in Command 118 are used to draw a mesh surface of functions in three dimensions.

Command 118   THREE-DIMENSIONAL GRAPHICS, PART 2

mesh(Z)	plots the values in the matrix **Z** as height values above a rectangular grid, and connects neighboring points, into a mesh surface.
mesh(Z,C)	plots the values in the matrix **Z** as height values above a rectangular grid, in the color specified for each point by the elements of the matrix **C**.
mesh(U,V,Z,C)	draws a function mesh surface of the elements in the matrix **Z**, that is a figure where neighboring points are connected with lines. The graph is drawn in a three-dimensional perspective, with the elements z_{ij} as height values over the grid points (u_{ij}, v_{ij}).

Command 118	THREE-DIMENSIONAL GRAPHICS, PART 2 (continued)

	The viewpoint is set automatically, and can be changed with the command `view`. **U:** matrix with the x-coordinates **V:** matrix with the y-coordinates **Z:** matrix with the z-coordinates, usually $z_{ij} = \mathbf{f}(u_{ij}, v_{ij})$ **C:** matrix with the color for each point. If **C** is left out, **C** = **Z** is used. If u and v are vectors of length m and n respectively, **Z** has to be a matrix of size m x n, and the surface is defined by (u_j, v_i, z_{ij})
`meshc( ... )`	draws a mesh surface like the command `mesh`, but also draws a contour plot under the graph.
`meshz( ... )`	draws a mesh surface like the command `mesh`, but also draws a reference grid down to the (x,y) plane.
`waterfall( ... )`	is like `meshz`, but the reference grid is only drawn in one direction.
`hidden on`	keeps MATLAB from drawing lines that are hidden behind the mesh surface drawn by the command `mesh`. The command `hidden` by itself toggles between `on` and `off`. This command is only applicable to the command `mesh`.
`hidden off`	makes MATLAB draw lines behind the mesh surface.

The graph can be rotated using the command `rot90` on the defining matrix. Also, see the command `view` in Section 13.5.

Command 119	MATRIX ROTATION

`rot90(A)`	returns the matrix **A** rotated *90* degrees counter-clockwise. Often used together with the command `mesh`.
`rot90(A,k)`	returns the matrix **A** rotated $k*90$ degrees counter-clockwise.

We would also like to stress that the command `mesh` can be very useful to get an image of a matrix. This can be useful in understanding for instance how numerical methods work.

■ **Example 13.15**

(a) The matrix **Matlabmatrix** consists of ones and zeroes, where the ones form the letters MATLAB. Unfortunately, the matrix is too big to be shown here. The following commands draw a mesh surface of the matrix, and also draw a spy plot (see Section 9.3) of the matrix. The commands are stored in the file **meshplot.m**:

```
clf                                    % Clears the figure.

subplot(2,2,1); mesh(Matlabmatrix);    % Draws the standard mesh.
title('Standard view');                % Gives the title.

subplot(2,2,2); mesh(Matlabmatrix)     % Draws the mesh surface.
view([1 -4 2]); axis([0 200 0 20 0 3]);% Adjusts the view.
title('Viewed from position [1,-4,2]');% Title.

subplot(2,2,3); mesh(Matlabmatrix);    % and so on...
view([-1 -2 -7]);
title('Viewed from beneath');

subplot(2,2,4); spy(Matlabmatrix);     % The command spy shows
title('This is the matrix structure'); % the non-zero elements.
```

Running the program with `meshplot;` gives us Figure 13.24 (a)–(d).

When we use the command `spy` (see Section 9.3) we notice that the origin is placed in the upper left-hand corner. This is the best way to illustrate a matrix, since we write and define matrices in this way.

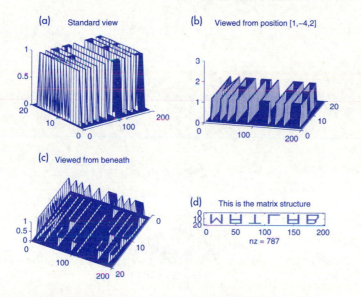

Figure 13.24 Matlabmatrix drawn in different ways.

(b) We now want to write a MATLAB program to draw a mesh grid of the following functions:

$$z_1 = f(x,y) = \sin x \cdot \sin y$$
$$z_2 = f(x,y) = x - 0.5x^3 + 0.2y^2 + 1$$
$$z_3 = f(x,y) = \sin (x^2 + y^2)^{0.5} / (x^2 + y^2)^{0.5}$$

These are the same functions as the ones in Example 13.13 (a), and we now assume that the same matrices **Z1**, **Z2**, and **Z3** are already defined by that program. The following statements:

```
% The matrices Z1, Z2, and Z3 are already defined.
clf                      % Draws the graphs.
subplot(2,2,1), mesh(Z1)
title('sin(x)*sin(y)');
subplot(2,2,2), meshz(Z2)
title('x - 0.5*x^3 + 0.2*y^2 + 1');
subplot(2,2,3), waterfall(Z2)
title('x - 0.5*x^3 + 0.2*y^2 + 1')
subplot(2,2,4), meshc(Z3)
title('sin(r)/r')
```

When this is executed, we obtain Figures (a)–(d).

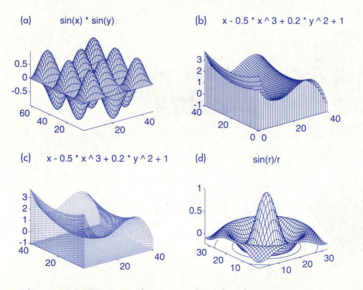

Figure 13.25 Some functions plotted with various mesh commands.

(c) The following MATLAB program performs the LU and the QR factorization of a given matrix **A**, and also plots the matrices **L**, **U**, **Q**, **R** in four subplots in the graphics window. These commands are stored in **luqrmesh.m**:

```
if ~ exist('A')
    A = input('Give a matrix A: ')
else
    disp('OK, this is the matrix')
    A
end
[L,U] = lu(A);
[Q,R] = qr(A);
disp('Press any key when you are ready!')
pause, clf
subplot,mesh(A); title('The matrix A');
pause,clf
subplot(221), mesh(L), title('The matrix L')
subplot(222), mesh(U), title('The matrix U')
subplot(223), mesh(Q), title('The matrix Q')
subplot(224), mesh(R), title('The matrix R')
```

The program runs with the command:

luqrmesh

OK, this is the matrix

A =

30	1	7	2	6	5
4	24	9	4	0	1
9	9	21	6	1	7
8	3	7	21	3	9
4	9	1	6	27	9
1	6	4	2	3	9

Press any key when you are ready!

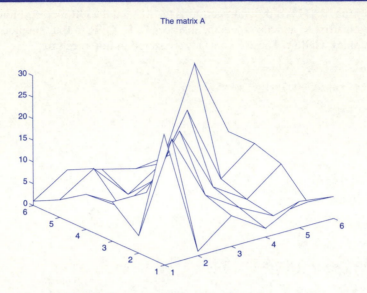

Figure 13.26 The matrix **A** drawn with `mesh`.

First we get Figure 13.26 and after another key is pressed, we get Figure 13.27 (a)–(d).

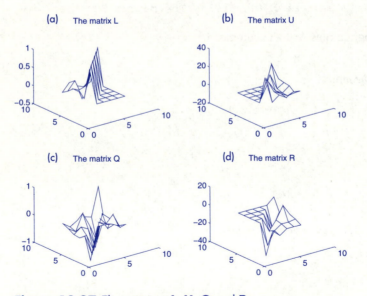

Figure 13.27 The matrices **L**, **U**, **Q** and **R**.

Earlier in this section we discussed how to draw a mesh surface graph. A shaded surface graph is drawn in the same way: create two matrices with the *x* and *y* coordinates of each point, evaluate the function, and draw the graph with a suitable command.

Surface graphs can be received with the commands `fill`, `fill3`, `surf`, `surfc` and `surfl`. The command `surfl` shows a shaded surface plot with lighting. It is based on a combination of diffuse, specular, and ambient lighting models. These kind of surfaces are viewed with a grayscale and by the use of the command `shading interp`, defined in Command 123. It is also possible to create the normal vector components of a surface and obtain diffusive or specular reflectance using these data.

| Command 120 | **SURFACE GRAPHS** |

`surf(X,Y,Z,C)`	draws a surface graph of the surface specified by the coordinates (x_{ij}, y_{ij}, z_{ij}). If **x** and **y** are vectors of length *m* and *n* respectively, **Z** has to be a matrix of size $m \times n$, and the surface is defined by (x_j, y_i, z_{ij}). If **X** and **Y** are left out, MATLAB uses a uniform rectangular grid. The colors are defined by the elements in the matrix **C**, and if left out **C** = **Z** is used.
`surfc(X,Y,Z,C)`	does the same as `surf(...)`, except that MATLAB also draws a contour plot beneath the surface.
`surfl(X,Y,Z,ls)`	does the same as `surf(...)`, but also places a light in the direction **ls** = [*v, h*] or **ls** = [*x, y, z*], where the parameters are the same as for the command `view`.
`surfl(X,Y,Z,ls,r)`	does the same as above, but the user may give the relative contributions due to ambient light, diffuse reflection, specular reflection, and the specular spread coefficient using the vector **r** = [*ambient, diffuse, specular, spread*].
`surfnorm(X,Y,Z)`	is the same as `surf`, but also draws normals.
`[Nx,Ny,Nz] =` `surfnorm(X,Y,Z)`	gives the normals to the surface defined by the matrices **X**, **Y**, **Z**, but does not draw the graph. Thus $(nx_{ij}, ny_{ij}, nz_{ij})$ is a vector defining the normal in the point (x_{ij}, y_{ij}, z_{ij}). The normals have length = *1*.
`diffuse(Nx,Ny,Nz,ls)`	returns the reflectance of a diffuse surface with normal components given by **Nx**, **Ny**, **Nz,** using Lambert's law. **ls** is the three-component vector defining the light source position.

Command 120	SURFACE GRAPHS (continued)
`specular(Nx,Ny,Nz,ls,v)`	returns specular reflectance of a surface with normal components **Nx, Ny, Nz,** using the positions of the light source **ls** and the viewer **v.**
`pcolor(Z)`	draws a pseudocolor plot of the matrix Z as a rectangular array of cells with colors determined by the values of the elements of Z.
`pcolor(X,Y,Z)`	the same as `surf(X,Y,Z); view(2)` (see Command 121).
`fill(x,y,c)`	draws the polygon with the corners specified by the coordinate vectors **x** and **y.** The polygon is filled with the color specified in the string **c** (see Table 13.1), or by the values in a vector **c** of the same length as **x** and **y.** If **x** or **y** are matrices, a polygon is drawn for each column.
`fill3(x,y,z,c)`	draws the polygon specified by **x, y,** and **z.** The polygon is filled with the color in the string **c**, or in the values in the vector **c** (see Section 13.6). If the arguments are matrices, a polygon is drawn for each column.

The color scales used by these commands can be adjusted (see Section 13.6).

■ **Example 13.16**

(a) Let us draw $\dfrac{\sin r}{r}$ with a contour plot shown beneath:

```
x = -8:0.5:8; y = x;
[Xx Yy] = meshgrid(x,y);
R = sqrt(Xx.^2 + Yy.^2) + eps;
Z = sin(R)./R;
surfc(Xx,Yy,Z); title('(sinr)/r');
```

and we get Figure 13.28.

(b) We now draw the same function with normals plotted. We assume that **Xx, Yy** and **Z** have been computed as in (a). The following statement gives us Figure 13.29.

```
surfnorm(Xx,Yy,Z)
```

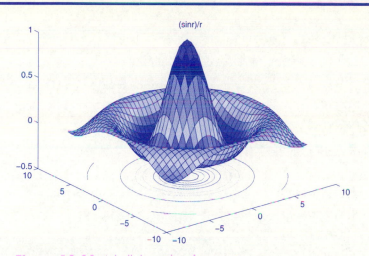

Figure 13.28 A bell-shaped surface, with contour lines beneath.

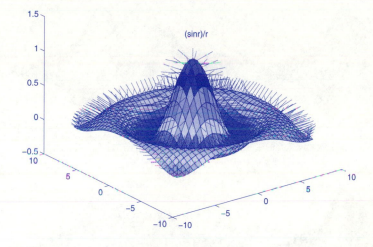

Figure 13.29 A bell-shaped function with normals. ■

■ **Example 13.17**

Let us study the commands `surfl` and `surf` using different weights for the ambient light, diffuse reflection and specular reflection. We will use a built-in function `peaks`, which is commonly used for demonstration of the three-dimensional graphics commands. For better visualization, we have manipulated the axes, according to Chapter 14, but these specific commands are omitted here, and we will only show some parts of the program. Let us now study the program:

```
[X,Y] = meshgrid(-3:1/8:3);
Z = peaks(X,Y) .* sin(X);
[Nx,Ny,Nz] = surfnorm(Z);

s = [-3 -3 2];              % The light source position.
k1 = [0,1,0,0];            % Diffuse.
k2 = [0,0,1,1];            % Specular.
```

The commands resulting in (a)–(d) in Figure 13.30 are:

```
surfl(X,Y,Z,s);        shading interp;  % Leftmost upper (a)
surfl(X,Y,Z,s,k1);     shading interp;  % Rightmost upper (b)
surfl(X,Y,Z,s,k2);     shading interp;  % Leftmost lower (c)
DD = diffuse(Nx,Ny,Nz,s);
surf(X,Y,Z,DD);        shading interp;  % Rightmost lower (d)
```

(a) surfl(X,Y,Z,s)   (c) surfl(X,Y,Z,s,k1)

(b) surfl(X,Y,Z,s,k2)   (d) surf(X,Y,Z,DD)

Figure 13.30 Three-dimensional shaded surface graphs with different lighting models.

In parts (a)–(d), the following commands are used:

```
colormap(gray);

axis( [ -3 3 -3 3 min(min(Z)) max(max(Z))]);
```
■

A graph might be easier to grasp if it is viewed from a different angle. The command `view` is used to change the view of the graph. It is both possible to specify a viewpoint, and to specify the angles of azimuth and elevation. It is also possible to change the perspective with the command `viewmtx`.

Command 121	VIEWPOINT AND PERSPECTIVE

`view(v,h)`	sets the view angle. The scalar *v* is the azimuth angle, that is the angle in the (*x,y*) plane counterclockwise. The elevation above the plane is set by the scalar *h*. Both *v* and *h* are in degrees.
`[v,h] = view`	returns the angles *v* in the *x,y* plane and *h* above the *x,y* plane, currently in use by `view`.
`view(r)`	places the viewer in position **r** = [*x y z*].
`view(n)`	sets the view angles according to *n = 2* the standard two-dimensional viewpoint, that is straight down from above. *n = 3* the standard three-dimensional viewpoint.
`view`	gives the *4 × 4*-matrix used to transform the data when drawing the graphics.
`view(T)`	makes MATLAB use **T**, a *4 × 4* matrix, when drawing the graphics.
`viewmtx(v,h,s,r)`	returns a *4 × 4* matrix that defines a viewpoint and a view direction. Type `help viewmtx` to obtain more information.

■ **Example 13.18**

(a) Suppose Figure 13.28 is in the graphics window. The command:

```
view([1 0 0]);
```

gives the same bell-shaped surface viewed straight from the side in Figure 13.31.

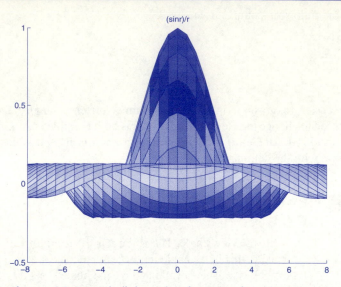

Figure 13.31 A bell-shaped surface seen from the side.

(b) Although the command `view` is mostly useful in connection with three-dimensional graphics, it is possible to apply `view` to two-dimensional graphics. If we have Figure 13.14 in the graphics window, which is created with the two-dimensional command `plot`, then the command:

```
view([1 0.6 0.35])
```

shows the same circle drawn in three dimensions, seen from position (1, 0.6, 0.35) in Figure 13.32.

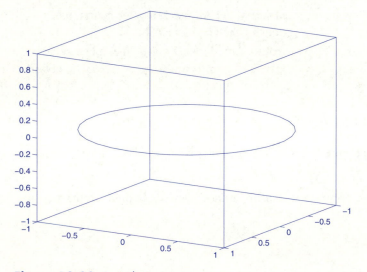

Figure 13.32 A circle in space.

Also, see examples in Section 13.5

The commands `surf` and `mesh` can be used to plot a function in a non-uniform grid. We now have to include the matrices with the coordinates in the call to the graphics routine.

■ Example 13.19

Suppose we want to study the Mach numbers around a section of an aircraft wing. The calculations and generation of the grid are beyond this text, but the figure is easy to draw in MATLAB. The grid is stored in **X1, Y1**, and the matrix **Mach** is the Mach numbers. The following statements generate Figure 13.33.

```
surf(X1,Y1,Mach);              % Draws the surface.
view(2);                       % Sets the view.
axis([-0.5 1.5 -1 1]);         % Zooms in on the wing.
shading interp                 % Interpolates the colors.
```

To see the grid, we use the command `mesh`, for a constant matrix:

```
mesh(X1,Y1,ones(size(X1)))     % Draws the grid.
view(2);                       % Sets the view.
axis([-0.5 1.5 -1 1]);         % Zooms in on the wing.
```

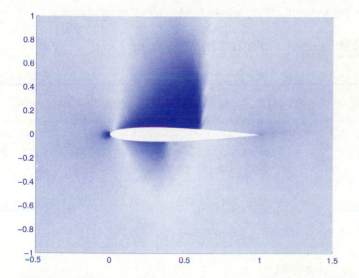

Figure 13.33 A section of an aircraft wing. The darker areas indicate a higher Mach number.

We get Figure 13.34.

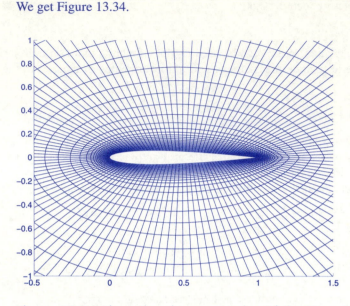

Figure 13.34 The grid used to generate the airfoil in Figure 13.33. ■

To investigate functions of three variables graphically, MATLAB has the command `slice`. This command draws surfaces in three dimensions, and the colors in points on the surfaces are proportional to the values of the function in these points.

Command 122	SLICES IN THREE DIMENSIONS

`slice(V,xs,ys,zs,nx)`	draws slices of the functions in three variables defined by the matrix **V**. The matrix **V** is in itself a set of *nx* layers, evaluated over three matrices obtained from `meshgrid` with three arguments. The vectors **xs**, **ys**, and **zs** specify which slices to plot.

■ **Example 13.20**

Let us try to get an idea of what the function $f(x,y,z) = x^2 + y^2 + z^2$ looks like in the cube:

$$\begin{bmatrix} -1 & 1 \end{bmatrix} \times \begin{bmatrix} -1 & 1 \end{bmatrix} \times \begin{bmatrix} -1 & 1 \end{bmatrix}$$

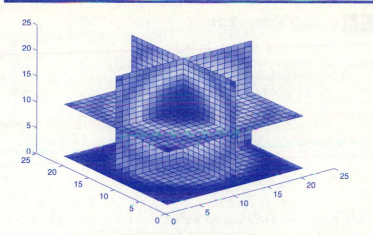

Figure 13.35 A function of three variables illustrated with the command `slice`.

We first define a three-dimensional grid with `meshgrid` and evaluate the function over the grid:

```
[X,Y,Z] = meshgrid(-1:.1:1,-1:.1:1,-1:0.1:1);
V = X.^2 + Y .^ 2 + Z.^2;
```

Notice that the function is evaluated at 21^3 points. We can now decide which of the slices parallel to the axes we want to draw. A vector *[1 3 21]*, for instance, indicates that we want to draw slice *1*, *3*, and *21*. The command

```
slice(V,[11],[11],[1 11],21)
```

gives Figure 13.35, where the slices are defined by the planes `x = 11, y = 11, z = 1`, and `z = 11`. This is also shown in Figure C.7 in the color plate section.

As expected, this function is constant along spheres. This is more obvious in colors than in black and white. ■

13.6 Color control

In MATLAB the user can control colors and illumination of the three-dimensional surface graphs.

The command `shading` configures how the surfaces are plotted. The surface can be drawn with or without the mesh, and with flat or interpolated color scales.

Command 123	SURFACE PROPERTIES

shading type	redraws the surface with the following properties according to type:
faceted	draw the mesh in the surface; this is the default
interp	use interpolated colors on the surface
flat	all facets are drawn in constant colors from the corners of the facets

■ **Example 13.21**

In Example 13.16 we plotted a bell-shaped surface with the mesh visible. If we want Figure 13.28 with the colors interpolated, we give the following command with Figure 13.28 in the graphics window:

    shading interp

and now we obtain Figure 13.36.

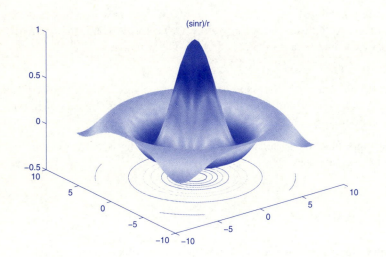

Figure 13.36 The bell-shaped surface with interpolated colors.   ■

MATLAB uses color maps to draw surface plots. A color map is an $m \times 3$-matrix, in which the rows form the colors, specified by the amount of red in the first column, the amount of green in the second column, and the amount of blue in the last column. Thus the map specifies m colors.

The color on the surface is specified by an index to the color map. This index is usually calculated relative to the minimum and maximum of the surface. The command `colormap` is used to set which color map MATLAB uses.

| **Command 124** | **COLOR MAPS** |

`colormap(Cm)`	sets the current color table to **Cm**. The matrix **Cm** can be one of MATLAB's own tables, or a user-defined table.
`colormap`	returns the current graphics table in an $m \times 3$-matrix.
`colorbar`	draws a vertical color scale in a bar in the current graphics window. See also `help colorbar`.
`colorbar('horiz')`	draws horizontal color scale in a bar in the current graphics window.

There are 11 predefined color maps in MATLAB:

`gray(m)`	returns a linear gray color scale with *m* shades
`hsv(m)`	returns bright saturated colors from red over blue to red again
`hot(m)`	returns a hot color mix of black, over red, to yellow and white
`cool(m)`	returns cold colors of cyan and magenta
`bone(m)`	returns a bluish gray color scale
`copper(m)`	returns a copper color scale
`pink(m)`	returns variations of pink colors
`flag(m)`	returns the colors of the UK and US flags, red, white, and blue, but also black, repeated cyclically
`prism(m)`	returns the six colors red, orange, yellow, green, blue, and violet, cyclically repeated
`jet(m)`	returns an alternative hsv color table from red to blue, that is from hot to cold
`white(m)`	returns an all white color map.

In the color plate section, these different types of colormaps are shown in Figure C.1. Furthermore, the Cosine Mountain highway shown in Figure C5 is defined by

```
colormap('jet');
```

■ Example 13.22

Suppose we have Figure 13.31 in the graphics window. The command:

```
colorbar
```

gives Figure 13.37.
■

There are a few additional commands to manipulate the color maps.

Command 125	MANIPULATION OF COLORS
rgb2hsv(Cm)	returns an hsv-map from the $m \times 3$ rgb color map **Cm**. The hsv map contains the same colors as the rgb map, but now saturated.
hsv2rgb(Cm)	returns an $m \times 3$ rgb color map from the hsv color map **Cm**.

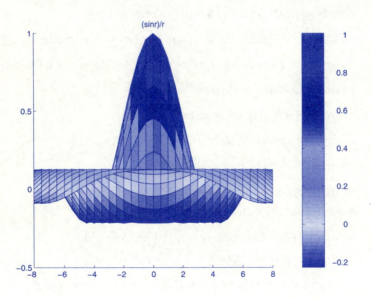

Figure 13.37 The bell-shaped curve with a color bar.

Command 126	**MANIPULATION OF COLORS (continued)**
`rgbplot(Cm)`	draws a graph of the columns of the color map **Cm**. The lines are drawn in red, green, and blue respectively.
`caxis(v)`	sets the current interval of the color map to be $v = [v_{min}\ v_{max}]$ where the components v_{min} and v_{max} are the lower and upper index bounds of the color map.
`caxis`	returns the current interval of the color map.
`caxis('auto')`	resets the scaling to the MATLAB automatic scaling.
`spinmap(t,s)`	rotates the colormap for t seconds using the step s. If s is not specified, $s = 2$ is used, and if t is not specified, $t \approx 3$ is used.
`spinmap(inf)`	rotates the color map forever.
`brighten(s)`	brightens the current colormap if $0 < s < 1$ and darkens the color map if $-1 < s < 0$. The figure is redrawn.
`nt = brighten(Cm,s)`	returns a brighter/darker color map of **Cm**, but does not redraw the current plot.
`contrast(Cm,m)`	returns a color table of length m from the color table **Cm**, with increased contrasts on a black-and-white monitor. If m is omitted, a table of the same size as **Cm** is returned.
`whitebg`	toggles the background color in the graphics window between black-and-white. The colors of scales and so on are changed if necessary to remain visible.
`whitebg(str)`	set the background color according to **str**, which is either a string (see Table 13.1), or an rgb-vector.
`graymon`	sets parameters for black-and-white monitors.

■ **Example 13.23**

We study the hsv color map with the command `rgbplot`:

```
rgbplot(hsv);
title('rgbplot of hsv');
axis([0 70 -0.1 1.1])
```

and obtain Figure 13.38.   ■

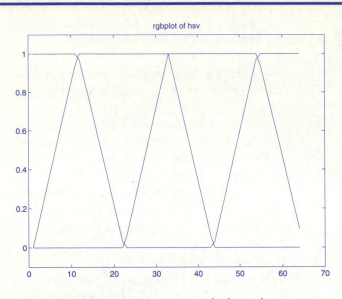

Figure 13.38 An `rgbplot` over the hsv color map.

13.7 Hard copy of the graphics window

Assuming that necessary hardware and software are installed, it is possible to get hard copies from the MATLAB graphics window. The command `print` can be used to get a hard copy either to a file, or to a printer, and is applied to the current figure.

On a PC or Macintosh system, the print alternative under the file menu is the easiest way to print graphics.

Command 127	**PRINT HARD COPIES**

`print`	sends a high resolution copy of the current graphics window to a printer. This requires that the print command is assigned to a printer, type `help print` for more information.
`print filename`	sends a copy of the current graphics window to the file **filename**.
`print -deps filename`	sends a copy in eps-format, encapsulated postscript, to the file named **filename**. This file can later be imported to a document. To see more options, type `help print`.

Command 127   **PRINT HARD COPIES (continued)**

`[str,dev] = printopt`	gives the command string and device used by `print`. It is possible to modify this M-file, type `help printopt`.

If no printer is specified to MATLAB when it is installed, then print the graphics to a file and send this file to the printer using a systems command.

The command `orient` can be used to set the orientation of the hard copy. This command should be given prior to `print` if the orientation is to be changed.

Command 128   **ORIENTATION**

`orient landscape`	sets the orientation MATLAB uses in the next `print` to landscape.
`orient portrait`	sets the orientation MATLAB uses in the next `print` to portrait.
`orient tall`	sets the orientation of next `print` to portrait, but also sets the scale to fill the whole paper.
`orient`	returns the current orientation in a string.

■ **Example 13.24**

This book includes many figures from MATLAB. They were created with various MATLAB commands and printed to hard copies with a statement like:

```
print C13/fig10 -deps
```

The pictures have then been imported directly into this book. This is an example of MATLAB working in cooperation with other programs, in this case FrameMaker.   ■

The command `orient` sets attributes of the current figure. The use of graphical objects (see Chapter 14) gives a more detailed control of the properties of hard copies. Paper size, position on the paper, background colors, and lots of other properties can be set.

13.8 Sound

MATLAB can make a vector sound with the command `sound`.

Command 129   **SOUND**

`sound(y)`	sends the vector **y** to the speaker. The vector is scaled to maximize the amplitude.
`sound(y,f);`	does the same as the above, but the sample rate used to play the sound is set to *f* Hz. This is not applicable on Sun SPARC stations.
`saxis`	returns the limits of the sound axis, in a row vector.
`saxis([min max])`	sets the sound axis scale. Increasing the span makes the sound lower, and decreasing makes the sound louder. Note that the auto scaling is optimal, a louder sound is probably distorted.
`saxis(str)`	sets the scale according to the string **str**. Even though all options of the axis command are valid, only `'auto'` is relevant to sound.

■ **Example 13.25**

(a) A sine wave might sound like this:

```
x = sin(linspace(0,10000,10000)); % A pure sine wave.
sound(x);
```

(b) There are a few predefined sounds, that can be loaded with the command `load`. Here we try two of them:

```
load train;        % A train whistle, loaded into y.
sound(y);
load chirp;        % Bird chirps.
sound(y);
```
■

There are additional sound commands on some systems, type `help sounds` to check for specific systems.

Sun SPARC stations use sound files with the sound vector stored as mu-law encoded data.

Command 130   SOUND COMMANDS ON SPARC STATIONS

`auread(fstr)`	reads and returns a vector from the file named **fstr**.
`auwrite(sv,fstr)`	writes the vector **sv** to a Sun audio file named **fstr**.
`lin2mu(sv)`	converts the linear sound vector **sv** to a mu-law encoded vector.
`mu2lin(sv)`	converts the mu-law encoded sound vector **sv** to a linear vector.

Microsoft Windows use sound files in wav format.

Command 131   SOUND COMMANDS SPECIFIC FOR MS-WINDOWS

`wavread(fstr)`	returns the sampled data in the file named **fstr**. Type `help wavread` for more information.
`wavwrite(sv,f,fstr)`	writes the sampled sound vector **sv** with the sampling rate *f* to a file named **fstr**.

Advanced Graphics

The graphics system in MATLAB is object-orientated, that is a graphical output, such as a curve, is built of graphical objects. The high-level MATLAB commands are usually advanced enough that users do not have to concern themselves about including objects. However, it is possible to use low-level MATLAB commands in order to adjust the objects.

In MATLAB it is possible to introduce graphical user interface to the applications. For instance radio buttons, slides and menus. With these an application can be controlled easily by the user.

Movies can be created in MATLAB by joining a sequence of pictures. These movies can be used to make interesting demonstrations.

14.1 Construction of a figure

A picture consists of a number of **graphical objects** which are stored in hierarchical order. To understand the connections we use an example:

■ **Example 14.1**

Graphical example with plot regions.

```
x  = 0.1:0.1:4*pi;      % Creates the vector x.
y1 = sin(x);            % Creates y1 values.
y2 = sin(x)./x;         % Creates y2 values.
figure;                 % Creates a new window.
subplot(1,2,1);         % Defines the first subplot area.
plot(x,y1);             % Plots the curve with a line.
subplot(1,2,2);         % Defines a second subplot area.
plot(x,y2,'*');         % Plots the curve with symbols.
```

The commands given above plot the two vectors **y1** and **y2** as functions of **x** in two subregions of the graphics window. The result is illustrated in Figure 14.1 (a) and (b).

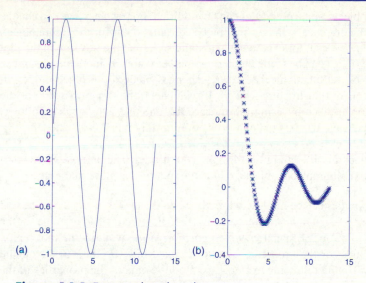

Figure 14.1 Figures plotted in plot regions.

The graphs are composed of five graphical objects arranged in a hierarchical structure. First, there is the window which is a **figure object**. Then there are two objects defining plot regions with corresponding axes, called **axes object.** These were created with the `subplot` commands. Finally, there are two **line objects** created with the `plot` commands. The hierarchical structure of the objects in Example 14.1 is shown in Figure 14.2.

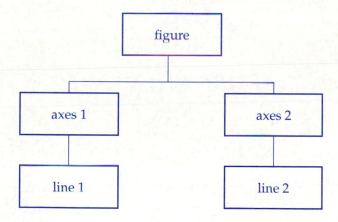

Figure 14.2 The hierarchical structure of the objects.

For each of the objects, some properties can be modified. For instance, we can change the position of the graphical window and the background color for the figure object. For an axes object we can, for example, change the scale and the position in the plot region. The line object can be made thicker, in another color, in another style and so on. As a result of the hierarchical structure, changes made to an object affect all underlying objects in the structure as well. If we change the screen position of the figure object, for instance by using the mouse, the line and axes objects follows. However, if we change the axis scale of axes object *2* only line *2* is affected.

There is one object missing in Figure 14.2, the **root object.** The purpose of this root is to be the root of all graphical objects, that is the root of the entire hierarchy.

Some of the properties can be modified directly when the object is created. When **y2** was plotted, the "*"-sign indicated that stars were to be used instead of a line for the curve. The call to subplot specifies which position of the window the plot region has. However, most of the properties can be changed only by the set command described below. In the following example we modify some of the properties of the figure from the previous example:

■ **Example 14.2**

```
clear;

x  = 0.1:0.1:4*pi;
y1 = sin(x);
y2 = sin(x)./x;

fg = figure;            % Creates window and figure handle.

r1 = subplot(1,2,1);    % Creates subplot and axis handle.

l1 = plot(x,y1);        % Creates line and line handle.

r2 = subplot(1,2,2);
l2 = plot(x,y2,'*');

disp('The previous example');
```

```
pause;
set(r1,'Position',[0.1 0.1 0.3 0.3]);   % Changes position.
set(l1,'LineWidth',5);                   % Thickens line width.
set(r2,'XTick',[ 1 4 11 ]);              % Changes x axis.
set(l2,'LineStyle','+');                 % Changes marks.
pause;
delete(fg);                              % Deletes window.
```

By specifying a variable name when the commands figure, subplot and plot are used, we create a handle or identifier to the object. By using this handle we can modify the object using the set command. In the example each object has one property changed. The position of the first plot region is changed and the second gets a different *x* axis scale. Our window looks like Figure 14.3.

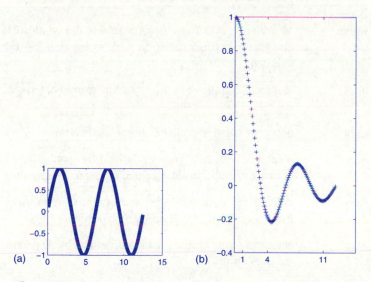

(a)   (b)

Figure 14.3 Same example as in Figure 14.1 but with changed properties.

14.2 Graphical objects

The different objects which exists in MATLAB are listed in the following table.

Command 131	GRAPHICAL OBJECTS

Object	Parent	Description
root	-	the screen is the root object. All other graphical objects are children to the root. The object handle is zero.
figure	root	a window on the screen is a figure object. The object handle is an integer, which is indicated in the window title.
axes	figure	an axes object defines a plot region in the window. It also describes the position and orientation of the children.
line	axes	graphical primitive used by, for example, `plot`, `plot3`, `contour` and `contour3`.
patch	axes	polygons filled in solid or interpolated colors.
surface	axes	a surface with four corners defined by input. Can be drawn with solid or interpolated colors or as a mesh.
image	axes	defined by a matrix who uses current color map. Images can also have their own color map.
text	axes	character string whose position is defined by its parent, the axes object.
uicontrol	figure	user interface controls. When the user clicks with the mouse on a control object, MATLAB performs a task specified by the chosen control.
uimenu	figure	create menus on top of the window. The user can control the program with these menus.

A parent influences all their children, and these children influence their children, and so on. Consequently, an **axes** influences an image, but does not affect a **uicontrol.** According to the table, the object handles of the root and the figure objects are integers. The other objects use floating points as object handles and these contain information to MATLAB. To plot an object, the low-level command of the same name as the object is used, for example the command `line` to draw a line.

14.2.1 General functions

To handle graphical objects, MATLAB has two basic commands, `get` and `set`. By using these the properties of all objects can be inspected and manipulated.

■ **Example 14.3**

We create a graphical window and its handle *gfp*:

```
gfp = figure;
```

First we control what unit the window uses:

```
get(gfp,'units')
```
ans =
pixels

Now we change the size and position of the window:

```
set(gfp,'Position',[100 500 400 400])
```

The lower left-hand corner is moved to position (*100, 500*) and the windows size is *400 × 400* pixels.   ■

Command 132	SET AND GET

`set(h,prstr,val, ...)`	sets the property **prstr** to the value *val* for object with handle *h*.
`set(h,prstr)`	lists all accepted values of the property **prstr** for object with handle *h*.
`set(h)`	lists all changeable properties for the object with handle *h*.
`get(h)`	lists all properties and their values for the object with handle *h*.
`get(h,prstr)`	returns the current value of the property **prstr.**
`findobj(prstr, prval,...)`	returns a list of all objects with the property **prstr** set to **prval**.
`findobj(hlist,prstr, prval,...)`	returns a list of handles to all objects in the list **hlist** and their descendants with the property **prstr** set to **prval**.
`findobj(hlist,'flat', prstr,prval, ...)`	returns a list of handles to all objects in the list **hlist** with the property **prstr** set to **prval**. Their descendants are not searched.

■ **Example 14.4**

In some high-level commands, for example `plot`, one can set these properties directly. For instance, the lines drawn in Example 14.2 could have been made by:

```
plot(x,y1,'LineWidth',5);
plot(x,y2,'LineStyle','+'); or plot(x,y2,'+');   ■
```

■ **Example 14.5**

If we want to know what kind of pointers there are to choose between, `set` can be used.

```
set(gcf,'Pointers')
```
[crosshair | {arrow} | watch | topl | topr | botl | botr |
circle | cross | fleur]

In this example, arrow is the current value.   ■

Further, there are three functions which return the handle of the current graphical object:

Command 133	CURRENT OBJECT

`gcf`	returns the handle of the current figure object.
`gca`	returns the handle of the current axes object.
`gco`	returns the handle of the current object, that is the object last clicked on with the mouse.

■ **Example 14.6**

The following commands return the properties of the current window and axes:

```
get(gcf);  % Shows the properties of the current
           % figure object.
get(gca);  % Shows the properties of the current axes
           % object.                                   ■
```

There are also functions for deleting objects and for restoring the defaults as shown in Command 134.

Command 134   OTHER GENERAL FUNCTIONS

`clf`	clears the current window.
`close`	closes the current window.
`close(h)`	closes the window *h*.
`cla`	deletes the current plot region.
`rotate(h,ax,a,o)`	computes new values of the object *h* so that it is rotated by angle *a* around axis *ax*. The optional parameter *o* gives start position of the rotation. The default is [*0 0 0*].
`reset(h)`	resets the window or the plot region *h* to the defaults.
`delete(h)`	deletes the object *h*.

14.2.2 The root object

The root is the same as the screen and has no parent. Its sole task is to be a parent to all other objects. In MATLAB the properties can be examined, and in some cases also changed and defined, using the commands `set` and `get`.

■ **Example 14.7**

The root object has the object handle *0*, consequently the command to obtain the screen size is:

```
scrsize = get(0,'ScreenSize')
```

scrsize =

     0   *0*   *1152*   *900*

To obtain all properties of the root object we type the command:

```
get(0);
```

CaptureMatrix = [1]
CaptureRect = [1 1 0 0]
CurrentFigure = [1]
Diary = off
DiaryFile = diary
Echo = off

Format = short

FormatSpacing = loose

PointerLocation = [712 224]

PointerWindow = [0]

ScreenDepth = [8]

ScreenSize = [1 1 1152 900]

TerminalOneWindow = yes

TerminalProtocol = x

Units = pixels

ButtonDownFcn =

Children = [1]

Clipping = on

Interruptible = no

Parent = []

Type = root

UserData = []

Visible = on   ■

14.2.3 Figure objects

A figure object is a graphical window. The parent is the screen, the root object, and the figure inherits a lot of the roots properties. Properties can be changed either when the figure is created or with the `set` command.

A figure object can be created in several ways as shown in Command 135.

Command 135   **THE FIGURE FUNCTION**

`figure`	opens a window and returns the figure handle.
`figure(fp)`	sets the current figure object to the window with handle *fp*. All graphics commands are applied to the current figure.
`figure(prstr,val...)`	sets the property **prstr** to the value *val*.
`refresh(fp)`	forces MATLAB to redraw the figure object with handle *fp*. If just `refresh` is written, the current figure object is redrawn.

Command 135   THE FIGURE FUNCTION (continued)

```
drawnow
```
forces MATLAB to draw an object. For instance, MATLAB will not draw objects from plot commands in a loop until the loop is finished unless `drawnow` is given after each plot command.

```
newplot
```
opens a new figure/axes or clears the current figure/axes depending on the value of the NextPlot property. Write `help newplot` for more information.

■ Example 14.8

(a) To replace the numbered title of the window with a name of your own, the following commands can be used:

```
fp = figure;
set(fp,'NumberTitle','off');
set(fp,'Name','ExampleWindow');
```

(b) To change the position and size of the window:

```
set(fp,'Position',[100 100 400 400]);
```

(c) To obtain all the properties of the current window:

```
get(gcf);
```

BackingStore = on

Color = [0 0 0]

Colormap = [(64 by 3)]

CurrentAxes = [56.0001]

CurrentCharacter =

CurrentMenu = [1]

CurrentObject = []

CurrentPoint = [0 0]

FixedColors = [0 0 0]

InvertHardcopy = on

KeyPressFcn =

MenuBar = figure

MinColormap = [64]

Name =

NextPlot = add

NumberTitle = on

PaperUnits = inches

PaperOrientation = portrait

PaperPosition = [0.25 2.5 8 6]

PaperSize = [8.5 11]

PaperType = usletter

Pointer = arrow

Position = [296 420 560 420]

Resize = on

SelectionType = normal

ShareColors = yes

Units = pixels

WindowButtonDownFcn =

WindowButtonMotionFcn =

WindowButtonUpFcn =

ButtonDownFcn =

Children = [56.0001]

Clipping = on

Interruptible = no

Parent = [0]

Type = figure

UserData = []

Visible = on   ■

14.2.4 Axes objects

A plot region is an area defined within the window. The parent is the figure object and its children are the line, image, patch, surface, and text objects.

The properties of the axes object define not only the position, but also orientation and size of the figure to be plotted.

Command 136 AXES OBJECTS

axes	creates an axes object that covers all of the window with properties according to default values. Returns the handle to the plot region.
axes(h)	sets the current axes object to *h*.
axes(prstr,val,...)	creates an axes object with the property **prstr** set to *val*. Returns a handle to the plot region.

Since it is possible to define the size of the axes object, it is also possible to have several axes objects in the same figure object (compare with the subplot command). When a graphical command is used it performs in the current axes object.

■ **Example 14.9**

Suppose we want to construct a picture which cannot be displayed with the limited options of the subplot command. Here we create five plot regions by using the axes command.

```
[X,Y] = meshgrid(-2:0.3:2,-2:0.3:2);
ZS    = cos(X).*sin(Y);
                                    % Position:
a(1) = axes('Position',[0.1 0.1 0.2 0.2]); % Lower left (d).
a(2) = axes('Position',[0.8 0.1 0.2 0.2]); % Lower right (e).
a(3) = axes('Position',[0.8 0.8 0.2 0.2]); % Upper right (b).
a(4) = axes('Position',[0.1 0.8 0.2 0.2]); % Upper left (a).
a(5) = axes('Position',[0.3 0.3 0.5 0.5]); % Middle (c).
for i = 1:5,
      axes(a(i));% Plots the picture in the different
   surf(ZS);% plot areas.
   if i == 1
      view(37.5,30);% Changes the viewpoint of the
   elseif i == 2% different plot areas. The
      % middle plot
      view(-37.5,70);% keeps the default angle
      % (-37.5,30)
   elseif i == 3
      view(10,30);
   elseif i == 4
      view(0,-20);
   end;
end;
```

Note that the first two numbers define the position of the lower left-hand corner and the last two the width and height of the plot region. Within the current window the position is normalized in the interval *[0,1]*. The result is displayed in Figure 14.4 (a)–(e). We see the same surface in all plot regions but from different angles. ∎

■ Example 14.10

It is also possible to move the axis made by the subplot command. Suppose that we have these two subplots, a toothbrush and toothpaste.

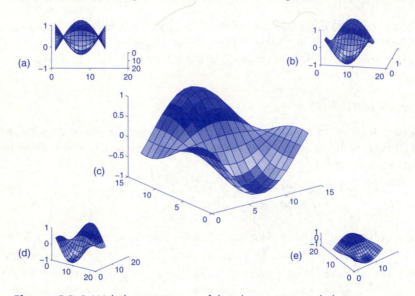

Figure 14.4 With the positioning of the plot regions made by `axes`.

(a)

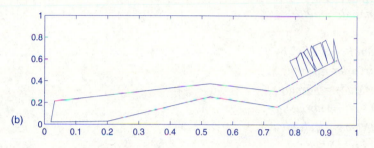

(b)

Figure 14.5 Two axis objects made by `subplot`.

We can get the positions of the lower subplot by typing `subplot(2,1,2);`
`get(gca,'Position')`:

> *ans =*
>
> *0.1300   0.1100   0.7750   0.3400*

To move the object we type
`set(gca,'Position',[0.15 0.49 0.775 0.34])`. Then we make the axis invisible with `axis off`. The result can be seen in Figure 14.6.

Thus axis objects can be positioned on top of each other.

Figure 14.6 Manipulation puts the toothpaste on the toothbrush.

■ **Example 14.11**

To obtain the properties of current axes object one gives the following command:

```
get(gca);
```

AspectRatio = [NaN NaN]
Box = off
CLim = [0 1]
CLimMode = auto
Color = none
CurrentPoint = [(2 by 3)]
ColorOrder = [(6 by 3)]
DrawMode = normal
FontAngle = normal
FontName = Helvetica
FontSize = [12]

FontWeight = normal
GridLineStyle = :
LineStyleOrder = –
LineWidth = [0.5]
NextPlot = replace
Position = [0.1 0.1 0.6 0.8]
TickLength = [0.01 0.025]
TickDir = in
Title = [62.0001]
Units = normalized
View = [0 90]
XColor = [0 0 0]
XDir = normal
Xform = [(4 by 4)]
XGrid = off
XLabel = [63.0001]
XLim = [2 10]
XLimMode = auto
XScale = linear
XTick = [2 4 6 8 10]

XTickLabels =
> *2*
> *4*
> *6*
> *8*
> *10*

XTickLabelMode = auto

XTickMode = auto

YColor = [0 0 0]

YDir = normal

YGrid = off

YLabel = [64.0001]

YLim = [−1 1]

YLimMode = auto

YScale = linear

YTick = [(1 by 11)]

YTickLabels = [(11 by 4)]

YTickLabelMode = auto

YTickMode = auto

ZColor = [0 0 0]

ZDir = normal

ZGrid = off

ZLabel = [65.0001]

ZLim = [−1 1]

ZLimMode = auto

ZScale = linear

ZTick = [−1 0 1]

ZTickLabels =

ZTickLabelMode = auto

ZTickMode = auto

ButtonDownFcn =

Children = [(4 by 1)]

Clipping = on

Interruptible = no

Parent = [1]

Type = axes

UserData = []

Visible = on ■

The axes are scaled after the maximum and minimum of the given data with *1*, *2* or *5* units between each mark as default. If we want to manipulate the marks and the grid lines, this can be done through the properties `'XTick'` and `'YTick'`.

■ **Example 14.12**

The following program shows how the grid lines can be changed:

```
x = [1 3 7];             % Creates x-vector
y = [6 9 2];             % and y-vector.

s1 = subplot(2,2,1);     % Upper left-hand corner (a).
plot(x,y);
grid;                    % Uses default grid lines.
title('Default');

s2 = subplot(2,2,2);     % Upper right-hand corner (b).
plot(x,y);
set(s2,'XTick',x);       % Changes x axis marks.
set(s2,'XGrid','on');    % Plots x axis grid lines.
title('X scale manipulated');

s3 = subplot(2,2,3);     % Lower left-hand corner (c).
plot(x,y);
set(s3,'YTick',y);       % Changes y axis marks.
set(s3,'YGrid','on');    % Plots y axis grid lines.
title('Y scale manipulated');

s4 = subplot(2,2,4);     % Lower right-hand corner (d).
plot(x,y);
set(s4,'XTick',x);       % Changes both axes marks.
set(s4,'YTick',y);
grid;                    % Plots grid lines for both axes.

title('Both scales manipulated');
```

This returns Figure 14.7(a)–(d). ■

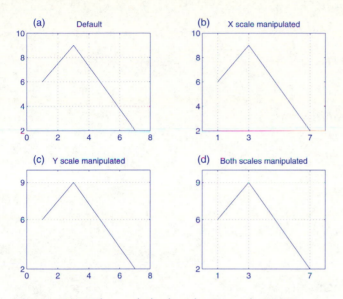

Figure 14.7 The result displayed in Example 14.12.

14.2.5 Line objects

Usually, the low-level command `line` is not used directly to create a line object. Instead a high-level command is used, for example `plot`. It is possible, however, to manipulate lines already drawn with the `line` command.

Command 137	LINE OBJECT

`line(x,y)`	adds the line defined by the vectors **x** and **y** to current figure. If **x** and **y** are two matrices of the same size, a line is drawn for each column.
`line(x, y, z)`	plots a line in three dimensions.
`line(prstr,val,...)`	plots a line with the given properties.

■ **Example 14.13**

To obtain all the properties of a line object:

```
l1 = line;
get(l1);
```

Color = [1 1 1]
EraseMode = normal
LineStyle = –

LineWidth = [0.5]
MarkerSize = [6]
Xdata = [0 1]
Ydata = [0 1]
Zdata = []

ButtonDownFcn =
Children = []
Clipping = on
Interruptible = no
Parent = [58.0004]
Type = line
UserData = []
Visible = on   ■

14.2.6 Text objects

When text is displayed in a window, a text object is created. This is done by the
`text` command. One specifies where the text is to be written, and it is also
possible to change the objects' properties.

Command 138	TEXT IN FIGURES

`text(x,y,txt)`	returns the handle to the text object. Writes the string **txt** to the current two-dimensional plot region starting at *(x, y)*. The coordinates are specified in the scale of the current axes.
`text(x,y,z,txt)`	writes the string **txt** to the current three-dimensional plot region like the previous.
`text(prstr,val,...)`	creates a text object with the properties **prstr** set to *val*.

■ **Example 14.14**

(a) To obtain the properties of a text object:

```
t1 = text;
get(t1);
```

Color = [0 0 0]
EraseMode = normal

Extent = [−0.00230947 −0.00293255 0 0]

FontAngle = normal

FontName = Helvetica

FontSize = [12]

FontWeight = normal

HorizontalAlignment = left

Position = [0 0 0]

Rotation = [0]

String =

Units = data

VerticalAlignment = middle

ButtonDownFcn =

Children = []

Clipping = off

Interruptible = no

Parent = [58.0004]

Type = text

UserData = []

Visible = on

(b) In this example, we want to have the line and the corresponding text in the same color. In addition, the line width and the text font are changed.

```
x = linspace(2,10,100);
y1 = sin(x);
y2 = bessel(1,x);
ha = axes('Position',[0.1 0.1 0.6 0.8]);
l1 = line(x,y1);
t1 = text( x(100),y1(100),'Sine');
l2 = line(x,y2);
t2 = text( x(100),y2(100),'Bessel');
set(l1,'Color','Blue');        % Sets color and width of
set(l1,'LineWidth',3);         % Line 1.
set(t1,'Color',Blue);          % Sets color, weight, and size
set(t1,'FontWeight','bold');   % of text 1
set(t1,'FontSize',18);
set(l2,'Color','Red');         % Line 2, color and width.
set(l2,'LineWidth',10);
set(t2,'Color','Red');         % Text 2, color, angle, font,
```

```
set(t2,'FontAngle','italic') % and size.
set(t2,'FontName','palatino'');
set(t1,'FontSize' ,18);
set(ha,'Box','off');             % Do not draw the box, draw only
                                 % the axes.
```

The result is displayed in Figure 14.8, but unfortunately without the colors.

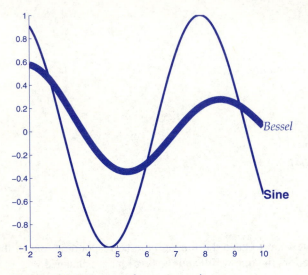

Figure 14.8 Lines with corresponding text. ■

14.2.7 Patch objects

A patch object is an area defined by a filled polygon. The corners of the polygon are defined by two or three vectors, **x, y** and **z**, depending on the number of dimensions. The corners are defined in the order of the vector elements. The polygon is filled with the color specified by the patch command.

Command 139	**FILLED POLYGONS**

`patch(x,y,c)`	creates a polygon, filled with the color *c* and defined by the vectors **x** and **y** in current plot. Returns the handle to the patch object.
	If **x** = **X** and **y** = **Y** are matrices, a polygon for each column is drawn. In this case *c* could be: a matrix of the same size as **x** and **y** for interpolated shading. a column vector of the same size as the number of rows in **x** and **y** for flat shading.
`patch(x,y,z,c)`	the polygon is defined in three dimensions.
`patch(prstr,val,...)`	creates a polygon with the properties **prstr** set to *val*.

The shape and the properties of a polygon can be redefined by `set` and read by `get`.

■ **Example 14.15**

An example with a sphere and a polygon specified by us:

```
sphere(10);          % Plots a sphere with 121 "corners".
x = [-2 -2  2  2];   % Defines x-positions of our polygon.
y = [-2  2  2 -2];   % Defines y-positions of our polygon.
z = [-2 -2 -2 -2];   % Defines z-positions of our polygon.
c = [-2 -1  1  2];   % Defines colors of our polygon.
p1 = patch(x,y,z,c); % Plots the polygon and keeps a handle.
```

The commands results in Figure 14.9.

To obtain the properties of our patch object *p1*, we write:

```
get(p1);
```
CData = [−2 −1 1 2]
EdgeColor = [0 0 0]
EraseMode = normal
FaceColor = interp
LineWidth = [0.5]
XData = [−2 −2 2 2]

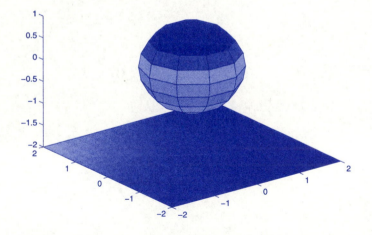

Figure 14.9 A sphere and our polygon created with `patch`.

YData = [−2 2 2 −2]

ZData = [−2 −2 −2 −2]

ButtonDownFcn =

Children = []

Clipping = on

Interruptible = no

Parent = [69.0006]

Type = patch

UserData = []

Visible = on

14.2.8 Surface objects

A surface object creates "flying carpets" in three dimensions.

Command 140　**SURFACES**

```
surface(x,y,z,c)
```
creates a filled polygon defined by the vectors **x**,**y** and **z**, in the current plot. The parameter *c* defines the color. Returns a handle to the surface object.

```
surface(x,y,z)
```
as previous command but **z** are also used as *c*.

```
surface(prstr,val..)
```
creates a polygon with the properties **prstr** set to *val*.

■ **Example 14.16**

(a) In the previous example we could have created the sphere according to this:

```
[x,y,z] = sphere;   % Position of sphere.
ss = surface(x,y,z);% Creates and plots surface object.
view(3);
```

List the properties of the surface object:

```
get(ss);
```

CData = [(21 by 21)]

EdgeColor = [0 0 0]

EraseMode = normal

FaceColor = flat

LineStyle = –

LineWidth = [0.5]

MarkerSize = [6]

MeshStyle = both

XData = [(21 by 21)]

YData = [(21 by 21)]

ZData = [(21 by 21)]

ButtonDownFcn =

Children = []

Clipping = on

Interruptible = no

Parent = [115.001]

Type = surface

UserData = []

Visible = on

Remark: The object property `'FaceColor'` can be changed to be defined as `'interp'` instead of `'flat'` using the following statement:

```
set(ss,'FaceColor','interp')
```

To see the possible properties, write

```
set(ss,'FaceColor')
```

which results in

[none | {flat} | interp | texturemap] –or–a ColorSpec.

The property `'texturemap'` can in general be chosen as an alternative to `'interp'` and `'flat'` when, for example, the `patch`, `surface`, or `mesh` command is given. The property `'none'` is used in Example 14.16(b) and in the upper part of Figure C.2 in the color plate section.

(b) The command `mesh` is a high-level function that uses `surface`. We can get a handle to a plot that `mesh` makes in the same way. This program uses both `patch` and `mesh` and changes properties for the obtained objects.

```
% The vectors xl, yl and xl represent a cube in three dimensions.
zl = [1 1 -1 -1 1 1 -1 -1 -1 -1 1 1 1 1 -1 -1];
yl = [1 -1 -1 1 1 1 1 1 1 -1 -1 1 -1 -1 -1 -1];
xl = [1 1 1 1 1 -1 -1 1 -1 -1 -1 -1 -1 1 1 -1];

clf                                      % Clears current
                                         % figure.
p = plot3(xl,yl,zl);                     % Draws lines of a
                                         % cube,
                                         % keeps a handle.
set(p,'LineWidth',3,'Color','b')         % Changes line
                                         % properties.
[XX,YY,ZZ] = sphere(15);                 % The matrices XX,
                                         % YY and ZZ
                                         % define unit
                                         % sphere.
hold
h1 = mesh(XX,YY,ZZ);                     % Draws sphere,
                                         % keeps handle.
set(h1,'EdgeColor','b','FaceColor','c')  % Changes sphere
                                         % properties.
h2 = mesh(2.*XX,2.*YY,2.*ZZ);            % Draws sphere
                                         % with radius 2,
                                         % keeps handle.
set(h2,'EdgeColor','r','FaceColor','none') % Changes
                                         % properties.
set(gca,'Visible','off')                 % Change property
                                         % visible
                                         % for current axes.

axis square                              % Makes sphere
                                         % round.
```

The result is the plot shown in Figure 14.10. ■

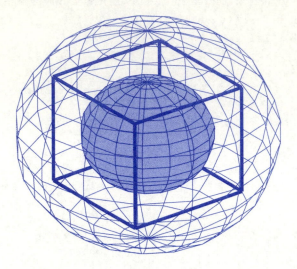

Figure 14.10 A unit sphere inscribed in a cube that is inscribed in a larger sphere.

14.2.9 Image objects

It is also possible to display images in MATLAB. An image in MATLAB is defined as a matrix whose elements correspond to points in the picture and the element values correspond to the colors of the points.

The command `image`, which is both a high-level and low-level command, plots a matrix as a picture on the screen. The corresponding function to capture the image of a graphical window is the command `capture`. Note that `capture` and `image` often give a lower resolution than MATLAB's internal representation, and that they also require more memory.

Command 141	IMAGES

`image(C)`	plots the matrix **C** as an image. Each element of **C** is a point of the image and the value defines the color. The handle of the image is returned.
`image(x,y,C)`	**x** and **y** are two vectors containing minima and maxima values of the *x*- and *y*-axis; otherwise as previously.
`image(prstr,val)`	creates an image whose appearance and properties are defined by **prstr** and *val*. These properties can be changed with the `set` command.

Command 141 **IMAGES (continued)**

`imagesc(...)`	is the same as `image` but the data is scaled to use the full color map.
`capture(h)`	creates a new window with the same content as the window with handle *h*.
`[C,Cm] = capture`	returns an image matrix **C** with corresponding color map **Cm** without displaying the image.

■ **Example 14.17**

To obtain the properties of an image object:

```
ip = image;
get(ip);
```

CData = [(63 by 40)]

XData = [1 40]

YData = [1 63]

ButtonDownFcn =

Children = []

Clipping = on

Interruptible = no

Parent = [74.0004]

Type = image

UserData = []

Visible = on

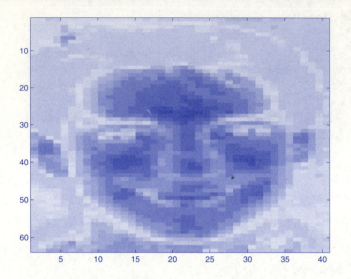

Figure 14.11 What MATLAB displays if no arguments are given to `image`.

The command `image` without arguments, returns a predefined image and the example gave us Figure 14.11. ■

14.3 Callback functions

To all the graphical objects one can define callback functions. Such a function is activated when the object is clicked on with the mouse button.

■ **Example 14.18**

Let us add some commands to Example 14.14b:

```
set(l1,'ButtonDownFcn','answer1');
set(l2,'ButtonDownFcn','answer2');
```

When we click on the first line, the sine function, the M-file **answer1.m** is called. If we click the Bessel function the M-file **answer2.m** is called. To make something happen when we click on the curves we let **answer1.m** and **answer2.m** be the following:

```
% file answer1.m
load train;
sound(y);
```

and

```
% file answer2.m
load chirp;
sound(y);
```

When the sine function is clicked on, a train can be heard from the speaker of the computer and when the Bessel function is clicked on, a bird chirp. Unfortunately this medium does not allow an illustration! ■

14.4 Graphical user interface

To make MATLAB programs even more easy to use there are two objects, `uicontrol` and `uimenu`.

Command 142	GRAPHICAL USER INTERFACE
`uicontrol(prstr, v,...)`	returns a handle to the created control window in current figure object. With **prstr** and *v* the properties are manipulated: what kind, buttons, slides, and so on. The property `'CallBack'` controls the consequence of the choice of the user.
`uimenu(prstr,v)`	creates a pull-down menu with the returned handle at the top of current window. Its properties, name, what to do in case of a choice, and so on are given in **prstr** and *v*.
`uimenu(um,prstr,v)`	creates a menu option to the menu *um*. If *um* is a menu option, a submenu of *um* is created, that is hierarchical menus can be created.

It is easy to understand and use the program with these controls.

■ **Example 14.19**

Suppose we want to write an M-file that plots an optional matrix. As a starting point the following commands could be used:

```
fp = figure;
h1 = uimenu('Label','Archive');
uimenu(h1,'Label','New matrix','CallBack','menuans = 11;Ans;');
uimenu(h1,'Label','Quit','CallBack','menuans = 12;Ans;');
h2 = uimenu('Label','Plot');
uimenu(h2,'Label','Mesh Plot','CallBack',...
'menuans = 21; Ans;');
uimenu(h2,'Label','Carpet','CallBack',...
'menuans = 22; Ans;');
```

The result becomes a window with two pull-down menus on top, an 'Archive' and a 'Plot'. The archive menu has two options, 'New matrix' and 'Quit'. When one of these is chosen, two things happen, the variable *menuans* is set to *11* or *12*, and the M-file **Ans.m** is executed. The property 'CallBack' decides the action when an option is chosen.

To make the example complete we need the M-file **Ans.m**:

```
% Name: Ans.m
if menuans == 11
    Matrix = input('Give a matrix to be plotted ');
end
if menuans == 12
    delete(fp);
    break;
end
if menuans == 21
    eval(['mesh(' Matrix ')']);
end
if menuans == 22
    eval(['surf(' Matrix ')']);
end
```

Each possible menu option is taken care of by the value of *menuans* that is defined in the property CallBack. The options *21* and *22* evaluate a figure command with the variable **Matrix,** which is a string defined by the user in option *11*. If the matrix **X** is to be plotted we write 'X' because eval handles strings.

The properties of the 'Archive' menu are obtained by:

```
get(h(1));
```
Accelerator =
BackgroundColor = [0.701961 0.701961 0.701961]
CallBack =
Checked = off
Enable = on
ForegroundColor = [0 0 0]
Label = Archive
Position = [1]
Separator = off
ButtonDownFcn =
Children = [(2 by 1)]
Clipping = on

Interruptible = no

Parent = [2]

Type = uimenu

UserData = []

Visible = on

The window with menus looks like Figure 14.12.

Figure 14.12 A window with pull-down menus in the XView environment. ■

■ **Example 14.20**

Some different kinds of `uicontrol` objects:

```
hf = figure;
h1 = uicontrol('Position',[10,10 100, 100]);
set(h1,'CallBack','Ans1');
set(h1,'BackGroundColor','Yellow');
set(h1,'String','Train');
h2 = uicontrol('Position',[200,200 10, 10]);
set(h2,'CallBack','Ans2');
set(h2,'Style','checkbox');
h3 = uicontrol('Position',[10,200 100, 10]);
set(h3,'CallBack','get(h3,''value'')');
set(h3,'Style','slider');
h4 = uicontrol('Position',[200,10 20, 20]);
set(h4,'BackGroundColor','White');
```

```
set(h4,'CallBack','delete(hf)');
set(h4,'Style','radiobutton');
```

The example produces four different controls in the window, as shown in Figure 14.13.

Figure 14.13 Four controls displayed in an XView environment.

To obtain the properties of *h3* we type:

get(h3);

BackgroundColor = [0.701961 0.701961 0.701961]

CallBack = get(h3,'value')

ForegroundColor = [0 0 0]

HorizontalAlignment = center

Max = [1]

Min = [0]

Position = [10 200 100 10]

String =

Style = slider

Units = pixels

Value = [0.327621]

ButtonDownFcn =

Children = []

Clipping = on

Interruptible = no

Parent = [1]

Type = uicontrol

UserData = []

Visible = on

```
When the user moves the slider control to a value the
CallBack property returns it.
```

14.5 Movies

14.5.1 An introductory example

Let us see what happens if we let the function generating the bell-shaped surface of
Example 13.16 oscillate.

■ **Example 14.21**

```
x = -8:0.5:8; y = x;              % Defines surface.
[XX,YY] = meshgrid(x,y);
r = sqrt(XX.^2 + YY.^2) + eps;
Z = sin(r)./r;
surf(Z);                          % Plots frame.
anaxes = axis;                    % Saves values
                                  % of axes.
                                  % Later used to make
                                  % all frames in
                                  % same scale.
fmat = moviein(20);               % Creates matrix
                                  % storing the
                                  % movie. It takes
                                  % 20 frames.

for j = 1:20                      % Loops the snapshots.
    surf(sin(2*pi*j/20)*Z,Z)      % Plots surface
                                  % of each step.

    axis(TheAxes)                 % Uses same axes
                                  % all the time.

    fmat(:,j) = getframe;         % Copies frame
                                  % to matrix.
end
movie(fmat,10);                   % Shows movie.
                                  % 10 times.
```

We see that the movie is saved picture by picture in the columns of the matrix,
and then it is displayed. Before it is recorded, the maxima and minima of the
axes are stored so all pictures have the same axis size.   ■

14.5.2 Storing a picture in a matrix

The `getframe` command is used in MATLAB to store a snapshot of the window in a matrix.

Command 143	PICTURE TO MATRIX

`getframe`	copies the current window to a column vector.
`getframe(p)`	copies the picture in the object with the handle *p*. The object can be the screen, a window or a plot region.
`getframe(p,r)`	copies a rectangle, specified by **r**, of the object with handle *p* to a vector. The form of **r** is [*left bottom width height*].

14.5.3 Creating the movie matrix

Before recording the movie, all the pictures have to be stored. This is done columnwise in a matrix created with the `moviein` command.

Command 144	CREATE THE MOVIE MATRIX

`moviein(n)`	creates a matrix which can store *n* pictures. One of the pictures has to be drawn first since the size of the picture is defined by the current window. (See Example 14.21.)

14.5.4 Show the movie

By the `movie` command the recorded movie is shown. Different arguments can be added for specification of the movie.

Command 145	SHOWING THE MOVIE

`movie(mat)`	shows the movie stored in matrix **mat** once.
`movie(mat,n)`	shows the movie *n* times. If *n* is negative the movie is shown once as recorded and then backwards.
`movie(mat,v)`	shows the recorded pictures in the order defined by the integer vector **v**.
`movie(mat,n,pps)`	shows the movie in *pps* pictures/second.
`movie(p,...)`	shows the movie in object *p*.

Command 145	SHOWING THE MOVIE (continued)

`movie(p,mat,n,` `pps,pos)`	shows the movie in position **pos** = *(x,y)*. The coordinates *x* and *y* are given in units defined by the property `Units` from the lower left-hand corner of *p*.

15 MATLAB in Combination with Other Programs

MATLAB can be used together with other programs. FORTRAN or C routines can be called from MATLAB. The opposite is also possible, that is MATLAB can be called from FORTRAN or C. Thus fast compiled programs can utilize the powerful matrix or graphical commands of MATLAB, and bottlenecks in MATLAB programs can be avoided by writing these parts in C or FORTRAN and compiling them.

MATLAB can also cooperate with other applications, for instance Microsoft Word for Windows. This is briefly discussed in the last section of this chapter.

The Student Edition of MATLAB cannot be dynamically linked with FORTRAN and C, so this chapter can be skipped for such users.

15.1 MATLAB and FORTRAN or C, an introduction

MATLAB can be called from FORTRAN or C programs, and C or FORTRAN programs can be called from MATLAB. The latter can be useful if a MATLAB program is too slow. Since MATLAB is an interpreting language, the commands are interpreted as they are executed. This results in, for instance, for-loops sometimes being slow.

The libraries included with MATLAB are written in FORTRAN 77 and C, but it is possible to link them with FORTRAN 90 or C++ as well.

It is not recommended to write FORTRAN or C routines unless it is really necessary. The advantage of MATLAB is the possibility to express the operations on a high level, relieving the programmer of worries about index loops and other unimportant trouble-makers.

A compiled routine that can be called from MATLAB is termed a MEX-file. MATLAB keeps track of how they are called. They can, when compiled, be used like an M-file.

A MATLAB compiler and C Math Library are also commercially available by The MathWorks, Inc. The former can be used either as an automatic MEX-file generator or as a C source code generator for stand-alone applications together with the C Math Library.

Table 15.1 Pointers in connection with external programming.

MATLAB-Pointer		Type in C
ep	pointer to a MATLAB process	Engine
fp	file pointer	MATFile
mp	matrix pointer	Matrix
pr, pi	pointer to the real and imaginary parts of a full matrix	double
ir, jc	pointer to a vector with row and column indices of sparse matrices	int

In Chapter 2 we encountered the binary files MATLAB creates. These are called MAT-files, and there are routines in the libraries to read and write them in C or FORTRAN programs. In Section 15.4 we also show how to read or write other binary or text files in MATLAB. This can be useful when a specific format is required by another program.

MATLAB is written in C, and data is referenced by **pointers**. Thus using MATLAB together with other programming languages requires the use of pointers. Throughout this chapter we use the notation in Table 15.1, basically consistent with the notation in the MATLAB External Interface Guide.

Often when a name of a pointer is quoted, the object pointed at is really referenced. How these types should be declared in C and FORTRAN can be seen in the examples in the next sections.

Pointers are natural in C, but FORTRAN does not use pointers. The above pointers are in FORTRAN represented by 4-byte integers, and all operations on matrices in FORTRAN must be carried out using conversion routines.

The commands are only listed once, since they are almost identical in C and FORTRAN. The languages are separated when some examples are presented in the next two sections. These examples which are the same in both languages, should give a basic understanding of how MATLAB and C or FORTRAN can interact. They have been compiled on a workstation running Solaris 2.3, but the basic idea is the same for any system. Some important details may, however, vary between platforms. This is why the examples shipped together with MATLAB can be of great interest. They can be found in the library /matlab/extern/src. (See the MATLAB External Interface Guide if more information is required, or talk to a systems administrator.)

There are four main categories of routines to use in C or FORTRAN programs communicating with MATLAB.

    mx   matrix commands

    mat   MAT-file commands

    eng   MATLAB process commands

    mex   MEX commands

The first letters of the command indicate what kind of command it is. First the commands named the MAT-file commands are listed. These can be used to read and write MATLAB's binary files in C or FORTRAN programs.

Command 146	**READING AND WRITING MAT-FILES IN C OR FORTRAN**

`matOpen(filename, mode)`	opens the MAT-file in the string **filename**, and returns a *fp*. The string **mode** can take the values "r" as in reading, "w" as in writing and "u" as in updating.
`matClose(fp)`	closes the MAT-file *fp*.
`matGetDir(fp)`	returns a matrix pointer that can be used to find the names of all the variables in the MAT-file *fp*.
`matGetMatrix(fp, namestr)`	reads the matrix in **namestr** from the MAT-file *fp*, and returns an *mp*.
`matPutMatrix(fp,mp)`	writes the matrix *mp* to the MAT-file *fp*.
`matGetNextMatrix(fp)`	reads the next matrix in the MAT-file *fp*, and returns an *mp*. Do not use this command if MAT commands other than `matOpen` have been used.
`matDeleteMatrix(fp, namestr)`	removes the matrix in **namestr** from the MAT-file *fp*.
`matGetFull(fp, namestr,m,n,pr,pi)`	reads the $m \times n$ matrix named in the string **namestr** from the MAT-file *fp*. The result is returned in *pr* and also in *pi* if the matrix is complex.
`matPutFull(fp, namestr,m,n,pr,pi)`	writes an $m \times n$ matrix named in the string **namestr** to the MAT-file *fp*. The pointers *pr* and *pi* point to the real and imaginary parts of the matrix.
`matGetString(fp, namestr,str,strlen)`	reads the string named in **namestr** to the string **str** from the MAT-file *fp*.
`matPutString(fp, namestr,str)`	writes the string **str** to the MAT-file *fp* under the name **namestr**.

We want to be able to access the elements of a matrix after reading it from a MAT-file. This can be done with the routines given in Command 147.

Command 147	**MATRIX COMMANDS IN C OR FORTRAN**

`mxGetM(mp)`	returns the number of rows in *mp*.
`mxGetN(mp)`	returns the number of columns in *mp*.
`mxGetPr(mp)`	returns a *pr* to the matrix *mp*.
`mxGetPi(mp)`	returns a *pi* to the matrix *mp*.
`mxSetPr(mp,pr)`	sets the real part of *mp* to point at *pr*. This is a subroutine in FORTRAN.
`mxSetPi(mp,pi)`	sets the imaginary part of *mp* to point at *pi*. This is a subroutine in FORTRAN.
`mxGetName(mp)`	returns a pointer to the name of *mp*, that is a pointer to a string.
`mxSetName(mp,name)`	sets the namepointer of *mp* to the string **name**. This is a subroutine in FORTRAN.
`mxGetNzmax(mp)`	returns the maximum number of non-zero elements of the sparse matrix *mp*.
`mxSetNzmax(mp,nzmax)`	sets the maximum number of non-zero elements in the sparse matrix *mp* to *nzmax*. This is a subroutine in FORTRAN.
`mxGetIr(mp)`	returns *ir*, a pointer to the vector containing the row indices of the sparse matrix *mp*.
`mxGetJc(mp)`	returns *jc*, a pointer to the vector containing the column indices of the sparse matrix *mp*.
`mxSetIr(mp,ir)`	sets a pointer *ir* to the row indices of a sparse matrix *mp*. This is a subroutine in FORTRAN.
`mxSetJc(mp,jc)`	sets a pointer *jc* to the column indices of a sparse matrix *mp*. This is a subroutine in FORTRAN.
`mxIsFull(mp)`	returns a *1* if *mp* is stored as a full matrix otherwise a *0*.
`mxIsSparse(mp)`	returns a *1* if *mp* is stored as a sparse matrix, otherwise a *0*.
`mxIsString(mp)`	returns a *1* if *mp* is a string, otherwise *0*.
`mxIsNumeric(mp)`	returns a *1* if *mp* is a numeric, otherwise *0*.
`mxIsTypeDouble(mp)`	returns a *1* if *mp* is stored in double precision. In the current version of MATLAB this is always true, but future versions of MATLAB are likely to include more numerical types.

Command 147	MATRIX COMMANDS IN C OR FORTRAN (continued)
`mxIsComplex(mp)`	returns a *1* if *mp* is complex, otherwise *0*.
`mxCreateFull(m,n,cf)`	returns a full $m \times n$ matrix. This matrix is real if *cf = 0* otherwise complex.
`mxCreateSparse(m,n, nzmax,cf)`	creates a sparse $m \times n$ matrix with nzmax spaces for non-zero elements. The matrix is real if *cf = 0* otherwise it is complex.
`mxFreeMatrix(mp)`	gives back the memory of the matrix *mp*. This is a subroutine in FORTRAN.
`mxCalloc(nm,size)`	reserves a memory space and returns a pointer to it. The *size* is given in size per element, and *nm* is the number of elements. The allocated workspace is thus *size*nm* bytes.
`mxFree(pointer)`	gives back the memory previously reserved with `mxCalloc`. This is a subroutine in FORTRAN.
`mxGetString(mp,str, strlen)`	reads a string into **str** of length less than or equal to *strlen* from *mp*. Notice that **str** must be assigned memory prior to the call. In FORTRAN **str** is a normal string, that is an array of characters.
`mxCreateString(str)`	creates an *mp* containing **str**.
`mxGetScalar(mp)`	returns the element (*1,1*) of the matrix *mp*, that is the value for scalars.

When MATLAB is called from other programs, it is sometimes referred to as a "MATLAB Computation Engine". The call is made with the following commands.

Command 148	CALLS TO MATLAB FROM C OR FORTRAN
`engOpen(startstr)`	opens a MATLAB engine, and returns an *ep* to it. The string **startstr** should contain the command starting MATLAB, including the path if necessary.
`engClose(ep)`	closes the MATLAB engine *ep*. Returns *0* if the engine was closed without problems, and the value *1* if an error occurred.
`engGetMatrix(ep, namnstr)`	gets the matrix named in the string **namestr** from the MATLAB engine *ep*'s workspace, and returns an *mp*.

Command 148	**CALLS TO MATLAB FROM C OR FORTRAN (continued)**

`engPutMatrix(ep,mp)`	stores the matrix *mp* in the MATLAB workspace *ep*.
`engGetFull(ep, namestr,m,n,pr,pi)`	gets the full $m \times n$ matrix from the MATLAB engine workspace *ep*. Instead of returning an *mp*, this routine gives a *pr* and a *pi*, that is pointers to the real and imaginary parts of the matrix.
`engPutFull(ep, namestr,m,n,pr,pi)`	writes the $m \times n$ matrix **namestr**, defined by the real and imaginary parts from *pr* and *pi*, to the MATLAB workspace *ep*.
`engEvalString(ep, commandstr)`	executes the commands in the string **commandstr**. These are given as in the MATLAB command window. The commands are executed in the MATLAB engine *ep*.
`engOutputBuffer(ep, p,n)`	defines a buffer and a pointer *p* to it. This buffer is used by the MATLAB engine *ep* for its output. The maximum number of characters is *n*.

We conclude these lists with the commands used in the MEX-files.

Command 149	**CALLS TO C OR FORTRAN FROM MATLAB**

`mexFunction(nls,nrs, pls,prs)`	the routine called by MATLAB when the user calls the MEX function. We write this routine with four arguments. The first two parameters are the number of parameters in and out, *nls* and *nrs* respectively. These are followed by two pointers to lists of pointers with these arguments, *prhs* and *plhs*, input arguments and output arguments respectively.
`mexCallMATLAB(nls, nrs,pls,prs,namnstr)`	calls the built-in MATLAB command, M-file, or MEX-file named in **namestr**. The same arguments as above, but notice that this function is calling, that is the interpretation of the arguments are reversed.
`mexEvalString(str)`	executes the MATLAB commands in the string **str**.
`mexGetMatrixPtr( namestr)`	returns an *mp* to the matrix in the MATLAB workspace with the name in the string **namestr**.

Command 149	CALLS TO C OR FORTRAN FROM MATLAB (continued)
`mexErrMsgTxt(errstr)`	outputs the error message in the string **errstr** and returns the control to MATLAB.
`mexGetMatrix( namestr)`	copies the matrix with the name in the string **namestr** from the MATLAB workspace and returns an *mp* to it.
`mexPutMatrix(mp)`	stores the matrix *mp* in the MATLAB workspace.
`mexGetFull(namestr, m,n,pr,pi)`	gives a simplified access to full matrices from the MATLAB workspace in the same way as the command `matGetFull` from MAT-files.
`mexPutFull(namestr, m,n,pr,pi)`	gives a simplified way to put full matrices to the MATLAB workspace. Puts the matrix defined by *pi* and *pr* with the name in **namestr**.
`mexPrintf(formatstr, str1,...,strn)`	writes the strings **str1**, **str2**, and so on, according to the format in the string **formatstr**. Works like the `sprintf` command in MATLAB. It is not available in the FORTRAN library.

There are also the routines `mexAtExit` and `mexSetTrapFlag`. For more information about these, see the MATLAB External Interface Guide.

A good habit for programmers is to always explicitly deallocate memory no longer used. For those less interested in 'correct' behavior it is a relief to know that this is unnecessary if we only allocate memory with the MATLAB routines, since MATLAB handles the memory for us.

15.2 MATLAB and C

To call MATLAB from C, a MATLAB engine must first be started. On platforms other than UNIX this requires MATLAB version 4.2c. This is easily done by a call to `engOpen`.

The next phase is to transfer the matrices we want to use to MATLAB. This is accomplished in two steps. We can either choose to work with the matrices in the MATLAB format from the start, creating them with `mxCreateFull` or `mxCreateSparse`, and name them with `mxSetName`. Alternatively we can use an arbitrary format, and first convert it to the MATLAB format. An important distinction of the standard C format and the MATLAB format is that C stores matrices row by row, while MATLAB stores them column by column. Thus a transposition might be necessary.

In the second step, the matrices are placed in the MATLAB workspace with the command `engPutMatrix`. MATLAB is now ready to receive commands. These are given just like in the command window, but now in a string passed to `engEvalString`. Finally, a conversion and transfer from MATLAB to C might be necessary. This may sound very complicated, but a few examples make it more clear.

■ **Example 15.1**

Suppose we have a matrix we want to see drawn in a C program. It is a good idea to use MATLAB for the visualizations. We write the following MATLAB program stored in the file **plotm.c**:

```c
#include <stdlib.h>
#include <stdio.h>
#include <string.h>
#include "/opt/matlab/extern/include/engine.h"
void main()
{
Engine*ep;
Matrix*mp;
double*Ar;
int i,j;
                                    /*Creates the matrix.*/
mp = mxCreateFull(10,10,0);
mxSetName(mp,"A");
Ar = mxGetPr(mp);

for (i = 1;i < 11;i++)
{
    for (j = 1;j < 11;j++)
    {
        Ar[i-1 + 10*(j - 1)] = j*j*i*i;
    }
}
                /*Starts the MATLAB Engine.*/
ep = engOpen("");
engPutMatrix(ep,mp);
                /*Gives the command mesh(A).*/
engEvalString(ep,"mesh(A);");
engClose(ep);
mxFreeMatrix(mp);
exit(0);
}
```

This is compiled with:

```
cc -o plotm plotm.c /opt/matlab/extern/lib/sol2/libmat.a
    -lnsl -lm
```

The users must find the library **libmat.a** on their own systems, or ask a systems administrator where it is stored. Usually, it should be stored in:

```
.../matlab/extern/lib/..machinedependent../libmat.a
```

where **libmat.a** contains all the routines supporting the communication between C and MATLAB. Notice that both the path `/opt/matlab/../sol2/` and the compiler directive `-lnsl` are machine dependent. This is also true for the path to the included header file **engine.h,** given at the beginning of the program. When this program is run, we obtain Figure 15.1. ■

To read from and write data to a MAT-file in a C program the matrices must be converted to the MATLAB format in the same way as in Example 15.1, but we do not have to start a MATLAB engine this time. Instead we open a MAT-file.

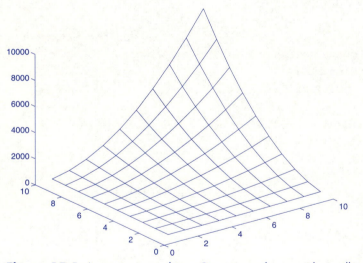

Figure 15.1 A matrix created in a C program drawn with a call to MATLAB.

■ **Example 15.2**

Suppose we need a matrix with normally distributed random elements in a C program. This apparently simple matrix can be quite difficult to generate, so instead we create it in MATLAB and store it in a file. This file can be read from our C program. The following MATLAB statements create a 10×10 random matrix and store it in the file **data.mat**:

```
Random = randn(10);          % Creates a random matrix.
save data Random             % Saves Random to data.mat.
```

The following C program reads **Random** from the file **data.mat**, does something with it, and stores the result as a matrix in **data.mat.**

```c
#include <stdio.h>
#include <string.h>
#include "/opt/matlab/extern/include/mat.h"

void main()
{
MATFile*fp;
Matrix*mp,*mp2;
double*Ar,*Br;
int i,j;

        /* Creates an area and read the matrix to it. */
mp2 = mxCreateFull(10,10,0);
mxSetName(mp2,"Newmatrix");
fp = matOpen("data.mat","u");
mp = matGetMatrix(fp,"Random");
Ar = mxGetPr(mp);
Br = mxGetPr(mp2);

        /*Multiplies with 2 to the new matrix.*/
for (i = 1;i < 11;i++)
{
    for (j = 1;j < 11;j++)
    {
        Br[i-1+10*(j-1)] = 2*Ar[i-1+10*(j-1)];


    }
}
        /*Store Newmatrix and close the file.*/
matPutMatrix(fp,mp2);
matClose(fp);
exit(0);
}
```

When this program is running, the file **data.mat** is expanded with the matrix **Newmatrix**, which is *2*****Random***. ■

Finally, we describe calls to C routines from MATLAB. These routines are called MEX-files, and the call in MATLAB looks exactly like a call to a function file, that is an M-file.

We use the same commands and matrix types in a MEX-file as we do when we call MATLAB from C. Now we must include the special MEX commands.

The file should have a main function called `mexFunction`, which is the routine called by MATLAB. This routine takes four arguments: the number of in and out parameters, and two pointers to lists of pointers to these parameters.

■ **Example 15.3**

We create a MEX file that from a given matrix returns a matrix where the elements have been multiplied with their row indices. The following C routines are stored in the file **rmult.c**.

```c
#include <math.h>
#include "mex.h"
#define element(i,j) pr[i+m*j]

/* A routine multiplying the elements with their row indices

static void rowMult(double* pr,int m,int n)
{
    int i,j;

    for (i = 0;i < m;i++)
    {
        for (j = 0;j < n;j ++)
        {
            element(i,j) = element(i,j)*(1+i);
        }
    }
}
                /*This routine is called by MATLAB.*/

void mexFunction(int nlhs,Matrix*plhs[],int nrhs,Matrix*prhs

{
    int   mrhs, mlhs,m,n;
    Matrix*lhs[1],*mp;
                /*Gets the size of the matrix.*/...
    m = mxGetM(prhs[0]);
    n = mxGetN(prhs[0]);

/*Creates a matrix of the same size and copies the elements.*

    mp = mxCreateFull(m,n,REAL);
    memcpy((char*)mxGetPr(mp),(char*)
        mxGetPr(prhs[0]),sizeof(double)*m*n);
```

```
      /*Calls a routine that operates on the matrix.*/...
      rowMult(mxGetPr(mp),m,n);

           /*Returns the new matrix */...
      plhs[0] = mp;
}
```

To compile this, we type `!cmex  rmult.c` at the MATLAB prompt and
MATLAB supplied script file **cmex** takes care of all compilation and linking.
Macintosh users are referred to the relevant manuals. ■

15.3 MATLAB and FORTRAN

To call MATLAB from FORTRAN, a MATLAB engine must first be started. This is easy, and requires only a call to `engOpen`.

The next phase is to transfer the matrices we want to use to MATLAB. This is accomplished in two steps. In the first we create a MATLAB matrix of desired size with the command `mxCreateFull` or `mxCreateSparse`, and we name the matrix with a call to `mxSetName`. Next we have to copy the matrix from FORTRAN format to the MATLAB format. This is something that is not necessary in C, and is done with the `mxCopy...` commands listed below in Command 150. In the second step, the matrices are placed in the MATLAB workspace with the command `engPutMatrix`.

MATLAB is now ready to receive commands. These are given just like in the command window, but now in a string passed to `engEvalString`.

Finally, a conversion and transfer from MATLAB to FORTRAN might be necessary.

The routines in Command 150 are used to convert the pointers in FORTRAN to the objects pointed at.

Command 150	**CONVERTING POINTERS IN FORTRAN**

`mxCopyPtrToReal8(pr,x,n)`	copies *n* values from a *pr* (or a *pi*), see Table 15.1, to an ordinary FORTRAN array **x**.
`mxCopyReal8ToPtr(x,pr,n)`	copies *n* values from an ordinary FORTRAN array to a *pr*, or to a *pi*.
`mxCopyPtrToCharcter(px, str,n)`	copies *n* characters from *px* to a FORTRAN string **str**.
`mxCopyCharacterToPtr(str, px,n)`	copies *n* characters from a FORTRAN string **str** to a pointer *px*.
`mxCopyPtrToInteger4(x, px,n)`	copies *n* integers from a pointer *px* to an ordinary FORTRAN array **x**.
`mxCopyInteger4ToPtr(x, px,n)`	copies *n* integers from a FORTRAN array **x** to a pointer *px*.
`mxCopyPtrToComplex8(pr, pi,z,n)`	copies *n* complex numbers from a *pr* and a *pi*, to a complex FORTRAN array **z**.
`mxCopyComplex8ToPtr(z, pr,pi,n)`	copies *n* complex numbers from a complex FORTRAN array **z** to *pr* and *pi*.

This may sound very complicated, but a few examples make it more clear.

■ Example 15.4

Suppose we have a matrix we want to see drawn in a FORTRAN program. It is a good idea to use MATLAB for the visualizations, and we type the following MATLAB program stored in the file **plotm.f**:

```fortran
      program plotm
      integer engOpen,engClose,engEvalString,mxCreateFull
      integer engPutMatrix,mp,ep,stat,i,j
      double precision A(10,10)
C                     Creates a test matrix.
      do 100 i = 1,10
         do 110 j = 1,10
            A(i,j) = j*j*i*i
110      continue
100 continue
C                     Starts a MATLAB engine.
      ep = engOpen("")
C                     Stores it as A in MATLAB format.
      mp = mxCreateFull(10,10,0)
      call mxSetName(mp,"A")
      call mxCopyReal8ToPtr(A,mxGetPr(mp),100)
C                     Copies the matrix to the engine.
      stat = engPutMatrix(ep,mp)
C                     Draws the matrix A.
      stat = engEvalString(ep,"mesh(A);")
C                     Prints the figure to a file.
      stat = engEvalString(ep,"print Images/ex152 -deps")
C                     Closes the MATLAB engine.
```

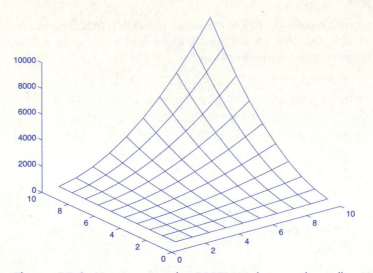

Figure 15.2 A matrix created in FORTRAN drawn with a call to MATLAB.

```
stat = engClose(ep)
stop
end
```

This is compiled with:

```
f77 -o plotm plotm.f /opt/matlab/extern/lib/sol2/libmat.a -lnsl
```

The users must find the library **libmat.a** on their own systems, or ask a systems administrator where it is. Usually it should be stored in:

```
.../matlab/extern/lib/..machinedependent../libmat.a
```

where **libmat.a** contains all the routines supporting the communication between FORTRAN and the MATLAB Engine. Notice that `/opt/matlab/../sol2/` and the compiler directive `-lnsl` are machine dependent. If the library is not found, consult the manuals or ask a systems administrator.

When this program is run, we obtain Figure 15.2.

To read from and write data to a MAT file in a FORTRAN program the matrices must be converted to the MATLAB format in the same way as in Example 15.4, but we do not have to start a MATLAB engine this time. Instead we open a MAT file.

■ **Example 15.5**

Suppose we need a matrix with normally distributed random elements in a FORTRAN program. This apparently simple matrix can be quite difficult to generate, so instead we create it in MATLAB and store it in a file. This file can be read from our FORTRAN program. The following MATLAB statements create a *10 × 10* matrix and store it in the file **data.mat**:

```
Random = randn(10)     % Creates a random matrix.

save data Random       % Saves Random data.mat.
```

We now create a FORTRAN program that reads this file, operates on the matrix, and stores it as a new matrix on the file **data.mat**:

```
      program readwrite
      integer mxCreateFull
      integer mp,mp2,fp,matOpen,matClose,i,j
      double precision A(10,10)
C           Opens the MAT file.
      fp = matOpen("data.mat","u")
C           Copies Random to MATLAB format.
      mp = matGetMatrix(fp,"Random")
      call mxCopyPtrToReal8(mxGetPr(mp),A,100)
C           Multiplies all elements in the Matrix with 2.
      do 100 i = 1,10
         do 110 j = 1,10
            A(i,j) = A(i,j)*2
110      continue
100 continue
C           Saves the matrix A, under a new name.
      mp2 = mxCreateFull(10,10,0)
      call mxSetName(mp2,"Newmatrix")
      call mxCopyReal8ToPtr(A,mxGetPr(mp2),100)
      stat = matPutMatrix(fp,mp2)
C           Closes the file and quits.
      stat = matClose(fp)
      stop
      end
```

When this program is running, the file **data.mat** is expanded with the **Newmatrix**, which is *2*Random*. ■

Finally, we describe calls to FORTRAN routines from MATLAB. These routines are called MEX-files. A call in MATLAB to a MEX-file looks just like a call to a function file, an M-file.

We use the same commands and matrix types in a MEX-file as we do when we call MATLAB from FORTRAN. Now we must also include the special MEX commands.

The MEX-file in FORTRAN must be built by at least two separate files. One file should have a main function called `mexFunction`, which is the routine called by MATLAB. This routine takes four arguments: the number of in and out parameters, and two pointers to lists of pointers to these parameters. This function calls routines that perform the actual operations on the matrices.

■ **Example 15.6**

First, we type the main routine, and store it as **rmultg.f**:

```
C               This routine is called by MATLAB.
      subroutine mexFunction(nlhs,plhs,nrhs,prhs)
      implicit none
      integer nlhs,plhs,nrhs,prhs,mxCreateFull
      integer mp,mxGetPr,mxGetM,mxGetN,mp2
      mp = prhs
      mp2 = mxCreateFull(mxGetM(mp),mxGetN(mp),0)
C         Call a routine to operate on the matrix.
      call operate(mxGetPr(mp),mxGetpr(mp2),
      mxGetM(mp),mxGetN(mp))
C         Return the new matrix.
      plhs = mp2
      return
      end
```

Next, we type the routine **operate.f**, that performs the computations:

```
      subroutine operate(pr,pr2,m,n)
      implicit none
      integer  pr,pr2,m,n,i,j
C               Worst case workspace required in FORTRAN.
      double precision A(1000)
C               Copies the matrix to A.
      call mxCopyPtrToReal8(pr,A,m*n)
C               Multiplies every row with their indices.
      do 100 i = 1,m
```

```
        do 110 j = 1,n
          A(i+(j-1)*m) = real(i*A(i+(j-1)*m))
110     continue
100 continue
C           Copies A to the return matrix.
      call mxCopyReal8ToPtr(A,pr2,m*n)
      return
```

These files are compiled and linked with the command `!cmex  rmultg.f operate.f` or with the equivalent command `fmex`.

When this is compiled, we can type the following MATLAB commands:

```
New = rmultg([1 2 3;1 2 3;1 2 3])
```

New =

1	*2*	*3*
2	*4*	*6*
3	*6*	*9*

■

15.4 Binary files and text files in MATLAB

Sometimes it might be necessary to use binary files in MATLAB. Therefore it must be possible to read and write files in any format if another program requires or generates files in a special format. We begin this section with an example.

■ **Example 15.7**

Suppose we want to store the Hadamard matrix on a file. This can be done with the command `save`, as discussed in Section 2.8. However, it is not possible to control the format the matrix is stored in when the commands `save` and `load` are used. Using the low level file handling commands in MATLAB the format and precision can be controlled in detail.

We can write the following to export a *64 × 64* Hadamard matrix to the file **hada.mtl**:

```
fp = fopen('hada.mtl','w');
antok = fwrite(fp,hadamard(64),'int8');
[err,msg] = ferror(fp,'clear');
if err ~= 0
    disp('An error occurred when writing to the file:')
    disp(msg)
end
```

```
err = fclose(fp);
if err ~= 0
      disp('Could not close the file.')
end
```

■

As can be seen in the example, the file must first be opened in writing mode. We also have to close the file. This was not necessary using the commands `save` and `load`.

The commands `fopen` and `fclose` are used to open and close files in MATLAB.

Command 151	**OPENING AND CLOSING BINARY FILES IN MATLAB**

`fopen(filename,op)`	opens the file named in the string **filename** and returns a file pointer, or *-1* if an error occurred.
	The string **op** indicates which operations are possible to the file, and can take the following values:
	`'r'` read only.
	`'r+'` read and write.
	`'w'` overwrite old file, or create new if the file does not exist. Read only.
	`'w+'` overwrite old file, or create new if the file does not exist. Read and write.
	`'a'` append an old file, or create new if the file does not exist. Write only.
	`'a+'` append an old file or create a new if it does not exist. Read and write.
	PC- and VMS users must separate between binary files and text files. This is done with an additional `'t'` in the string **op**, see `help fopen`.
`[fp,msg] = fopen(filename,op,arch)`	if an error occurs as above, *fp* is assigned the value −1 and an error message is stored in the string **msg** to interpret the error message, see a textbook on C. The string **arch** determines the machine format the data is stored in, type `help fopen` to get more information.

Command 151	OPENING AND CLOSING BINARY FILES IN MATLAB (continued)
`[filename,op,arch]` `= fopen(fp)`	returns information about the file *fp* is referring to. The string **filename** is the name of the file, the string **op** the mode the file was opened in, and the string **arch** in what machine format the file was opened.
`fclose(fp)`	closes the file *fp*. Returns *−1* if it failed, or *0* if everything went well.
`fclose('all')`	closes all open files. Returns *−1* if it failed, or *0* if everything went well.

■ **Example 15.8**

(a) We open the file **hada.mtl** created in Example 15.7, for reading and appending:

```
[fp, msg] = fopen('hada.mtl','a+');
if fp == -1
    disp(msg)
end
[f,op,ark] = fopen(fp)
```

  f =

  hada.mtl

  op =

  a+

  ark =

  ieee−be

(b) We close the file opened in (a):

```
err = fclose(fp)
```

  err =

  0

There are two commands, `fwrite` and `fread`, to write and read data from the files.

Command 152	**WRITING TO AND READING FROM BINARY FILES**

`fwrite(fp,A,prec)`	writes the matrix **A** column by column to the file *fp*. The function returns the number of written elements. The string **prec** determines the precision used. There are more than *20* different precisions available. Type `help fwrite` for more information. A fourth argument can be used to write empty bytes between the elements of **A**.
`fread(fp)`	reads and returns data from the file *fp*.
`[A,c] = fread(fp,s,prec)`	reads data from the file *fp* to the matrix **A**. The size of **A** is determined by *s* according to

$$s = n \qquad \text{a column vector of length } n.$$
$$s = \texttt{inf} \qquad \text{all the data from } fp \text{ is read into a column vector.}$$
$$\mathbf{s} = [m, n] \qquad \text{an } m \times n \text{ matrix is read column by column from } fp.$$

The scalar *c* returns the number of elements read from the file.

`feof(fp)`	returns *1* if the end of the file *fp* is reached, and *0* if not.

■ **Example 15.9**

We type the following to read the file **hada.mtl** created in Example 15.7:

```
fp = fopen('hada.mtl','r');
A = fread(fp,[64,64],'int8');
fclose(fp);
nnz(A - hadamard(64))
```

gives

ans =
        0

that is it is the same Hadamard matrix that we wrote to the file.   ■

MATLAB can create and read formatted text files. In these operations MATLAB reads and writes the elements column by column. However, text files are always read row by row, thus a transposition might be necessary.

Command 153	WRITING AND READING FORMATTED TEXT FILES

`fprintf(` `fp,fstr,A,...)`	writes the elements of the matrix or matrices **A**,... to the file *fp* in the format according to the string **fstr**. This string can contain format characters like in the C programming language. (See Table 15.1 for a list of the most important codes, see a textbook in C or type `help fprintf` for more information.)
`fprintf(fstr,A,..)`	writes formatted data to the screen.
`[A,c] = fscanf(` `fp,fstr,s)`	reads data from the file *fp* to the matrix **A**. If *s* is a scalar, then **A** becomes a column vector. If **s** = [*m,n*], then **A** becomes an $m \times n$ matrix read column by column from *fp*. The string **fstr** determines the format of the data to be read, and uses the same format characters as `fprintf`.
`fgetl(fp)`	reads the next line from the file *fp* to a string.
`fgets(fp)`	reads the next line from the file *fp* to a string including eol (end of line) characters.

The characters used in the format string of the commands `fprintf` and `fscanf`, but also in the commands `sprintf` and `sscanf` are listed in Table 15.2.

Table 15. Format codes to the commands `fprintf` and `sprintf`.

Control characters		Format codes	
\n	new line	%e	scientific format, lower case e
\r	beginning of the line	%E	scientific format, upper case E
\b	back space	%f	decimal format
\t	tab	%s	string
\g	new page	%u	integer
' '	apostrophe	%i	follows the type
\\	back slash	%X	hexadecimal, upper case
\a	bell	%x	hexadecimal, lower case

In addition to these, the width, the number of decimals, and the justification can be specified. MATLAB usually aligns the numbers with right justification, but a minus sign between the percentage sign and the format code changes this to left justification. The field width and the number of decimals are also specified between the percentage sign and the format code, according to %[-][#.#]F, where the brackets indicate that the entry is optional, and the F is the format code (see Table 15.2).

■ **Example 15.10**

(a) Let us write the number π in different formats with the command sprintf:

```
twodec = sprintf('%4.2f',pi)       % Two decimals.
twodec =
    3.14
ninedec = sprintf('pi = %11.9f',pi)  % Nine decimals,
                                      % and text.
ninedec =
    pi = 3.141592654
scfform = sprintf('%E',pi)         % Scientific
                                    % large E.
scfform =
    3.141593E+00
```

(b) The following program writes a formatted table of the function $f(x) = 1/x$ in the interval $[0, 4]$, to the text file **tab.txt**:

```
% Write a formatted table of the function f(x) = 1/x.
x = 1:4; y = zeros(4,2);
y(:,2) = 1./x';
y(:,1) = x';
fp = fopen('tab.txt','w+');
% The left column is an integer in four positions, and the
% right is written with three decimals in six positions.
fprintf(fp,'%4.0f \t %6.3f\n',y')
fclose(fp);
```

When run, these statements generate the file **tab.txt**. We can check the contents of this file with:

```
type tab.txt
    1    1.000
    2    0.500
    3    0.333
    4    0.250
```

(c) To read the file created in (b) we type:

```
fp = fopen('tab.txt','r');
[Tab,c] = fscanf(fp,'%f %f',[2,4]);
fclose(fp);
Tab = Tab'
```

Tab =

1.0000	1.0000
2.0000	0.5000
3.0000	0.3330
4.0000	0.2500

Again, note that the read matrix must be transposed, since MATLAB creates matrices column by column, while the file is read row by row. ■

In every file operation, an error can occur. This should generally be controlled after every file operation, something we have not done except in Example 15.7. The control is done by a call to the function `ferror` that generates an error code, and an error message if an error occurred in the last file operation.

Command 154   **ERROR MESSAGES**

`ferror(fp)`	returns an error message if an error occurred during the latest operation on the file *fp*.
`[msg,errn] = ferror(fp,'clear')`	returns an error message as in the previous, but also returns an error code that can be checked with a C language reference manual. If `'clear'` is specified, the error message buffer is cleared.

■ **Example 15.11**

Preferably an error check should be done after each file operation:

```
fp = fopen('tab.txt','r');
[a,c] = fscanf(fp,'%f %f',[2,5]);
[msg, errn] = ferror(fp);
if errn ~= 0
    disp('An error occurred reading from tab.txt!')
    disp(msg)
end
```

If **tab.txt** is the file created in Example 15.10b the statements above give:

An error occurred reading from tab.txt!

At end-of-file.   ■

There are three functions to control the position of the file pointer *fp*: `fseek`, `ftell`, and `frewind`. These can be used to move around in the file, and to check the position of the file pointer.

Command 155   **POSITION OF THE FILE POINTER**

`frewind(fp)`	moves the file pointer *fp* to the beginning of the file.
`fseek(fp,nb,u)`	moves the file pointer to the position determined by *u* and *nb*, where *nb* is the number of bytes from the start specified by *u* as:

-1   the beginning of the file
0   the current position
1   the beginning of the file

If

$nb < 0$ move the pointer *nb* bytes from *u* towards the beginning of the file.

$nb = 0$ move the pointer to *u*.

$nb > 0$ move the pointer *nb* bytes from *u* towards the end of the file.

`ftell(fp)`	returns the position of the file pointer as the number of bytes read from the beginning of the file. A negative number indicates that an error has occurred.

15.5 Cooperation with other programs

The possibilities to use MATLAB together with other programs are machine dependent. To see what is possible, read the manuals to the systems. We mention a few examples in this section.

It is possible to read and write files in the Lotus 123 spreadsheet format WK1. Type `help wk1read` and `help wk1write` for more information.

If MATLAB is run under Microsoft Windows, it is possible to exchange data with other programs using DDE, Dynamic Data Exchange. This is specially developed between MS-Word and MATLAB. Users who have access to the MATLAB Notebook Suite can write their own MATLAB commands interactively in Word, and mix the code with plain text and graphics generated by MATLAB.

In UNIX networks it is possible to start MATLAB processes on other computers, and thus perform computations on the computer with the most free computer capacity, while having the graphics and command windows on one's own computer.

There are many toolboxes to MATLAB. Here we mention a few important ones:

the Signal Processing Toolbox	used for signal processing
the Optimization Toolbox	used for optimization
the Symbolic Math Toolbox	used for symbolic mathematics, by a link to Maple V

More information about these and other toolboxes, can be found in Appendix C. Some information can also be obtained by typing `expo` and then choosing TOOLBOXES.

The existing possibilities for using MATLAB together with other programs are useful and are likely to be further developed in future versions of MATLAB.

Appendix A
Step-by-Step Introduction

This is a short introduction to MATLAB. We recommend that the commands are tried while reading. For detailed information about the commands used see references given for each subsection and/or try to use help for the command. All commands appear in Appendix E and the List of Command Tables.

A.1 Starting and quitting MATLAB

MATLAB is started by clicking on an icon or by typing `matlab`, depending on the computer in use. For more information read Section 2.1. The following appears in the MATLAB Command Window:

> *< M A T L A B (R) >*
> *(c) Copyright 1984-94 The MathWorks, Inc.*
> *All Rights Reserved*
> *Version 4.2c*
> *Dec 31 1994*

> *Commands to get started: intro, demo, help help*
> *Commands for more information: help, whatsnew, info, subscribe*

>>

It is a good idea to try some of these commands. The commands `intro` and `demo` should prove worthwhile. A command is given after the MATLAB prompt, and is processed when the return key is hit.

    >> intro ↵

To quit MATLAB simply type `quit` and press return (from here on we do not stress the return at the end of the command lines).

    >> quit

If you want to abort current computations in MATLAB press the "CTRL" button and the "c" button simultaneously. MATLAB stops whatever it is doing and the screen prompter returns indicating MATLAB is ready to start running:

    >>

A.2 Basic assignments and calculations

MATLAB can be used as an ordinary calculator in a natural way:

```
>> 5011 + 13
```

ans =
     5024

```
>> 2^5, 2*(3+2)
```

ans =
     32
ans =
     10

The variable *ans* is assigned the previous result if no assignment is made. Normally variables are used and assigned values or results:

```
>> x = 14
```

x =
     14

```
>> y = 3*x
```

y =
     42

All the elementary mathematical functions are defined (see Section 2.4):

```
>> sin(x)
```

ans =
     0.9906

Parentheses can be used as in mathematics.

```
>> u = 2*x - y;
>> w = 2*(x-y);
>> exp((2-u)/(w-2))
```

ans =
0.7589

Note that a semicolon at the end of the command makes MATLAB do the assignment 'quietly', nothing is typed to the screen.

Variables in MATLAB are usually vectors or matrices:

```
>> vcol = [1; 2; 3; 4], vrow = [ 5 6 7 8]
```

vcol =

            1
            2
            3
            4

vrow =

            5   *6*   *7*   *8*

```
>> A = [1 2 3 4; 5 6 7 8; 9 10 11 12]
```

A =

            1   *2*   *3*   *4*
            5   *6*   *7*   *8*
            9   *10*   *11*   *12*

Note that the rows are separated by semicolons.

Functions can be applied to vectors or matrices in a single command:

```
>> sqrt(vcol)
```

ans =

        1.0000

        1.4142

        1.7321

        2.0000

By now we have several variables defined. To see them we can type:

```
>> who
```

Your variables are:

A   u   vrow   x

ans   vcol   w   y

The command `whos` will also show current variables but with some additional information about each variable. Try the command and see how to distinguish if the variable is a scalar or a vector.

During a session MATLAB remembers all variables defined. To make MATLAB forget, type:

```
>> clear
```

All previous variables are now deleted. If `who` is typed nothing is returned.

Vectors can be generated by the colon operator (see Section 4.2):

```
>> vector = 0:8
vector =
    0   1   2   3   4   5   6   7   8

>> vector2 = 0:0.5:2
vector2 =
    0   0.5000   1.0000   1.5000   2.0000
```

or with the commands `linspace` and `logspace` (see Section 4.2). Computations can be carried out on the vectors:

```
>> 2.^vector
ans =
    1   2   4   8   16   32   64   128   256
```

Note the period prior to the operator ^. It indicates that the operation should be carried out for each element in the vector (see Section 3.5).

It is possible to repeat previously given commands with the help of the arrow keys (see Section 2.1). It is very time-saving to avoid rewriting a long statement if a typing error was made.

Vectors or matrices can be included inside the brackets defining a new expression (of course the sizes must now match):

```
>> table = [vector; vector.^ 2;vector=.^=3]
table =
    0   1   2   3    4    5    6    7    8
    0   1   4   9   16   25   36   49   64
    0   1   8  27   64  125  216  343  512
```

A.3 Simple graphics

To draw graphics in MATLAB the data has to be computed and stored in vectors or matrices. To plot a graph of the first powers of 2 for example, there are three steps. First, generate a vector of values. Second, evaluate the function for these values. Third, plot the vectors versus each other (see Section 13.1).

```
>> vector = 0:8
```

vector =

   0 1 2 3 4 5 6 7 8

```
>> values = 2.^vector
```

values =

   1 2 4 8 16 32 64 128 256

```
>> plot(vector,values)
```

The result is a simple graph where the scaling is automatically done (Figure A.1).

To obtain a smoother graph, use more values, for example *100* values between *0* and 8. Try typing:

```
>> vector = linspace(0,8,100);
>> values = 2.^ vector;
>> plot(vector,values);
```

Now let us try different line types. Give the command `plot` as above, now including the extra argument `':'` or `'+'`. These can be combined with colors, for example `'b-1.'` for a blues dash-dotted curve:

```
>> plot (vector, values, b -');
```

Figure A.1 The function 2^x.

Other line styles and colors can be found in Section 13.1.

Three-dimensional graphics are drawn in much the same way. Generate the data into matrices and plot them, now using, for example the `surf` or the `mesh` commands. To generate values to plot a function of two variables is a little bit more tricky. These values, or grid points, are discrete points in a plane. The best way to generate this grid is to use the command `meshgrid`, as described in Section 13.4.

```
>> vector2 = 0:0.5:8;
>> [X,Y] = meshgrid(vector2,vector2);
>> mesh(X,Y,2.^X+2.^Y)
```

The brackets are used to receive more than one return argument. Recollect that the semicolon supresses the echoing of the result. This is worth remembering if the matrix is big. The resulting mesh plot can be seen in Figure A.2.

A surf plot is quite similar to a mesh plot, but now the actual surface is drawn instead of the grid lines (see Figure A.3). Surf plots are generated with the command `surf`.

```
>> surf(X,Y,cos(X./2).*sin(Y./2))
```

To draw statistical diagrams, use the command `hist` (see Section 6.5). To illustrate, we generate a random vector of numbers in *[0,1]* with the command `rand` which is described in Section 4.1.

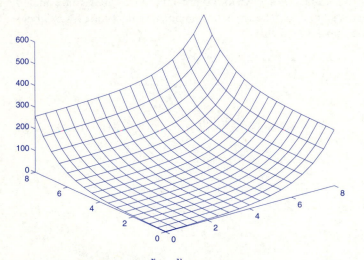

Figure A.2 The function $2^x + 2^y$ plotted with `mesh`.

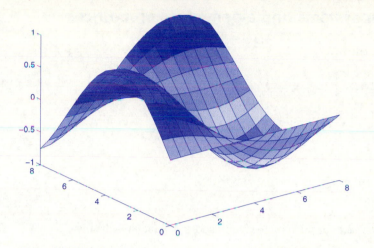

Figure A.3 The function $cos(x/2)sin(y/2)$ plotted with `surf`.

```
>> random = rand(1,7)
```
random =

     0.4553   0.3495   0.4523   0.8089   0.9317   0.6516   0.2152

```
>> hist(random)
```

The result is shown in Figure A.4. Try other commands on the same vector, for example `stairs` and `bar` (see Section 6.5).

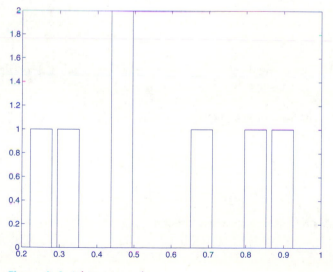

Figure A.4 A histogram plot.

A.4 Linear systems and eigenvalues of matrices

We define the matrices

$$\mathbf{A} = \begin{bmatrix} 3 & 4 & 5 \\ 5 & 2 & 2 \\ 1 & 2 & 3 \end{bmatrix} \qquad \mathbf{B} = \begin{bmatrix} 1 & 2 & 3 \\ 1 & 1 & 1 \end{bmatrix}$$

with the following statements:

```
>> A = [3 4 5; 5 2 2; 1 2 3];
>> B = [1 2 3; 1 1 1];
```

The matrices can be multiplied by the command `B*A` which results in:

ans =

16	*14*	*18*
9	*8*	*10*

But `A*B` results in:

??? E.rror using ==> *

Inner matrix dimensions must agree.

since this matrix multiplication is not defined! (See Section 3.2.) To compute the determinant of **A**, use the command `det`:

```
>> det(A)
```

ans =
   −6

The determinant of **B** is not defined. Also try `trace`, `null`, `orth` and `inv` on the same matrices. These commands are all defined in Section 7.1.

Now we focus on the linear system of equations:

$$3x_1 + 4x_2 + 5x_3 = 25$$
$$5x_1 + 2x_2 + 2x_3 = 18$$
$$x_1 + 2x_2 + 3x_3 = 13$$

or in matrix notation $\mathbf{A}\,\mathbf{x} = \mathbf{b}$, with **A** as above and **b**:

$$\mathbf{b} = \begin{bmatrix} 25 \\ 18 \\ 13 \end{bmatrix}$$

This system is solved with the back slash operator, \ :

```
>> A\b
ans =
    2.0000
    1.0000
    3.0000
```

Overdetermined systems are solved in the same way. Since these systems usually do not have straight forward solutions, MATLAB uses the method of least squares to solve them. (See Sections 7.2 and 7.7.)

Eigenvalues and eigenvectors are determined with the command `eig`, for example for the matrix **A** from above:

```
>> [Eigenvectors,Eigenvalues] = eig(A)
Eigenvectors =
    -0.7111   -0.4501   -0.0210
    -0.6185    0.8459   -0.7756
    -0.3342   -0.2863    0.6309
Eigenvalues =
    8.8291        0         0
        0   -1.3373         0
        0         0    0.5082
```

The columns of the matrix **Eigenvectors** form the eigenvectors, and the diagonal elements of the matrix **Eigenvalues** are the eigenvalues (see Section 8.1).

A.5 Curve fitting and polynomials

Polynomials are represented by vectors with the coefficients as components (see Section 10.1). The polynomial:

$$p(x) = 2x^3 + x^2 + 5x + 17$$

is represented by the vector **p** = [2 1 5 17], and can be evaluated for any value with the command `polyval`:

```
>> polyval(p,0), polyval(p,2)
```

```
ans =

    17

ans =

    47
```

Polynomials can be differentiated with the command `polyder`, and multiplied with the command `conv`:

```
>> pprim = polyder(p)
```

```
pprim =

    6   2   5
```

which represents $p'(x) = 6x^2 + 2x + 5$.

```
>> psquare = conv(p,p)
```

```
psquare =

    4   4   21   78   59   170   289.
```

which represents $p(x)^2 = 4x^6 + 4x^5 + 21x^4 + 78x^3 + 59x^2 + 170x + 289$.

Let us now plot all three polynomials in three subplots in the same figure. The command `subplot` is described in Section 13.3.

```
>> x = linspace(-2,2,50);
>> subplot(2,2,1); plot(x,2*x.^3+x.^2+5*x+17);
   xlabel('p(x)')
>> subplot(2,2,2); plot(x,6*x.^2+2*x+5);
   xlabel('p''(x)')
>> subplot(2,2,3);
>> plot(x,4*x.^6+4*x.^5+21*x.^4+78*x.^3 +
   59*x.^2+170*x+289)
>> xlabel('p(x)^2')
```

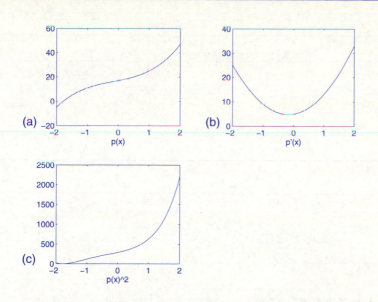

Figure A.5 The polynomial $p(x) = 2x^3 + x^2 + 5x + 17$, its derivative and the $p(x)^2$ polynomial.

The command `xlabel` writes a string below the current picture, at the x-axis (Figure A.5 (a)–(c)).

Polynomials can be used to fit curves to data. Assume that the following data has been acquired in an experiment, and entered into MATLAB:

```
>> x = 1:10;
>> y = [1 5 3 3 2 3 6 11 17 34];
```

Now the command `polyfit` returns the polynomial, that is the coefficients of the polynomial, of a specified degree that best fits the data in the least squares sense (see Section 10.4). As an example, the best polynomial of degree *4* is determined. Also, the original data is plotted in the same graph as the polynomial:

```
>> ypol = polyfit(x,y,4);
>> plot(x,y,'*',x,polyval(ypol,x),'-b')
>> legend(' Experimental data','Least square polynomial')
```

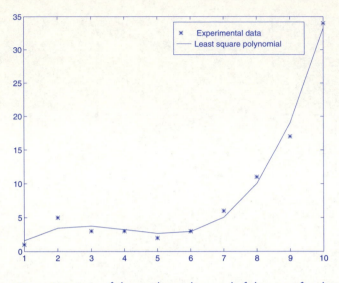

Figure A.6 A set of data with a polynomial of degree *4* fitted to it.

The result can be seen in Figure A.6.

Notice that several vectors can be plotted against each other with the same `plot` command. The command `legend` gives the box containing the explanation to the different vectors plotted. It is defined in Section 13.3. Try the `polyfit` and `polyval` commands for polynomials of different degrees and for different data sets.

Interpolation (and extrapolation) can be done with the different `interp` commands. To interpolate a value for $x = 4.3$ from the data set above we type:

```
>> interp1(x,y,4.3)
```

ans =

   2.7000

This is linear interpolation, also referred to as 'table look up'. Several other possibilities exist, type `help interp1` to see them. (Interpolation is described in Section 10.4.)

A.6 Simple programming

A program is a sequence of MATLAB statements, often controlled by conditional statements and repetitive statements. It is convenient to store these commands in an M-file, which is a text file with the extension .m.

Consider the MATLAB statements below stored in the file **draw.m**:

```
% Program plotting functions
% Comments can be made after %
% Displays explanatory text
disp('This program plots f(x) in the interval [a,b]');
% Reads from user
ftext = input('Give a function, e.g. sin(x) : ','s');
lb = input('Give lower bound : ');
ub = input('Give upper bound : ');
% Plot the function
clf; fplot(ftext,[lb ub]);
```

This program is run by typing `draw` after the MATLAB prompt. As an example:

```
>> draw
```

This program plots f(x) in the interval [a,b]

Give a function, e.g. sin(x) : 2.*x.*cos(x.^2)

Give lower bound, a : 0

Give upper bound, b : 2*pi

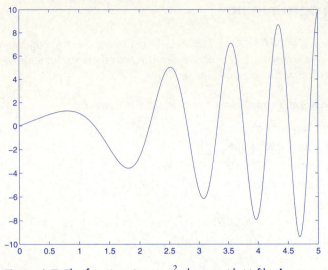

Figure A.7 The function $2x\cos x^2$ drawn with M-file **draw**.

The result of the program with these inputs can be seen in Figure A.7.

The program **draw.m** is an example of a command file. There are also function files. A function file must also have the extension .m, and have the keyword `function` in the first line. As an example, consider the following function:

```
function y = div(n,d);
% This function computes the integer division
% thus n = rem(n,d) + y.*d
y = (n-rem(n,d))/d;
```

This function can now be called as any other MATLAB function:

```
>> div(1234,7)
ans =
    176
```

Information about M-files can be found in Sections 2.9 and 12.3.

A.7 Analysis of functions

Finding a local minimum to a function of one variable is done with the command `fmin`, and for several variables with the command `fmins` (see Section 10.3).

We want to find a minimum to the function:

$$f(x) = \frac{x - 1.96}{x^2 + 1.15}$$

First, we create a function file that computes the function and stores it under the name
f.m.

```
function y = f(x);
y = (x-1.96)./(x.^2+1.15);
```

The command:

```
>> fmin('f',-1,1)
```

gives us the answer:

> *ans =*
>
> *-0.2742*

To see if this is correct we plot the function by giving the command:

```
>> fplot('f(x)',[- 10 10]);
>> title('f(x) = (x - 1.96)/(x^2+1.15)'),grid
```

The command `title` gave us a title to the figure. It is described in Section 13.3.
The command `grid` added the grid and it is also described in Section 13.3. We can
also find the exact location where the function *f(x) = 0*. This is done by the command

Figure A.8 An M-file function plotted with `fplot`.

`fzero` that requires a starting value for the iteration (see Section 10.2). In Figure A.8 we see that *2* is close to *f(x)=0* so we type:

```
>> fzero('f',2)
   ans =
        1.9600
```

A.8 Integrals

We can compute a definite integral by using the command `quad` described in Section 11.1. For computing:

$$\int_0^\pi func(x)dx$$

where *func(x) = sin(x)/x*, we must define:

```
function y = func(x)
y = sin(x)./x;
```

Now we simply type:

```
>> quad('func',1E-8,pi)
```

The result will be

```
   ans =
        1.8520
```

Note that this integral cannot be solved analytically. The function is shown in Figure A.9.

The marked area is the result of the integral. This area has been done with the graphical object `patch` described in Section 14.2. First we plot the function **func** with the `fplot` command and add a grid.

```
>> fplot('func',[- 10 10]); grid
```

Now we give the command `patch` and keep a 'handle' so that properties of the patch can be changed later on.

```
>> h = patch([0.001 0.001:0.01:pi pi],...
[0 func(0.001:0.01:pi) 0],'r')
```

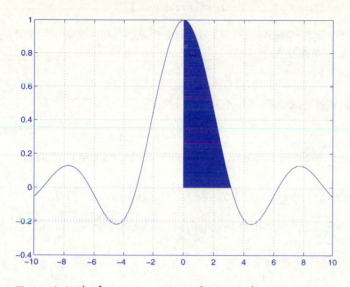

Figure A.9 The function *sin(x)/x* in the interval *−10 < x < 10.*

$$h =$$
$$85.0004$$

The first argument to `patch` defines the x-coordinates of the edges of the plot. The second argument defines the y-coordinates. The last argument defines in what color the patch is drawn, in this case "r" for red. We can now change the edge color of the patch by typing:

```
>> set(h,'EdgeColor',[0 0 1])
```

To see other properties that can be manipulated with the `set` command type `get(h)`. These commands are described in Section 14.2.

A.9 Ordinary differential equations

Suppose that we have a function **xprim** defined as:

```
function y = xprim(x,t);
y = (x-1.96)./(x.^3+1.15);
```

Besides the *x*, there is a *t* added as input argument even though the function does not depend on *t*. This is because we want to solve the ordinary differential equation:

$$\frac{dx}{dt} = \frac{x - 1.96}{x^3 + 1.15} \qquad (*)$$

with the MATLAB command `ode23` described in Section 11.2.

First let us solve (*) in the interval $0 < t < 10$ with initial condition $x(0) = 1$. The call of the `ode23` command looks like:

```
>> [x1,t1] = ode23('xprim',0,10,1);
```

The result is the two vectors **x** and **t** which we can plot:

```
>> plot(x1,t1)
```

Let us now solve (*) in the same *t*-interval but with a different initial value $x(0) = -1$:

```
>> [x2,t2] = ode23('xprim',0,10,-1);
```

We want this function to be plotted in the same figure so we give the command `hold` before plotting the new vectors.

```
>> hold; plot(x2,t2,':')
```

This gives us Figure A.10.

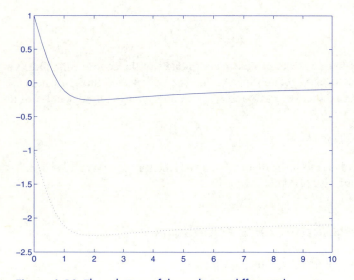

Figure A.10 The solutions of the ordinary differential equation with different initial values.

Appendix B
Definitions and Basic Concepts in Linear Algebra

This is a concise presentation of basics in linear algebra and matrix algebra. All concepts treated are also included in MATLAB.

B.1 Vectors

A **linear space** consists of **vectors** which can be added and multiplied by scalars.

The linear space $\mathbf{R}^n$ consists of column vectors:

$$\mathbf{x} = \begin{bmatrix} x_1 \\ x_2 \\ \vdots \\ x_n \end{bmatrix} \qquad \mathbf{y} = \begin{bmatrix} y_1 \\ y_2 \\ \vdots \\ y_n \end{bmatrix}$$

with real **elements** x_k and y_k and **length** n.

In the linear space $\mathbf{C}^n$, the elements can be complex.

Addition is defined element by element:

$$\mathbf{x} + \mathbf{y} = \begin{bmatrix} x_1 + y_1 \\ x_2 + y_2 \\ \vdots \\ x_n + y_n \end{bmatrix}$$

Multiplication by a scalar α is defined element by element:

$$\alpha\mathbf{x} = \begin{bmatrix} \alpha x_1 \\ \alpha x_2 \\ \vdots \\ \alpha x_n \end{bmatrix}$$

The null vector has all its elements equal to zero:

$$\mathbf{0} = \begin{bmatrix} 0 \\ 0 \\ \vdots \\ 0 \end{bmatrix}$$

A set of p vectors $\mathbf{x}_1, \mathbf{x}_2, .., \mathbf{x}_p$ in the linear space $\mathbf{R}^n$ are said to be **linearly dependent** if at least one of the vectors can be written as a linear combination of the others:

$$x_p = \alpha_1 \mathbf{x}_1 + ... + \alpha_{p-1} \mathbf{x}_{p-1}$$

where α_i are scalars.

If this is not possible, the vectors are said to be **linearly independent**. The most common definition of linear independence is that $\alpha_1 \mathbf{x}_1 + \alpha_2 \mathbf{x}_2 + ... + \alpha_p \mathbf{x}_p = \mathbf{0}$ holds only for $\alpha_1 = \alpha_2 = ... = \alpha_p = \mathbf{0}$.

■ **Example B.1**

The vectors

$$\mathbf{x}_1 = \begin{bmatrix} 1 \\ 0 \\ 0 \end{bmatrix} \qquad \mathbf{x}_2 = \begin{bmatrix} 1 \\ 1 \\ 0 \end{bmatrix} \qquad \mathbf{x}_3 = \begin{bmatrix} 1 \\ 1 \\ 1 \end{bmatrix}$$

are linearly independent in $\mathbf{R}^3$. ■

The maximum number of linearly independent vectors in a space is called the **dimension** of the space. The spaces $\mathbf{R}^n$ and $\mathbf{C}^n$ have the dimensions n. Note that in some cases it is convenient to say that $\mathbf{C}^n$ has the dimension $2n$, thus separating the real and imaginary parts.

A **basis** in a linear space is a set of vectors such that all vectors in that space can be written as a linear combination of these. The number of vectors in a basis is equal to the dimension of the space. There is an infinite number of bases in a linear space.

■ **Example B.2**

The vectors in Example B.1 form a basis in $\mathbf{R}^3$ and $\mathbf{C}^3$. The vectors:

$$\mathbf{e}_1 = \begin{bmatrix} 1 \\ 0 \\ 0 \end{bmatrix} \qquad \mathbf{e}_2 = \begin{bmatrix} 0 \\ 1 \\ 0 \end{bmatrix} \qquad \mathbf{e}_3 = \begin{bmatrix} 0 \\ 0 \\ 1 \end{bmatrix}$$

form a more common basis in the same space. We have:

$$\mathbf{x} = \begin{bmatrix} x_1 \\ x_2 \\ x_3 \end{bmatrix} = x_1 \mathbf{e}_1 + x_2 \mathbf{e}_2 + x_3 \mathbf{e}_3$$

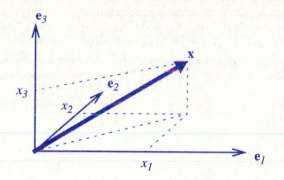

Figure B.1 A vector and its components.

that is an arbitrary vector in $\mathbf{R}^3$ can be expressed as a linear combination of the vectors of the basis. This is illustrated in Figure B.1. ■

The **scalar product** or **dot product** of two vectors $\mathbf{x}$ and $\mathbf{y}$ in $\mathbf{C}^n$, usually written $(\mathbf{x},\mathbf{y})$ or $<\mathbf{x},\mathbf{y}>$, is defined by:

$$(\mathbf{x}, \mathbf{y}) = \sum_{i=1}^{n} \overline{x_i}\, y_i$$

The complex conjugate of x_i is not necessary if we restrict ourselves to $\mathbf{R}^n$. Using notations introduced in the next section, it holds that $(\mathbf{x},\mathbf{y})=\mathbf{x}^H\mathbf{y}$.

The **Euclidean norm** $\|\mathbf{x}\|_2$ of a vector in $\mathbf{C}^n$ is defined by:

$$\|\mathbf{x}\|_2^2 = (\mathbf{x}, \mathbf{x}) = \sum_{i=1}^{n} |x_i|^2 = \mathbf{x}^H\mathbf{x}$$

The norm measures the size or the length of a vector. There are also other norms, and some of them are introduced in Section B.6.

Two vectors $\mathbf{x}$ and $\mathbf{y}$ are said to be **orthogonal** if $(\mathbf{x},\mathbf{y}) = 0$.

The angle θ between two vectors $\mathbf{x}$ and $\mathbf{y}$ is defined by:

$$cos\,\theta = \frac{(\mathbf{x}, \mathbf{y})}{\|\mathbf{x}\|_2\|\mathbf{y}\|_2}$$

We see that the angle between two orthogonal vectors is $\pi/2$ or *90* degrees, that is the vectors are perpendicular. The null vector is orthogonal to all vectors.

A set of non-zero vectors $\mathbf{x}_1, \mathbf{x}_2, ..., \mathbf{x}_p$ forms an **orthogonal system** if all vectors are mutually orthogonal. The vectors are also linearly independent, and thus orthogonality is stronger than linear independence. The vectors $\mathbf{x}_1, \mathbf{x}_2, ..., \mathbf{x}_p$ form an **orthonormal system** if they form an orthogonal system, and all have the Euclidean norm equal to one. The following holds for the vectors forming an orthonormal system:

$$(\mathbf{x}_j, \mathbf{x}_k) = \begin{cases} 0 & j \neq k \\ 1 & j = k \end{cases}$$

■ **Example B.3**

The vectors $\mathbf{e}_1$, $\mathbf{e}_2$ and $\mathbf{e}_3$ from Example B.2 form an orthonormal system in $\mathbf{R}^3$ (and in $\mathbf{C}^3$). They represent the **x, y, z** axes respectively in a normal Cartesian coordinate system.   ■

We could also have defined all the above concepts in terms of row vectors $\mathbf{v} = (v_1, v_2, ..., v_p)$ instead of in terms of column vectors. However, there are several advantages in working with column vectors.

B.2 Matrices, an introduction

A **matrix** is a rectangular array of numbers arranged in **rows** and **columns**. A matrix with m rows and n columns is referred to as an $m \times n$ matrix. For instance, this is a 2×3 matrix:

$$\begin{bmatrix} 2 & 1 & 3 \\ 3 & -2 & 0 \end{bmatrix} = \begin{bmatrix} a_{11} & a_{12} & a_{13} \\ a_{21} & a_{22} & a_{23} \end{bmatrix}$$

The numbers in the matrix are referred to as the **elements** or the **components** of the matrix. If the matrix is denoted $\mathbf{A}$, the elements of $\mathbf{A}$ are called a_{ij}, where i indicates the row index and j the column index, that is a_{ij} denotes the element in row i and column j.

An $n \times n$ matrix is said to be **square**.

The **size** of a matrix is given by the number of rows, m, and the number of columns, n. For square matrices, n is sometimes referred to as the **order** of the matrix.

The **main diagonal** starts in the top left-hand corner of the matrix and continues diagonally downwards to the right. The elements of the main diagonal are referred to as the **diagonal elements** a_{ii}. The **anti-diagonal** starts in the top right-hand corner, and continues diagonally to the left. The diagonals over and under the main diagonal are called the **super-diagonals** and **sub-diagonals** respectively.

Addition of two matrices of the same size is defined element by element. The matrix $C = A + B$ has the elements $c_{ij} = a_{ij} + b_{ij}$.

Multiplication of a matrix by a scalar is also defined element by element. The matrix αA has the elements $\alpha\, a_{ij}$.

Multiplication of matrices is only defined if the number of columns in the left matrix is equal to the number of rows in the right matrix. The matrix $C = A\,B$, where A is an $m \times p$ matrix and B is a $p \times n$ matrix, is an $m \times n$ matrix with the elements:

$$c_{ij} = \sum_{k=1}^{p} a_{ik} b_{kj}$$

The element c_{ij} is the scalar product of row i in A and column j in B.

Even if $B\,A$ is defined, $A\,B$ may not be. If both A and B are square matrices of order n, then $A\,B$ and $B\,A$ are both defined, but usually $A\,B \neq B\,A$. Matrix multiplication is **not commutative**.

The **identity matrix** of order n, denoted I or I_n, is an $n \times n$ matrix in which all the diagonal elements are 1 and all the off-diagonal elements are 0. A matrix multiplied with the identity matrix remains unchanged, thus it holds that $I\,A = A$ and $A\,I = A.$

A column vector can be seen as an $n \times 1$ matrix, and a row vector as a $1 \times n$ matrix. Sometimes it can be useful to regard a scalar as a 1×1 matrix.

If x is a column vector with n components, and A is an $n \times n$ matrix, then $A\,x$ is also a column vector with n components. This is called **matrix-vector multiplication**.

A **transposition** is a reflection in the main diagonal. The transposition operator is written ^{T}. If A is an $m \times n$ matrix with the elements a_{ij}, then the **transposed matrix** A^T is an $n \times m$ matrix with elements a_{ji}. A transposition can also be described as an interchange between rows and columns of a matrix in the sense that the first column of A is the first row in the transposed matrix, the second column of A the second row in the transposed matrix, and so on.

The **conjugate** of a matrix is a matrix in which all the elements are replaced by their complex conjugates. The result is written $\overline{A}$. A common operation is the conjugation and transposition, that is forming the matrix $\overline{A}^T$ or the equivalent $\overline{A^T}$. This matrix is usually written A^H, A^*, and in MATLAB A'.

The scalar product of two column vectors x and y can now be written:

$$(\mathbf{x}, \mathbf{y}) = \sum_{i=1}^{n} \bar{x}_i y_i = \mathbf{x}^H \mathbf{y}$$

and the Euclidean norm can be written $\|\mathbf{x}\|_2 = \sqrt{\mathbf{x}^H \mathbf{x}}$. Note that $\mathbf{x}^H \mathbf{y}$ is a scalar, since it is the product of a $1 \times n$ matrix and an $n \times 1$ matrix. On the contrary $\mathbf{x}\mathbf{y}^H$ is an $n \times n$ matrix.

B.3 Matrix concepts

Matrices are not only a set of numbers. A number of important and useful mathematical concepts are associated with matrices.

The **rank** of a matrix $\mathbf{A}$, *rank(A)*, is the number of linearly independent columns in the matrix $\mathbf{A}$, and this number is always equal to the number of linearly independent rows in $\mathbf{A}$. If $\mathbf{A}$ is an $m \times n$ matrix, then the rank is less than or equal to *min(m,n)*.

The **determinant** of a square matrix $\mathbf{A}$, *det(A)*, is a scalar that can be defined and computed in different ways. The following holds:

1. $det(\mathbf{A}) = det(\mathbf{A}^T)$

2. $det(\mathbf{A}^H) = \overline{det(\mathbf{A})}$

3. $det(\mathbf{A}) = 0$ if $\mathbf{A}$ has two rows that are equal, or a row that is a linear combination of the other rows. The same holds for the columns of $\mathbf{A}$.

4.   The determinant does not change if a row multiplied with a scalar is subtracted from another row. The same holds for the columns.

5.   The sign of the determinant changes if two rows are interchanged. The same holds for the columns.

6.   The determinant of an upper triangular matrix, that is a matrix where all the elements below the main diagonal are zero is the product of the diagonal elements. The same holds for a lower triangular matrix.

7.   The determinant of a matrix product is the same as the product of the determinants. This is the important multiplication theorem: $det(\mathbf{AB}) = det(\mathbf{A})det(\mathbf{B})$.

8.   Computation of the determinant is preferably carried out by Gaussian elimination.

A **system of n linear equations** can be written in the explicit form:

$$
\begin{cases}
a_{11}x_1 + a_{12}x_2 + \ldots + a_{1n}x_n = b_1 \\
a_{21}x_1 + a_{22}x_2 + \ldots + a_{2n}x_n = b_2 \\
\qquad\qquad \vdots \\
a_{n1}x_1 + a_{2n}x_2 + \ldots + a_{nn}x_n = b_n
\end{cases}
$$

or with $\mathbf{A} = (a_{ij})$, $\mathbf{x} = (x_1, x_2, \ldots, x_n)^T$ and $\mathbf{b} = (b_1, b_2, \ldots, b_n)^T$ in the compact form:

$$\mathbf{A}\,\mathbf{x} = \mathbf{b}$$

Introducing $\mathbf{a}_1, \mathbf{a}_2, \ldots, \mathbf{a}_n$ as the columns of $\mathbf{A}$, the system can be written in the semicompact form

$$x_1\mathbf{a}_1 + x_2\mathbf{a}_2 + \ldots + x_n\mathbf{a}_n = \mathbf{b}$$

The system has a unique solution if and only if $det(\mathbf{A}) \neq 0$.

The **range**, $\mathcal{R}(\mathbf{A})$, of an $m \times n$ matrix $\mathbf{A}$ is the set of all linear combinations of the columns $\mathbf{a}_1, \mathbf{a}_2, \ldots, \mathbf{a}_n$ of $\mathbf{A}$. This is a linear space, and the dimension of $\mathcal{R}(\mathbf{A})$ is the same as $rank(\mathbf{A})$.

The **null space**, $\mathcal{N}(\mathbf{A})$ of the matrix $\mathbf{A}$ is the set of vectors $\mathbf{x}$ such that $\mathbf{A}\,\mathbf{x} = \mathbf{0}$, that is all the solutions of the homogenous system. This is also a linear space, and its dimension is $m - rank(\mathbf{A})$.

The range and null space of $\mathbf{A}^T$ are defined in the same way.

The system $\mathbf{A}\,\mathbf{X} = \mathbf{I}$ where $\mathbf{A}$ is an $n \times n$ matrix and $\mathbf{I}$ is the identity matrix of order n is a **matrix equation.** Using the notation $\mathbf{x}_1, \mathbf{x}_2, \ldots, \mathbf{x}_n$ and $\mathbf{e}_1 = (1, 0, \ldots, 0)^T$, $\mathbf{e}_2 = (0, 1, \ldots, 0)^T, \ldots, \mathbf{e}_n = (0, 0, \ldots, 1)^T$ for the columns of $\mathbf{X}$ and $\mathbf{I}$ according to:

$$\mathbf{X} = \begin{bmatrix} \mathbf{x}_1 & \mathbf{x}_2 & \ldots & \mathbf{x}_n \end{bmatrix} \qquad \mathbf{I} = \begin{bmatrix} \mathbf{e}_1 & \mathbf{e}_2 & \ldots & \mathbf{e}_n \end{bmatrix}$$

we can write the matrix equation as the set of linear systems:

$$\mathbf{A}\mathbf{x}_k = \mathbf{e}_k \qquad k = 1, 2, \ldots, n$$

These have unique solutions if and only if $det(\mathbf{A}) \neq 0$. The solution $\mathbf{X}$ to $\mathbf{A}\,\mathbf{X} = \mathbf{I}$ is called the **inverse** of $\mathbf{A}$ and is denoted by $\mathbf{A}^{-1}$. It holds that $\mathbf{A}\,\mathbf{A}^{-1} = \mathbf{I}$ and $\mathbf{A}^{-1}\,\mathbf{A} = \mathbf{I}$.

The computation of the inverse is usually carried out by Gaussian elimination. A matrix that has an inverse is called **non-singular**, and otherwise it is said to be **singular**.

Eigenvalues and **eigenvectors** of a square matrix are defined by the equation:

$$\mathbf{A}\mathbf{x} = \lambda\mathbf{x}$$

This is equivalent to the homogenous system of equations:

$$(\mathbf{A} - \lambda\mathbf{I})\mathbf{x} = \mathbf{0}$$

For every $\mathbf{A}$ and every λ, the vector $\mathbf{x} = \mathbf{0}$ is a solution, but if $det(\mathbf{A} - \lambda\mathbf{I}) \neq \mathbf{0}$ there are also non-trivial solutions to the system. These solutions $\mathbf{x}_k \neq \mathbf{0}$ are called **eigenvectors** of $\mathbf{A}$ and the corresponding λ_k are called **eigenvalues** or **characteristic roots.** There are always n eigenvalues $\lambda_1, \lambda_2, ..., \lambda_n$ to $\mathbf{A}$ in the complex plane. An eigenvalue and its eigenvectors are called an **eigenpair**.

The function $\varphi(\lambda) = det(\mathbf{A} - \lambda\mathbf{I})$ is a polynomial in λ of exactly degree n, and is called the **characteristic polynomial** of $\mathbf{A}$. The **characteristic equation** is $\varphi(\lambda) = 0$.

It is always true that the matrix polynomial $\varphi(\mathbf{A}) = \mathbf{0}$. This is the **Cayley–Hamilton theorem**.

If $\mathbf{C}$ is a non-singular matrix, and $\mathbf{A}$ and $\mathbf{B}$ are defined as $\mathbf{B} = \mathbf{C}^{-1}\mathbf{A}\mathbf{C}$, then $\mathbf{A}$ and $\mathbf{B}$ are said to be **similar matrices**, and the transformation from $\mathbf{A}$ to $\mathbf{B}$ is called a **similarity transform.** Such a transform does not change the eigenvalues of the matrix.

The **spectral radius** $\rho(A)$ of a matrix $\mathbf{A}$ is defined as $\max_i |\lambda_i|$.

The following rules hold for the inverse, the transpose and the conjugate transpose:

$$(\mathbf{AB})^{-1} = \mathbf{B}^{-1}\mathbf{A}^{-1} \text{ if all the inverses exist.}$$

$$(\mathbf{AB})^{T} = \mathbf{B}^{T}\mathbf{A}^{T}$$

$$(\mathbf{AB})^{H} = \mathbf{B}^{H}\mathbf{A}^{H}$$

In the following chain of equivalences most of the above definitions appear. $\mathbf{A}$ is a square matrix of order n.

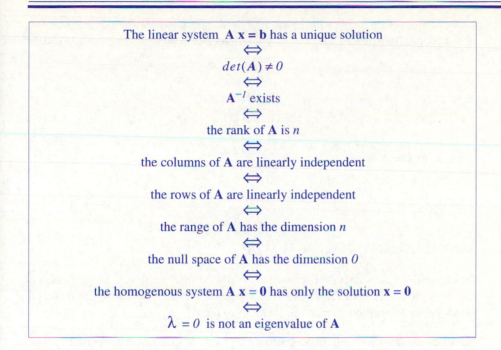

The linear system $\mathbf{A}\,\mathbf{x} = \mathbf{b}$ has a unique solution
$$\Longleftrightarrow$$
$$det(\mathbf{A}) \neq 0$$
$$\Longleftrightarrow$$
$\mathbf{A}^{-1}$ exists
$$\Longleftrightarrow$$
the rank of $\mathbf{A}$ is n
$$\Longleftrightarrow$$
the columns of $\mathbf{A}$ are linearly independent
$$\Longleftrightarrow$$
the rows of $\mathbf{A}$ are linearly independent
$$\Longleftrightarrow$$
the range of $\mathbf{A}$ has the dimension n
$$\Longleftrightarrow$$
the null space of $\mathbf{A}$ has the dimension 0
$$\Longleftrightarrow$$
the homogenous system $\mathbf{A}\,\mathbf{x} = \mathbf{0}$ has only the solution $\mathbf{x} = \mathbf{0}$
$$\Longleftrightarrow$$
$\lambda = 0$ is not an eigenvalue of $\mathbf{A}$

B.4 Matrix classes

Matrices can be classified in many ways. A matrix is said to be a **diagonal matrix** if all off-diagonal elements are zero. A matrix is said to be **upper triangular** if all elements below the main diagonal are zero. If all the elements on the diagonal are also zero, then the matrix is said to be **strictly upper triangular**. **Lower triangular** and **strictly lower triangular** are defined in the same way.

A matrix is said to be **tridiagonal** if non-zero elements only exist on the main diagonal, and in the first super-diagonal and sub-diagonal. More generally, a matrix is said to be a **band matrix** if all its non-zero elements are located to a band around the main diagonal.

A matrix is said to be in **upper Hessenberg form** if all the elements below the first sub-diagonal are zero.

A matrix is said to be **sparse** if most of its elements are zero; otherwise it is said to be **full**. Band matrices are examples of sparse matrices.

It is often useful to work with **block matrices**, that is where the elements of the matrices are also matrices. Arithmetic operations can in fact be carried out as usual.

Let **A** and **B** be defined by:

$$\mathbf{A} = \begin{bmatrix} \mathbf{A}_{11} & \mathbf{A}_{12} \\ \mathbf{A}_{21} & \mathbf{A}_{22} \end{bmatrix} \qquad \mathbf{B} = \begin{bmatrix} \mathbf{B}_{11} & \mathbf{B}_{12} \\ \mathbf{B}_{21} & \mathbf{B}_{22} \end{bmatrix}$$

this give us **C** = **A B** as:

$$\mathbf{C} = \begin{bmatrix} \mathbf{C}_{11} & \mathbf{C}_{12} \\ \mathbf{C}_{21} & \mathbf{C}_{22} \end{bmatrix}$$

where, for instance, $\mathbf{C}_{11} = \mathbf{A}_{11}\mathbf{B}_{11} + \mathbf{A}_{12}\mathbf{B}_{21}$.

Block matrices are sometimes referred to as **partitioned matrices.** In the previous example, the size of the submatrices must agree. Definitions like **block diagonal** and **block upper triangular** need no further explanation.

Matrices can also be classified according to their mathematical properties. Some concepts have already been introduced but are repeated here.

A matrix **A** is said to be **non-singular** if $det(\mathbf{A}) \neq 0$, and this means that all eigenvalues are non-zero. If $det(\mathbf{A}) = 0$ then the matrix is **singular** and at least one eigenvalue is zero.

A matrix **A** is said to be **Hermitian** if $\mathbf{A}^H = \mathbf{A}$. This is the same as **symmetric** for real matrices. The eigenvalues of **A** are real and the eigenvectors form an orthonormal basis.

A matrix **A** is said to be **skew-Hermitian** if $\mathbf{A}^H = -\mathbf{A}$. This is the same as **skew-symmetric** for real matrices. The eigenvalues are imaginary and the eigenvectors form an orthonormal basis.

A matrix **A** is said to be **normal** if $\mathbf{A}^H\mathbf{A} = \mathbf{A}\mathbf{A}^H$. The eigenvectors form an orthonormal basis.

A matrix **A** is said to be **unitary** if $\mathbf{A}^H\mathbf{A} = \mathbf{I}$. This is the same as **orthogonal** for real matrices. Thus it is true that $\mathbf{A}^{-1} = \mathbf{A}^H$. The columns of **A** form an orthonormal basis, and so do the rows. The eigenvalues have the absolute value *1* and the eigenvectors form an orthonormal basis.

A Hermitian matrix is said to be **positive definite** if $\mathbf{x}^H\mathbf{A}\,\mathbf{x} > 0$ for every $\mathbf{x} \neq 0$. All eigenvalues are positive.

Positive semidefinite is defined in the same way with the slightly weaker condition $\mathbf{x}^H\mathbf{A}\mathbf{x} \geq 0$ for every $\mathbf{x}$. The eigenvalues are non-negative.

A matrix is said to be **nilpotent** if $\mathbf{A}^p = \mathbf{0}$ for some integer p. It is said to be **idempotent** if $\mathbf{A}^2 = \mathbf{A}$.

It is **possible to diagonalize** if there exists a similarity transform $\mathbf{C}$ so that $\mathbf{C}^{-1}\mathbf{A}\mathbf{C}$ is diagonal and this happens if and only if $\mathbf{A}$ has n linearly independent eigenvectors.

A matrix is **defective** if it has less than n linearly independent eigenvectors.

B.5 Special matrices

A **zero matrix** has all components equal to zero. A **one matrix** has all components equal to one. An **identity matrix** has ones in the main diagonal, and all the other elements are zero. A **random matrix** has random elements.

A **Givens rotation** is a matrix which has the form:

$$
\begin{bmatrix}
1 & & & & \\
 & \ddots & & & \\
 & & \cos\theta & \sin\theta & \\
 & & & \ddots & \\
 & & -\sin\theta & \cos\theta & \\
 & & & & \ddots \\
 & & & & & 1
\end{bmatrix}
$$

that is it differs from the identity matrix in exactly four entries, $(i,i),(i,j),(j,i)$, and (j,j). Givens rotations are orthogonal.

Householder reflections are matrices defined by $\mathbf{I}-2\mathbf{w}\mathbf{w}^H$ where $\mathbf{w}^H\mathbf{w} = 1$. These matrices are unitary and Hermitian.

Gauss transforms have the form

where x denotes non-zero elements. They differ from the identity matrix in one column below the diagonal.

A **permutation matrix** has the same columns as the identity matrix, but in a different order. There is exactly one unit entry in each row and in each column.

B.6 Vector and matrix norms

We previously introduced the **Euclidean norm** or **two-norm** for vectors **x**.

$$\|\mathbf{x}\|_2 = \sqrt{\sum_{i=1}^{n} |x_i|^2} = \sqrt{\mathbf{x}^H \mathbf{x}}$$

It is also useful to introduce the **maximum norm**:

$$\|\mathbf{x}\|_\infty = \max_{1 \le i \le n} |x_i|$$

another norm is the **one-norm**:

$$\|\mathbf{x}\|_1 = \sum_{i=1}^{n} |x_i|$$

All these are special cases of the more general **p-norms**:

$$\|\mathbf{x}\|_p = \left(\sum_{i=1}^{n} |x_i|^p \right)^{1/p}$$

Norms are used to measure the size or length of vectors.

Matrix norms are defined by:

$$\|\mathbf{A}\| = \max_{\mathbf{x} \ne o} \frac{\|\mathbf{A}\mathbf{x}\|}{\|\mathbf{x}\|} = \max_{\|\mathbf{x}\| = 1} \|\mathbf{A}\mathbf{x}\|$$

and the following can de derived:

- the **one-norm** of **A**, that is, the maximum of the absolute values of the column sums,

$$\|\mathbf{A}\|_1 = \max_{1 \le j \le n} \sum_{i=1}^{n} |a_{ij}|$$

- the **two-norm** or **spectral norm** of **A**:

$$\|A\|_2 = \sqrt{\rho(A^H A)}$$

- and the **maximum norm** of **A**, that is, the maximum of the absolute values of the row sums,

$$\|A\|_\infty = \max_{1 \le i \le m} \sum_{j=1}^{n} |a_{ij}|$$

There is another common matrix norm, the **Frobenius norm** $\|A\|_F$ defined by:

$$\|A\|_F^2 = \sum_{i=1}^{m} \sum_{j=1}^{n} |a_{ij}|^2$$

The Frobenius norm cannot de defined by a vector norm, like the three other matrix norms.

The following inequalities hold:

1. $\rho(A) \le \|A\|$ for every matrix **A** and for all norms

2. $\rho(A) = \|A\|_2$ if **A** is Hermitian

3. $\|A\|_2 = 1$ if **A** is unitary

By matrix norms the sensitivity for perturbations in matrices can be estimated and measured.

The **condition number** for linear systems of equations **A x = b** is defined by:

$$cond(A) = \|A\| \cdot \|A^{-1}\|$$

and we have the relation:

$$\frac{\|\Delta x\|}{\|x\|} \le cond(A) \frac{\|\Delta b\|}{\|b\|}$$

where Δb is the perturbation in the right-hand side **b** and Δx the corresponding perturbation in the solution vector **x**. Notice that both vector and matrix norms occur in the relation. A similar relation exists for perturbations in **A**.

B.7 Matrix factorizations

1. **LU factorization** or **LU decomposition**
   P A = L U where **P** is a permutation matrix, **L** a lower triangular matrix with ones on the diagonal and **U** an upper triangular matrix.

2. **Cholesky factorization**
    A symmetric and positive definite matrix $\mathbf{A}$ can be factorized as $\mathbf{A} = \mathbf{G}\ \mathbf{G}^T$ where $\mathbf{G}$ is lower triangular.

3. **QR factorization**
    $\mathbf{A} = \mathbf{Q}\,\mathbf{R}$, where $\mathbf{A}$ is an $m \times n$ matrix, $\mathbf{Q}$ an orthogonal $m \times m$ matrix and $\mathbf{R}$ is upper triangular.

4. Suppose $\mathbf{A}$ has n linearly independent eigenvectors. Then a matrix $\mathbf{C}$ exists such that $\mathbf{C}^{-1}\ \mathbf{A}\ \mathbf{C} = \mathbf{D}$ is diagonal, that is $\mathbf{A} = \mathbf{C}\ \mathbf{D}\ \mathbf{C}^{-1}$. A sufficient condition is that all the eigenvalues are different.

5. **Schur decomposition**
    There exists a unitary matrix $\mathbf{U}$ for every matrix $\mathbf{A}$ so that $\mathbf{U}^H \mathbf{A}\ \mathbf{U} = \mathbf{T}$ is upper triangular, that is $\mathbf{A} = \mathbf{U}\ \mathbf{T}\ \mathbf{U}^H$.

6. For a Hermitian matrix $\mathbf{A}$ there exists a unitary matrix $\mathbf{U}$ so that $\mathbf{U}^H \mathbf{A}\ \mathbf{U} = \mathbf{D}$ diagonal, that is $\mathbf{A} = \mathbf{U}\ \mathbf{D}\ \mathbf{U}^H$.

7. **Murnaghan–Wintners theorem**
    For all real $\mathbf{A}$, there is a real orthogonal matrix $\mathbf{U}$ so that $\mathbf{U}^T \mathbf{A}\ \mathbf{U} = \mathbf{B}$ is a real block triangular matrix, where the diagonal blocks are either of size 2×2 or 1×1. Every block of order two represents a complex conjugate pair of eigenvalues.

8. **Jordan normal form**
    For every square matrix $\mathbf{A}$, there exists a non-singular matrix $\mathbf{S}$ such that $\mathbf{S}^{-1} \mathbf{A}\ \mathbf{S} = \mathbf{J}$, where $\mathbf{J}$ is a block diagonal matrix of the form:

$$
J = \begin{bmatrix} J_1 & & & \\ & J_2 & & \\ & & \ddots & \\ & & & J_p \end{bmatrix}
\qquad
J_k = \begin{bmatrix} \lambda_k & 1 & & \\ & \ddots & \ddots & \\ & & & 1 \\ & & & \lambda_k \end{bmatrix}
$$

If the block $\mathbf{J}_k$ is of order 1 it holds that $\mathbf{J}_k = (\lambda_k)$. One eigenvalue corresponds to every diagonal block, also called a **Jordan box**. The matrix $\mathbf{A}$ has p linearly independent eigenvectors, if the number of Jordan boxes is p.

9. **Singular value decomposition**
    Every $m \times n$ matrix $\mathbf{A}$ can be factorized by the two unitary matrices $\mathbf{U}$ and $\mathbf{V}$ such that $\mathbf{U}^T \mathbf{A}\ \mathbf{V} = \mathbf{D}$ is a diagonal $m \times n$ matrix. Here, $\mathbf{U}$ is an $m \times m$ matrix, $\mathbf{V}$ an $n \times n$ matrix, and $\mathbf{D}$ has the diagonal elements σ_k. These are ordered so that $\sigma_1 \geq \sigma_2 \geq \ldots \geq \sigma_p \geq 0$ where $p \leq min(m, n)$. All other σ_k, if any, are zero. The numbers σ_k are called **singular values** of $\mathbf{A}$.
    Thus $\mathbf{A} = \mathbf{U}\ \mathbf{D}\ \mathbf{V}^T$.

The singular values can be used to define the **pseudoinverse** $\mathbf{D}^+$ of $\mathbf{D}$. This is illustrated for the case $m \geq n$;

$$\mathbf{D} = \begin{bmatrix} \begin{matrix} \sigma_1 & & \\ & \ddots & \\ & & \sigma_p \end{matrix} & 0 \\ \hline 0 & 0 \end{bmatrix} \qquad \mathbf{D}^+ = \begin{bmatrix} \begin{matrix} \sigma_1 & & \\ & \sigma_p^{-1} & \\ \end{matrix} & 0 \\ \hline 0 & 0 \end{bmatrix}$$

but is defined in the same way if $m \leq n$. If $\mathbf{D}$ is of size $m \times n$, then $\mathbf{D}^+$ is of size $n \times m$. The pseudo-inverse $\mathbf{A}^+$ of $\mathbf{A}$ is also of size $n \times m$ and is defined by the singular value decomposition as $\mathbf{A}^+ = \mathbf{V} \mathbf{D}^+ \mathbf{U}^T$.

Appendix C
MATLAB toolboxes and SIMULINK

This information is given by the MathWorks, Inc., but edited to a form similar with the rest of The MATLAB Handbook.

MATLAB features a family of application-specific products, toolboxes, which build on the computational and graphical capabilities of MATLAB. These collections of M-files are implemented in the high-level MATLAB language in order to make it possible for the user to modify the source code for functions, and also to add new ones. One can easily combine the techniques in different toolboxes to design custom solutions for specific problems.

The toolboxes which are currently commercially available by The MathWorks, Inc. are listed and briefly described in Table C.1. The lists of toolboxes are not static, since in general, several new toolboxes are created every year.

The Student Edition of MATLAB, version 4, contains two toolboxes that are especially designed for this restricted version of MATLAB: the Signals and Systems Toolbox and the Symbolic Math Toolbox. These toolboxes contain subsets of the commercially available Signal Processing Toolbox, Control System Toolbox, and Symbolic Math Toolbox, listed in Table C.1. Note that the Student Edition of MATLAB is not designed for use with the professional toolboxes. A description of the Student Edition of MATLAB can be found in Appendix D.

Furthermore, there exists a powerful, visual, interactive environment, called SIMULINK, for simulating non-linear dynamic systems. SIMULINK provides a graphical user interface for construction of block diagram models of dynamic systems. One may create linear, non-linear, discrete-time, continuous, and hybrid models in a very simple way, since SIMULINK takes full advantage of windowing technology. By the use of click-and-drag operations and mouse interactions, components from a block library may be connected together. It is possible to change parameters during a simulation to do "what if" analysis. SIMULINK is fully integrated with MATLAB, and together with MATLAB and the MATLAB toolboxes it allows you to move among the various stages of modeling, design, analysis, and simulation.

It is possible to add extensions to SIMULINK. The environment includes a family of optional tools that, for example, enhance simulation speed, as shown in Table C.2. The toolboxes connected with SIMULINK are called blocksets, which extend the block library with specialized design and analysis capabilities, see Table C.3.

There is also a student version of SIMULINK for use with the Student Edition of MATLAB, called the Student Edition of SIMULINK.

For more information about the toolboxes and SIMULINK, use the MATLAB command `expo`, or take a look at The MathWorks Inc. World Wide Web Home Page:

http://www.mathworks.com

Furthermore, The MathWorks, Inc. maintains an archive on the anonymous FTP server **ftp.mathworks.com**. This site contains collections of M-files associated with books, user-contributed and MathWorks, Inc.-contributed software and documentation.

Other software commercially available by the MathWorks, Inc. are the MATLAB compiler and the C Math Library.

Table C.1 MATLAB toolboxes.

μ-*Analysis and Synthesis*	operates with MATLAB and the Signal Processing Toolbox, to be used for analysis and design of robust, linear control systems.
Chemometrics	for quantitative and qualitative analysis of data based on chemometric methods and techniques.
Control System	for automatic control system design and analysis. Functions from this toolbox are contained in the Signals and Systems Toolbox included with the Student Edition of MATLAB.
Extended Symbolic Math	for extended symbolic mathematics. Adds support for programming in Maple V and gives access to all Maple V libraries. Includes the Symbolic Math Toolbox.
Financial	for financial and quantitative analysis.
Frequency Domain System Identification	for accurate modeling of linear systems with or without delay based on frequency domain data.
Fuzzy Logic	for fuzzy logic modeling for development of intelligently-controlled products and processes. Is especially designed to work with SIMULINK.
Higher-Order Spectral Analysis	for advanced signal processing with higher order spectra.
Image Processing	operates with MATLAB and the Signal Processing Toolbox, to be used for advanced manipulation and analysis of images and two-dimensional signals.
LMI Control	for fast and efficient solution of linear matrix inequalities (LMIs).

Table C.1   MATLAB toolboxes. (continued)

MMLE3 Identification	operates with MATLAB and the Control System Toolbox, to be used for the estimation of continuous-time state-space models from observed input-output data.
Model Predictive Control	for control system design and applications involving contstraints on the manipulated and/or controlled variables.
NAG Foundation	provides interactive access to the mathematical and statistical routines in the NAG Foundation Library.
Neural Network	for design, implementation, and simulation of many kinds of neural networks and adaptive systems. Includes additional blocks to SIMULINK's extensive block library.
Non-linear Control Design (NCD)	operates with MATLAB and SIMULINK to be used for time-domain-based control design. Includes additional blocks to SIMULINK's extensive block library.
Optimization	for optimization of linear and nonlinear functions.
Partial Differential Equation (PDE)	for the study and solution of partial differential equations in time and two space dimensions, using the finite element method.
Quantitative Feedback Theory (QFT)	operates with MATLAB and the Control System Toolbox, to be used for practical design of robust feedback systems using QFT methods.
Robust Control	operates with MATLAB and the Control System Toolbox, to be used for advanced, robust, multivariable feedback control system design.
Signal Processing	for algorithm development, digital signal processing and time-series analysis. Functions from this toolbox are contained in the Signals and Systems Toolbox included with the Student Edition of MATLAB.
Spline	for the construction and use of piecewise polynomial functions, curve fitting, and approximation of functions.
Statistics	for statistical data analysis, modeling, and Monte Carlo simulation. Also provides GUI (graphical user interface) tools for fundamental concepts in statistics and probability, and building blocks for your own creation of statistical tools.

Table C.1 MATLAB toolboxes. (continued)

Symbolic Math	for symbolic mathematics, equation solving, variable-precision arithmetic, and special mathematical functions. The software is based on Maple V. An educational version is included in the Student Edition of MATLAB.
System Identification	for advanced signal processing and modelling, such as parametric modeling, system identification, and time-series analysis. Signal Processing Toolbox recommended.

Table C.2 Optional tools for SIMULINK.

SIMULINK Accelerator	for accelerated SIMULINK simulations. The accelerated model still provides full interactive access, for example, change of simulation parameters.
SIMULINK Real-Time Workshop	for automatic generation of C code for real-time implementation directly from SIMULINK block diagrams.

Table C.3 SIMULINK Blocksets.

DSP Blockset	operates with MATLAB, SIMULINK, and the Signal Processing Toolbox, to be used for extension of the use of SIMULINK and Real-Time Workshop to digital design.
Fixed-Point Blocksets	for extension of the SIMULINK block library to fixed-point applications, for example, choice of 8-, 16-, or 32-bit fixed-point results.

In this handbook some pictures have been generated by the PDE toolbox. See Figures 1.13 and 1.14 in Chapter 1.

Descriptions and examples of the educational version of the Symbolic Math toolbox are given in Appendix D.

D

Appendix D
The Student Edition of MATLAB, Version 4

This appendix is a brief summary of the Student Edition of MATLAB. The focus is on the Symbolic Math Toolbox, which is one of the two toolboxes included in this software package.

D.1 About the Student Edition

The Student Edition is in some respects a restricted version of the professional version of MATLAB 4.2, but it is also more extensive since it contains two toolboxes not included in the standard professional version.

The matrix size is limited to 8192 elements, and the number of rows and columns may not simultaneously be more than 32.

Both the Symbolic Math Toolbox and the Signals and Systems Toolbox are included. These contain subsets of the commercially available toolboxes (see Appendix C). No professional toolboxes can be used with the Student Edition of MATLAB, and the dynamical links to FORTRAN or C, that is the MEX-files described in Chapter 15, are not available.

The Student Version of MATLAB is only available on Macintosh or Windows personal computers.

The final major difference between the professional and student version of MATLAB is in the licensing agreements and the distribution of the program. Individual copies are sold to students through Prentice-Hall.

The Symbolic Math Toolbox contains functionality from the commercial software package Maple V. However, readers familiar with Maple will notice that the commands, as well as the syntax, are different from Maple. This toolbox is a useful complement to the numeric capabilities of MATLAB, and is especially useful to students in mathematical and engineering courses.

Section D.2 gives a presentation of the basic commands in the Symbolic Math Toolbox, together with a few examples. The approach is similar to the main part of the handbook. To get a full list of the commands available in the Symbolic Math Toolbox type `help toolbox\symbolic` at the MATLAB prompter. Section D.3 is a very brief overview of the Signals and Systems Toolbox, a toolbox very useful for signal processing and control theory.

D.2 The Symbolic Math Toolbox

A symbolic expression is defined by a string enclosed by quotation marks, for example,

```
fexpr = 'sqrt(5)'
```
fexpr =

sqrt(5)

```
gexpr = '2*sin(x)*cos(x)'
```
gexpr =

2*sin(x)*cos(x)

As in standard MATLAB the variables are matrices, but in this appendix we mainly consider the case of scalar symbolic expressions.

A symbolic expression can contain several variables, but normally only one of them can be the independent or free variable of the expression. This is called the **symbolic variable** and the default value is `'x'`. In fact, `'x'` is the symbolic variable also in cases where there is no variable in the expression, for example, `'sqrt(pi^2*13)'`. There are strict rules that determine which variable is the symbolic variable, and it can always be found by the command `symvar`. The user can explicitly specify the symbolic variable in several commands, thus overriding these rules.

The commands `numeric` and `eval` can be used to convert a symbolic expression to a numeric.

Command 156	NUMERIC EVALUATION OF SYMBOLIC EXPRESSIONS
`numeric(fexpr)`	evaluates the symbolic constant **fexpr**, to its numeric value. A symbolic constant is an expression with no variables.
`numeric`	evaluates the previous symbolic constant, which does not need to be *ans*, to its numeric value.
`eval(fexpr)`	evaluates the symbolic expression **fexpr**. All variables must have been assigned a value. Note that this is a standard MATLAB command, see Section 5.4.

■ **Example D.1**

```
x = numeric('pi')
```
x =

3.1416

```
y = eval('x^2+1')
```
y =

10.8696   ■

There are several commands for algebraic manipulations such as expanding and simplifying expressions.

Command 157	ALGEBRAIC MANIPULATIONS
`expand(fexpr)`	expands **fexpr** considering polynomial, trigonometric and other formulas. If **fexpr** represents a matrix, each element is expanded.
`simplify(fexpr)`	simplifies the expression using the rules in Maple.
`simple(fexpr)`	simplifies the expression **fexpr** to shortest form. This command also shows the different alternatives it is testing, therefore the printout is lengthy and `simplify` is to recommend.
`[fnew,descstr] = simple(fexpr)`	**fnew** is the expression **fexpr** simplified, and **descrstr** is a string describing the manipulations involved in the simplification.
`subs(fexpr,new,old)`	substitutes all occurrences of the string **old** with the string **new** in **fexpr**.

■ **Example D.2**

With the definitions

```
f = '(x-1) * (x+1)';
g = 'cos(x)^2-sin(x)^2';
h = '(x^2-1)/(x+1)-(x-1)';
```

the commands `expand`, `simplify` and `simple` give:

```
expf = expand(f)
```
expf =

x^2-1

```
[new,descr] = simple(g)
```

new =

cos(2*x)

descr =

combine(trig)

```
simph = simplify(h)
```

simph =

0

```
subsh = subs(h,'t','x')
```

subsh =

(t^2−1)/(t+1)−t+1   ■

As a complement to these commands there is the command `pretty` to tidy up the output, and the command `latex` to simplify transformation to LATEX documents.

Command 158   FORMATTED OUTPUT

`pretty(fexpr)`	tries to display the expression in **fexpr** as a standard mathematical expression.
`pretty(fexpr,n)`	the same as above, but now using *n* positions in each line, instead of the default value *79*.
`latex(fexpr)`	gives the LATEX representation of **fexpr** to be used in scientific reports, and so on.
`latex(fexpr,filestr)`	prints the LATEX representation of **fexpr** in the file *filestr.*

Notice that although the most common situation is that `pretty` is used with symbolic expressions, it is also possible to use `pretty` with numeric values or expressions.

■ **Example D.3**

```
pretty(27/54)
```
                    1/2

```
pretty('cos(x)^2-sin(x)^2')
```
                    2   2
         cos(x) − sin(x)

```
pretty('sin(x)/x')
```

$$\frac{sin(x)}{x}$$

∎

For polynomials and rational functions there are some special commands. Of course, the commands `expand`, `simplify`, `simple`, and `pretty` can also be used.

Command 159   **POLYNOMIALS AND RATIONAL FUNCTIONS**

`factor(pexpr)`	gives a factorization of the polynomial **pexpr**.
`factor(A)`	gives the prime number factorizations of the elements of **A**.
`collect(pexpr)`	collects the coefficients for each degree of the symbolic variables in **pexpr**.
`collect(pexpr,'s')`	does the same as above but now for the symbolic variable `'s'`.
`horner(pstr)`	transforms the polynomial **pexpr** to a nested representation, also named Horner representation.
`sym2poly(p)`	gives the coefficients of the polynomial as a vector (see Section 10.1). The first element is leading element.
`poly2sym(c)`	gives a symbolic polynomial from a coefficient vector, whose first element is taken as the leading coefficient.
`poly2sym(c,'s')`	gives the same as above, but in the symbolic variable `'s'`.
`[numexpr,denexpr]` `= numden(fexpr)`	returns an expression with a numerator **numexpr** and a denominator **denexpr**, approximating **fexpr**. The numerator and the denominator are relatively prime. If **fexpr** is a numeric expression, **numexpr** and **denexpr** are integers.

∎ **Example D.4**

```
factors = factor('x^2-7*x+12')
```

factors =

(x–3)*(x–4)

However, factorization in case of non-real factors cannot be obtained in this way:

```
nofact = factor('x^2+1')
```
nofact =
x^2+1

```
symb = poly2sym([1 2 −3 4])
```
symb =
*x^3+2*x^2−3*x+4*

```
horn = horner(symb)
```
horn =
*4+(−3+(2+x)*x)*x*

```
[n,d] = numden(0.76)
```
n =
19
d =
25

```
[nexpr,dexpr] = numden('x^2/(x*y)')
```
nexpr =
x
dexpr =
y   ■

As in the professional version, functions can be plotted with the standard MATLAB plot commands (see Section 13.1). However, the Symbolic Math Toolbox adds an easy-to-use plot command.

Command 160   PLOTTING IN TWO DIMENSIONS

`ezplot(fexpr)`	plots the function **fexpr** of the symbolic variable over the interval $-2\pi \leq x \leq 2\pi$.
`ezplot(fexpr,[xmin, xmax])`	plots the function **fexpr** over the interval $xmin \leq x \leq xmax$.

■ **Example D.5**

```
ezplot('x^2−5*x')
```

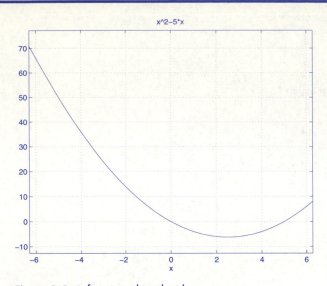

Figure D.1 A function plotted with `ezplot`.

Note that labels and a grid are included automatically by this command. ■

Symbolic expressions can be operated on in many ways. Most of these contain the prefix `sym`, as in symbolic expression.

Command 161   **BASIC SYMBOLIC OPERATIONS**

`symvar(fexpr)`	gives the symbolic variable in **fexpr**.
`symadd(fexpr,gexpr)`	adds the expressions **fexpr** and **gexpr**.
`symsub(fexpr,gexpr)`	subtracts the expressions **fexpr** and **gexpr**.

Command 161	**BASIC SYMBOLIC OPERATIONS** (continued)
`symmul(fexpr,gexpr)`	multiplies the expressions **fexpr** and **gexpr**.
`symdiv(fexpr,gexpr)`	divides the expressions **fexpr** and **gexpr**.
`sympow(fexpr,gexpr)`	computes the **gexpr** power of **fexpr**.
`symop(str1,str2,...)`	generates a new expression from **str1, str2** ...., by concatenation and performs the operations and minor simplifications.
`symsum(fexpr,min,max)`	gives the symbolic sum of the terms where the symbolic variable varies between *min* and *max*.

■ **Example D.6**

```
variable = symvar('x^2-4*x-4+4*y')
```

variable =

x

```
sumstr = symadd('x^2+4','x-3')
```

sumstr =

x^2+x+1

```
divstr = symdiv('x^2-1','x+1')
```

(x^2−1)/(x+1)

```
simplify(divstr)
```

x−1

The command `symop` can be used to perform operations of up to 16 different symbolic expressions. The actual operations are also of the form of a string:

```
expr = symop('a+b+c','+','x-c','+','2*b')
```

expr =

*a+3*b+x*

The Symbolic Math Toolbox can compute derivatives and integrals symbolically.

Command 162	DERIVATIVES AND INTEGRALS

`diff(fexpr)`	computes the first derivative symbolically of **fexpr** with respect to the symbolic variable.
`diff(fexpr,'s')`	does the same as above, but with respect to the variable `'s'`.
`diff(fexpr,n)`	computes the *n*th derivative of **fexpr** with respect to the symbolic variable.
`int(fexpr)`	computes the indefinite integral or anti-derivative of **fexpr** with respect to the symbolic variable.
`int(fexpr,'s')`	does the same as above but with respect to the variable `'s'`.
`int(fexpr,a,b)`	computes the definite integral, that is, a numeric value of **fexpr** over the interval [*a,b*].

■ Example D.7

(a) The following definitions

```
f = '(x-1)*(x+1)';

g = 'cos(x)^2-sin(x)^2';

h = '(x^2-1)/(x+1)-(x-1)';
```

differentiated give

```
fprime = diff(f), fsecond = diff(f,2)
```

   fprime =

   2*x

   fsecond =

   2

```
gprime = diff(g)
```

   gprime =

   −4*cos(x)*sin(x)

```
hprime = diff(h)
```

   hprime =

   2*x/(x+1)−(x^2−1)/(x+1)^2−1

```
shprime = simplify(hprim)
```

shprime =

0

(b) The indefinite integral of **f**

```
finteg = int(f)
```

finteg =

1/3*x^3−x

The integral of **f** in the interval [2,4]

```
finteginterval = int(f,2,4)
```

finteginterval =

50/3

```
tinteg = int('t*w^2−t^4','t')
```

tinteg =

1/2*t^2*w^2−1/5*t^5   ■

Note that the command `diff` used on numeric values is a standard MATLAB command (see Section 6.2).

We give some commands that can be used on functions.

| Command 163 | COMMANDS ON FUNCTIONS |

`taylor(fexpr)`	gives the six first terms in the Taylor expansion of the symbolic expression **fexpr** around $x = 0$.
`taylor(fexpr,n)`	gives the n first terms in the Taylor expansion of the symbolic expression **fexpr** around $x = 0$.
`finverse(fexpr)`	gives the inverse of the function **fexpr.**
`compose(fexpr,gexpr)`	gives the function **fexpr(gexpr(x)).**

■ **Example D.8**

(a) Define the expression `f = 'exp(−x^2)'`. The command `g = taylor(f)` results in

g =

1−1*x^2+1/2*x^4+O(x^6)

where O means ordo, that is, the error of term is of order x^6 for small values of x.

(b) Let us now graphically study some Taylor expansions of the function $f(x)=sin(x)$, using a different number of terms. Since the resulting functions contain the ordo term, for example, `O(x^6)`, we have to erase these characters in the function strings in order to be able to plot the functions.

```
f = 'sin(x)';
g2 = taylor(f,2); g2 = g2(1:length(g2)-7);
g5 = taylor(f,5); g5 = g5(1:length(g5)-7);
g8 = taylor(f,8); g8 = g8(1:length(g8)-7);

clf;
ezplot(f); hold on;
ezplot(g2); ezplot(g5); ezplot(g8);
title('Taylor expansion of sin(x): 2, 5, 8 terms')
grid
```

To obtain a more pedagogical figure with different marks representing different curves, the standard MATLAB commands can be used, for instance `plot`, `fplot` (see Section 13.1), `eval` (see Section 5.4), `feval` (see Section 12.4).

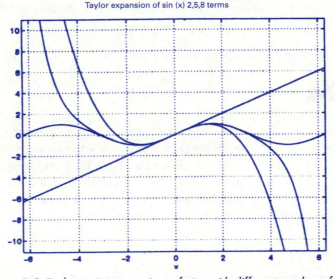

Figure D.2 Taylor series expansions of *sine* with different number of terms.

(c) If **f** is defined as `f='sin(x)'` the command `finv = finverse(f)` returns *finv =*

asin(x)

If the command is performed on a function without a unique inverse function a warning is given. If `g = 'x^2'` then

`ginv = finverse(g)` results in

Warning: finverse(x^2) is not unique

ginv =

x^(1/2)   ■

There is an interactive tool for manipulating functions of a single variable named `funtool`. It consists of three windows, two for displaying two functions and one window with buttons to change the functions. For instance, there are buttons to symbolically differentiate the functions, to get the inverse of the functions and to multiply the two functions with each other. If no functions **f** and **g** are defined before entering `funtool` the default functions $f = x$ and $g = 1$ are used.

Command 164	AN INTERACTIVE CALCULATOR FOR SYMBOLIC TREATMENT OF FUNCTIONS

`funtool`	starts an interactive calculator that treats functions of a single variable. Two functions, **f** and **g**, are displayed and a third window containing press buttons can manipulate these functions. Try the command `help funtool` for further information.

Non-linear equations can be solved by the command `solve`.

Command 165	NON-LINEAR EQUATIONS

`solve(fexpr)`	tries to solve the non-linear equation **fexpr** = *0*.
`solve(fexpr,'s')`	does the same as above, but in the variable `'s'`.
`solve(f1,f2)`	solves the system **f1** = **f2** = *0* where **f1** and **f2** represent functions of two variables.

Other versions of the command `solve` are also available, write `help solve` for more information.

■ **Example D.9**

(a) Define the function `fexpr = 'x^5−1'`. To find the *5* roots of $x^5−1=0$ we write

`frootssymb = solve(fexpr)` and get the result

frootssymb =

[1]

[1/4*5^(1/2)−1/4+1/4*i*2^(1/2)*(5+5^(1/2))^(1/2)]

[−1/4*5^(1/2)−1/4−1/4*i*2^(1/2)*(−5+5^(1/2))^(1/2)]

[−1/4*5^(1/2)−1/4+1/4*i*2^(1/2)*(−5+5^(1/2))^(1/2)]

[1/4*5^(1/2)−1/4−1/4*i*2^(1/2)*(5+5^(1/2))^(1/2)]

The MATLAB command to find zeroes of a polynomial is `roots`, see Section 10.1, and the command to find the roots of the polynomial $x^5−1$ is
`frootsnum = roots([1 0 0 0 0 −1])`

frootsnum =

   −0.8090 + 0.5878i

   −0.8090 − 0.5878i

    0.3090 + 0.9511i

    0.3090 − 0.9511i

    1.0000

(b) Let us find the solution of *2*x*sin(x)−1/exp(x)+x=0*. First we define the function.

`fexpr = '2*x*sin(x)−1/exp(x)+x'`

fexpr =

2*x*sin(x)−1/exp(x)+x

To see what the function looks like we write

`ezplot(fexpr)`

The result is Figure D.3.

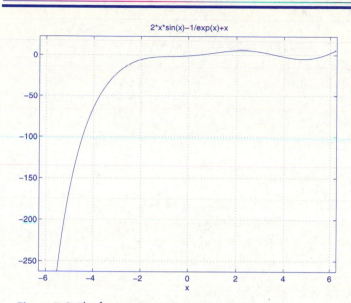

Figure D.3 The function *2*x*sin(x)–1/exp(x)+x.*

The function clearly has several zeroes. If we write `solve(fexpr)` the answer is one of them.

> *ans =*
>
> *5.759902388820633*

In this case we get a numeric value since the zeroes cannot be represented by formulas. The MATLAB command `fzero` (see Section 10.2) also finds a numeric value for a zero of a function but then the function must be defined in an M-file. ∎

To solve ordinary differential equations, the command `dsolve` can be used. Note that solutions of ordinary differential equations exist as a formula in special cases only. Numeric solutions can always be obtained in MATLAB by the commands `ode23` and `ode45`, see Section 11.2, if the initial values are given.

| Command 166 | ORDINARY DIFFERENTIAL EQUATIONS |

| `dsolve('ode')` | gives the solution of the ordinary differential equation specified. More general versions of the command are included in the toolbox. Write `help` `dsolve` for more information. |

■ **Example D.10**

(a) Suppose that we want to find the solution of $y''(x) = y$, where $y''(x)$ is

$\dfrac{d^2y}{dx^2}$ and with the initial conditions $y(0) = 12$ and $y'(0) = 2$.

Then we simply write `y = dsolve('D2y=y','y(0)=12','Dy(0)=2')` and get the result

y=

7*exp(x)+5*exp(−x)

If we do not specify the initial conditions and only write `y = dsolve('D2y=y')` the result is

y =

C1*exp(x)+C2*exp(−x)

The *C1* and *C2* stand for arbitrary constants that needs initial conditions to be specified.

(b) It is also possible to solve two first order equations with `dsolve`. The system

$$\begin{cases} x' = y \\ y' = -x \end{cases}$$

is solved with

`[x,y] = dsolve('Dx=y','Dy=-x')`

x =

C1*sin(t)−C2*cos(t)

y =

C2*sin(t)+C1*cos(t)

The constants *C1* and *C2* need initial conditions to be defined.   ■

The Symbolic Math Toolbox can also handle vectors and matrices symbolically. To create a symbolic matrix the command `sym` is used.

Command 167   SYMBOLIC OPERATIONS ON MATRICES, PART 1

`sym('[...]')`	returns a symbolic matrix defined by the quoted matrix.
`symadd, symsub, symmul`	adds, subtracts and multiplies symbolic matrices.

■ Example D.11

To create symbolic matrices of the type

$$\mathbf{A} = \begin{bmatrix} a & b \\ c & d \end{bmatrix} \qquad \mathbf{B} = \begin{bmatrix} 1 & 3 \\ d & a \end{bmatrix}$$

we write `A = sym('[a b; c d]'), B = sym('[1 3; d a]')`

   A =

   [a,b]

   [c,d]

   B =

   [1,3]

   [d,a]

These symbolic matrices can be added, subtracted and multiplied with each other. For instance `C = symmul(A,B)` gives

   C =

   [a+b*d, 3*a+b*a]

   [c+d^2, 3*c+d*a]

The command `D = symsub(A,B)` results in

   D =

   [b*d, 3*a+b*a−b]

   [d^2, 3*c+d*a−d]

Then there are a number of commands for matrix operations on symbolic matrices.

Command 168	SYMBOLIC OPERATIONS ON MATRICES, PART 2
`determ(A)`	computes the determinant of **A** symbolically. The matrix **A** can be symbolic or numeric.
`inverse(A)`	computes the inverse of **A** symbolically. The matrix **A** can be symbolic or numeric.
`linsolve(A,b)`	computes the solution of **Ax** = **b** in symbolic form. The right-hand side **b** is either a vector or a matrix. Both **A** and **b** can be numeric or symbolic.
`eigensys(A)`	computes the eigenvalues of **A** in symbolic form. The matrix **A** can be symbolic or numeric.
`[U,D] = eigensys(A)`	computes the eigenpairs of **A** in symbolic form and stores the eigenvectors as columns of **U** and the eigenvalues in the diagonal of **D**. The matrix **A** can be symbolic or numeric.
`jordan(A)`	computes the Jordan normal form of the matrix **A**. The components of the matrix must be known exactly, as an integer or a rational number.

■ **Example D.12**

(a) Let the rotation matrix **R** be defined as

$$\mathbf{R} = \begin{bmatrix} 1 & 0 & 0 \\ 0 & cos(th) & sin(th) \\ 0 & -sin(th) & cos(th) \end{bmatrix}$$

It is created with
`R = sym('[1 0 0; 0 cos(th) sin(th); 0 -sin(th) cos(th)]').`

R =

[1,   0,   0]
[0, cos(th),   sin(th)]
[0, -sin(th), cos(th)]

To find the inverse of this matrix we write `rotinverse = inverse(R)` which results in

rotinverse =

[1,   0,   0]

[0, cos(th)/(cos(th)^2+sin(th)^2), −sin(th)/(cos(th)^2+sin(th)^2)]

[0, sin(th)/(cos(th)^2+sin(th)^2), cos(th)/(cos(th)^2+sin(th)^2)]

We simplify the matrix by writing `simplify(rotinverse)`

ans =

[1,   0,   0]

[0, cos(th), −sin(th)]

[0, sin(th), cos(th)]

The eigenvalues of **R** are computed with `eigR = eigensys(R)`

eigR =

[1]

[cos(th)+1/2(−4*sin(th)^2)^(1/2)]*

[cos(th)−1/2(−4*sin(th)^2)^(1/2)]*

The command `simple(eigR)` helps us to find the shortest form of the expression. This command is a bit extensive so we only show the result

ans =

[1]

*[exp(i*th)]*

*[1/exp(i*th)]*

(b) Let the following symbolic matrix and vector be defined.

$$A = \begin{bmatrix} 1 & 1 \\ a & 1 \end{bmatrix} \qquad b = \begin{bmatrix} 2 \\ 1 \end{bmatrix}$$

The command `x = linsolve(A,b)` gives

x =

[−1/(a−1)]

*[(2*a−1)/(a−1)]*

The Symboblic Math Toolbox provides the option of variable accuracy in the computations. This can for instance be useful when studying error propagation in a computational process. The commands in question are `digits` and `vpa`.

Command 169	ACCURACY IN SYMBOLIC MATH COMPUTATIONS

`digits(n)`	makes the computations performed with *n* significant decimals. The command by itself gives current setting.
`vpa(A,n)`	computes the elements of A in variable precision defined by *n*. Without the optional *n* the current setting of digits is used for accuracy.

■ **Example D.13**

(a) Define the variable `a = 1 + 1E - 15`

> *a =*
>
> *1.0000*

If we give the command `digits` by itself we see that the default setting is *16*.

> *Digits = 16*

Note that what MATLAB displays does not depend on this variable. The command `longa = vpa(a)` that uses `Digits` gives

> *longa =*
>
> *1.000000000000001*

If we write `shorta = vpa(a,3)` or set `digits(3)` and then do `shorta = vpa(a)` the result is

> *shorta =*
>
> *1.00*

With these commands you can also compute operations with higher accuracy than MATLAB by itself allows. If we compute `1 + 1E - 23` in MATLAB the result is

> *ans =*
>
> *1.*

But if we use the Symoblic Math Toolbox for the same computation by using the command `vpa('1 + 1E-23',24)` the result is

ans =

1.00000000000000000000001

The rounding is avoided! ■

D.3 The Signals and Systems Toolbox

This toolbox is a subset of the commercial Signal Processing Toolbox and Control System Toolbox and is intended for teaching and engineering in the fields of control theory and signal processing. It can treat both continuous and discrete cases.

There are different commands and functions for representation of systems. The functions are represented in MATLAB by vectors or matrices.

There are also several filter functions and transformations and functions for Fast Fourier Transforms. Some of these are described in Chapter 10.

It is beyond the scope of this handbook to treat this toolbox. For the interested reader the `help` command or the manuals of the Student Edition and the commercial toolboxes can be used.

Appendix E
Quick Reference

This is a short presentation of the commands mainly following the structure of The MATLAB Handbook.

Editing and Special Keys

Some of the special keys are system dependent. Usually "or" in the following means keys on different systems. Some keys do not exist at all on some systems.

↑ or `Ctrl-P` and ↓ or `Ctrl-N`	Browse among and recall previous commands
← or `Ctrl-B`	Move left one character
→ or `Ctrl-F`	Move right one character
`Ctrl-L` or `Ctrl-←`	Move left to next word
`Ctrl-R` or `Ctrl-→`	Move right to next word
`Ctrl-A` or `Home`	Move to beginning of line
`Delete,` or `Backspace`	Delete character
`Ctrl-K`	Delete to end of line
`Ctrl-C`	Stop running calculations
`cedit`	Switch key modes

Basic System Commands

`exit, quit`	Leave MATLAB
`diary`	Diary of session
`save`	Save workspace on file
`load`	Load workspace from file
`type, dbtype`	List file
`what, dir, ls`	List contents of directory
`cd`	Change directory
`pwd`	Show current directory
`path`	Show and set current path
`!`	Command to the operating system follows

Help and Demonstration Commands

In the Macintosh and Windows versions, help is most easily obtained from the help menu.

`help`	Help on topic
`lookfor`	Search for text
`expo, demo`	Demonstration programs
`whatsnew`	List of new features
`info`	General information

Variables and Workspace

`who, whos`	List variables
`clear`	Clear variable
`size, length`	Size of matrix and vector
`exist`	Existence
`pack`	Restructure workspace
`format`	Output format
`casesen`	Differentiate on upper and lower case letters

Standard Constants and Variables

`ans`	Last unassigned answer
`pi`	π, 3.14159265358979
`eps`	Relative accuracy
`realmax, realmin`	Largest and smallest number
`inf`	Infinity, defined as 1/0
`NaN`	Not a number, e.g. 0/0

| `i, j` | Imaginary unit, $\sqrt{-1}$ |
| `nargin, nargout` | Number of arguments |

User I/O

The easiest way to obtain the value of a variable is to type the variable name and hit return.

`disp`	Display value or text
`input`	Input from keyboard
`ginput`	Read coordinates
`pause`	Pause execution
`waitforbuttonpress`	Wait for user action
`format`	Output format
`more`	Scroll format
`casesen`	Differentiate on upper and lower case letters
`menu`	Pop-up menu with choices
`lasterr`	Last error message string

For information on graphics commands and graphical user interface see the sections Graphics and Handle Graphics below.

Time-keeping Functions

`flops`	Number of flops
`tic, toc, etime`	Time keeping
`clock, date`	Time and date
`cputime`	Time since MATLAB start

Special System Commands

`computer, getenv`	Type of computer
`terminal`	Set terminal type
`ver`	Information on version etc.
`version`	MATLAB version
`hostid`	Server host id no.

Mathematical Functions

The standard mathematical functions are carried out elementwise.

Elementary Mathematical Functions

`abs`	Absolute value
`sign`	Sign function
`sqrt`	Square root
`pow2`	Power of 2
`exp`	Exponential function
`log, log2, log10`	Logarithmic functions
`sin, cos, tan, cot, sec, csc`	Trigonometric functions
`asin, acos, atan2, atan, acot, asec, acsc`	Inverse trigonometric functions
`sinh, cosh, tanh, coth, asinh, acosh, atanh, acoth, sech, csch, asech, acsch`	Hyperbolic functions and inverses

Advanced Mathematical Functions

`legendre`	Legendre functions
`bessel, bessely`	Bessel functions
`gamma, gammaln, gammainc`	Gamma function
`beta, betaln, betainc`	Beta functions
`expint`	Exponential integral
`erf, erfinv, erfc, erfcx`	Error functions
`ellipke, ellipj`	Elliptic integrals

Coordinate transformations

| `cart2pol, pol2cart,` | Cartesian and polar |
| `cart2sph, sph2cart` | Cartesian and spherical |

Integers and Floating Point Numbers

round, fix, floor, ceil	Rounding functions
rat	Rational approximation
rats	Rational number to string
rem	Remainder after division
gcd	Greatest common divisor
lcm	Least common multiplier

Complex Numbers

real, imag	Real and imaginary parts
conj	Conjugate
angle	Phase angle
unwrap	Adjust arguments
cplxpair	Complex pairs

Matrix Operations and Functions

A dot prior to the operator indicates an elementwise operation.

Matrix Operators

+, -	Addition and subtraction
, ., cross, dot, kron	Multiplication
/, \. ,/, .\	Division
' ,	
, .	Conjugation, transposition
^, .^	Power
>, <, >=, <=, ==, ~=	Relational operators
&, |, ~, xor	Logical operators

Matrix Functions

det, trace, rank	Determinant, trace and rank
inv, pinv	Inverse and pseudo-inverse
orth, null	Basic subspaces
subspace	Angle between subspaces
expm, logm, sqrtm, funm, polyvalm	Matrix functions
size, length	Size and length of matrices and vectors
any, all, isnan, isinf, isieee, issparse, isstr, isempty, finite	Logical functions
find	Find under condition

Defining Vectors and Matrices

The colon, :, is used to generate and extract vectors and matrices.

:	Index operator
linspace, logspace	Generate vectors
eye	Identity matrix
ones, zeros	Matrices of ones and zeros
rand, randn	Random matrices
diag	Diagonal matrices
triu, tril	Triangular matrices
fliplr, flipud, rot90, reshape	Changing matrices
hilb, invhilb, toeplitz, compan, gallery, hadamard, hankel, magic, pascal, rosser, vander, wilkinson	Special matrices

Strings

Strings are enclosed by apostrophes, "text".

strcmp	String compare
strtok, strrep	Extract strings
findstr	Search for a string

`isstr, isletter, isspace`	Logic on strings
`strmat`	Matrix of strings
`blanks, deblank`	Blanks in string
`lower, upper`	Case conversion
`abs, setstr, num2str, int2str, rats, hex2num, hex2dec, dec2hex`	String conversions
`sprintf, sscanf`	Formatted I/O
`eval, feval`	Evaluate strings

Data Analysis and Statistics

`sum, cumsum`	Sums
`prod, cumprod`	Products
`diff, gradient, del2`	Differences
`max, min`	Maxima and minima
`mean, median`	Mean and median values
`std`	Standard deviation
`cov`	Variance and covariance
`corrcoef`	Correlation matrix
`sort`	Sorting
`hist, bar, stairs`	Histogram plots, etc.

Linear Systems

Systems of linear equations are usually solved with the backslash operator, \.

`\`	Left divison, solution operator
`det, rank`	Determinant and rank
`inv`	Inverse of matrix
`norm, normest`	Norm of matrix
`cond, condest`	Condition numbers
`lu`	LU decomposition
`rref, rrefmovie`	Echelon form of matrix

`Chol`	Cholesky factorization
`qr`	QR factorization
`qrinsert, qrdelete`	QR manipulations
`planerot`	Givens rotations

Eigenvalues and Eigenvectors

`eig, polyeig`	Eigenvalues and eigenvectors
`poly`	Characteristic polynomial
`trace`	Trace of matrix
`balance`	Balance transform
`hess`	Upper Hessenberg form
`qr, qz`	QR and QZ decompositions
`schur`	Schur decomposition
`rsf2csf`	Real to complex Schur form conversion
`cdf2rdf`	Complex to real diagonal form conversion
`svd`	Singular value decomposition

Sparse Matrices

Most of the usual matrix commands can be applied directly to sparse matrices. Notable exceptions are the command `norm` and some of the graphics commands.

`sparse`	Full to sparse conversion
`full`	Sparse to full conversion
`find`	Find indices
`spconvert`	Indices to sparse
`nnz`	Number of non-zero elements
`spy`	Structure plot
`nonzeros`	Find non-zero elements
`speye`	Sparse identity matrix
`spones`	Ones in non-zero positions

`sprandn,sprandsym`	Sparse random matrices
`spdiags`	Sparse diagonal matrix
`issparse`	Logic on storage
`spalloc, nzmax`	Sparse allocation
`spfun`	Evaluate function
`sprank`	Rank of sparse matrix
`normest`	2-norm estimate
`condest`	Condition number estimate
`spaugment`	Create square matrix to compute least square solutions
`etree`	Elimination tree of matrix
`etreeplot`	Plot of elimination tree
`colmmd, symmmd`	Minimum degree orderings
`symrcm, colperm`	Column permutations
`randperm`	Permuted vector
`dmperm`	Dulmage–Mendelsohn decomposition
`spparms`	Sets sparse parameters
`symbfact`	Analyze `Chol` and `lu`
`gplot`	Graph plots

Polynomials and Curve Fitting

`polyval, polyvalm`	Evaluate polynomials
`conv, deconv`	convolution, product of polynomials
`residue`	Partial fractions
`polyder`	Derivative of polynomials
`poly`	Characteristic polynomial
`compan`	Companion matrix
`polyfit`	Polynomial approximation
`interp1-interp6`	Interpolation
`interpft`	Fourier interpolation
`spline`	Spline interpolation

`legendre, bessel, bessely`	Orthogonal functions
`fft, ifft`	Fast Fourier transform
`fft2, ifft2`	2D FFT
`fftshift`	Swap quadrants

Zeros, Maxima, and Minima

`roots`	Zeros of polynomials
`fzero`	Zeros of functions
`fmin, fmins`	Minima of functions

Integrals and Differential Equations

`trapz, quad, quad8`	Computation of definite integrals
`ode23, ode45, ode23p`	ODE solvers

Programming in MATLAB

Programs can be written by the prompter, or more conveniently, in an M-file. An M-file is a file of MATLAB commands, with the extension .m. The M-file is executed by giving the name of the file as a command. Blocks in MATLAB are closed by an end.

Conditional Statements

`if condition`
    `statement1`
    `statement2`
`...`
	The general form of an if-else block

`else`
    `statement3`
`end`
	The else part is optional, but an `if` always has an `end`

Loops

`for i=1:2:10`
    `statement1`
    `...`
`end`
	Loop i from 1 to 10 using step 2
	A block is closed by `end`

`while condition`
    `statement1`
    `...`
`end`
	Loop while condition is true

Control Statements			stem	Data sequence plot
%	Comment follows		hist, bar, stairs	Histogram plots, etc.
return	Leave M-file		*Graphics Control*	
pause	Pause execution		figure	Create or display a figure
break	Terminate current loop		clf	Clear figure
global	Declare variables global		hold	Hold the current plot
nargin	Number of arguments in		subplot	Divide current figure into
nargout	Number of arguments out			subplots
Debugging M-Files			clc	Clear command window
keyboard	Keyboard command mode		home	Put cursor home, i.e. top left
echo	Echo commands		axis	Scale of the axes
error	Terminate with error-message		zoom	Zoom in and out (2D only)
			grid	Show or hide gridlines
dbtype	Type M-file with line no.		title, xlabel,	
dbstop, dbclear	Set and clear breakpoints		ylabel, zlabel	Write basic text items
dbstatus	List current breakpoints		text	Write text anywhere
dbstep, dbcont	Execute statements		gtext	Place text with mouse
dbup, dbdown	Switch workspace		ginput	Read coordinates
dbstack	Show stack of workspaces		rbbox	Move rectangular region
dbquit	Quit debugging mode		hidden	Show or do not show hidden surfaces

Graphics

			view	Position and angle of view
2D- and 3D-Graphics			viewmtx	Matrix defining the view
plot	Plot in two dimensions		rot90	Rotate matrix
plot3	Plot in three dimensions		*Surface and Contour Plots*	
fplot	Plot function		contour	Contour plots
subplot	Divide current figure into subplots		contour3	Contour plots in 3D
errorbar	Plot with error bars		clabel	Mark contour lines
comet, comet3	Animated plot, 2D, 3D		meshgrid	Generate grid
polar	Plot in polar coordinates		cylinder, sphere	Special geometry grids
semilogx, semilogy			surf	Surface plot
loglog	Logarithmic plots		mesh	Mesh surface plot
quiver, feather,			meshc, meshz,	Mesh surface with reference
compass, rose	Complex graphics		waterfall	lines

surfl, surfc, surfnorm	Surface plots with special light, contours, and normals
pcolor	Surf plot seen from above
fill, fill3	Filled polygons
slice	Plot of functions of three variables

Color Control

shading	Surface color mode
colormap	Read or set color table
colorbar	Display a color bar
rgb2hsv, hsv2rgb	Conversion of color tables
caxis	Scale of the color axis
spinmap	Rotate colors
brighten	Change color map
contrast	Increase contrast
whitebg	Background color
graymon	Black and white parameters

Printing

print	Generate hardcopy
printopt	Print options
orient	Paper orientations

Sound

sound	Play sound
saxis	Sound axis
auread, auwrite	Sun au sound files
mu2lin, lin2mu	Sun sound conversion
wavwrite, wavread	Windows sound files

Handle Graphics

Graphics in MATLAB is object-orientated. First there is a root object that may have children, that is figures. These figures can contain one or more axes, plot regions. A plot is built by lines, surfaces, patches, and text objects drawn in the plot region.

Each object has a unique handle, and through this handle its properties may be changed.

get	Get properties
set	Set properties
gcf, gca, gco	Get handle to current figure, axis, or object.
clf, cla	Clear current figure or axes
close	Close figure
delete	Delete object
rotate	Rotate object
reset	Reset properties of an object
refresh	Refresh figure
drawnow	Flush graphics update
newplot	Set properties for next plot
figure	Set current or create figure
axes	Plot region
line	Line object
text	Text object
patch	Patch (filled polygon) object
surface	Surface object
image	Image object
capture	Bitmap copy
uimenu	User interface menu
dialog	Dialog box
errordlg, warndlg, helpdlg, questdlg	Inherited dialogs

Movies			
movie	Show movie		
getframe	Get movie frame		
moviein	Initialize movie		

Binary and Text Files

fopen	Open file		
fclose	Close file		
fwrite	Write to file		

fread	Read from file
fprintf	Formatted output to file
fscanf	Scan data from file
fegtl, fgets	Read line from file
ferror	Check for file error
feof	Check for end of file
frewind	Reset file
fseek	Set position in file
ftell	Get position in file

References

This list of references contains books in linear algebra, matrix algebra and applications. The basic MATLAB manuals are also listed.

Backstrom, G. (1995). *Practical Mathematics Using MATLAB*. Studentlitteratur (ISBN 91–44–49231–6) and Chartwell Bratt Ltd (ISBN 0–86238–397–8).

Golub, G. H. and Van Loan, C. F. *Matrix Computations* (2nd edition). The Johns Hopkins University Press, 1989 (ISBN 0–8018–3739–1).

Hager, W. W. *Applied Numerical Linear Algebra*. Prentice-Hall, 1988 (ISBN 0–13–041369–0).

Jennings, A. and McKeown, J. J. *Matrix Computation*. John Wiley, 1992 (ISBN 0–471–93527–1).

Lindfield, G. and Penny, J. *Numerical Methods Using MATLAB*. Ellis Horwood, 1995 (ISBN 0–13–030966–4).

Marcus, M. *Matrices and MATLAB: A Tutorial*. Prentice-Hall, 1993 (ISBN 0–13–562901–2).

Ogata, K. *Solving Control Engineering Problems with MATLAB*. Prentice-Hall, 1993 (ISBN 0–13–045907–0).

Strang, G. *Introduction to Linear Algebra*. Wellesley-Cambridge Press, 1993 (ISBN 0–9614088–5–5).

Strum, R. D. and Kirk D. E. *Contemporary Linear Systems Using MATLAB*. PWS Publishing, 1994 (ISBN 0–534–93273–8).

MATLAB manuals:

Building a Graphical User Interface, The MathWorks Inc., 1993.

External Interface Guide, The MathWorks Inc., 1992.

Reference Guide, The MathWorks Inc., 1992.

Release Notes Version 4.2, The MathWorks Inc., 1994.

User's Guide, The MathWorks Inc., 1992.

The Student Edition of MATLAB, Version 4, User's Guide, Prentice-Hall, 1995 (ISBN 0–13–184979–4).

References

List of Command Tables

This is a chapter-by-chapter list of all command tables. They are listed by table number under the title of the chapters. First the table number is given, followed by the table title and the page number.

14 Advanced Graphics

15 MATLAB in Combination with Other Programs

The Student Edition of MATLAB, Version 4

Index[†]

1. Page numbers in italics refer to Examples, and page numbers in roman refer to text references.